The Stock Index Futures Market

A Trader's Insights and Strategies

B. Thomas Byrne Jr.

PROBUS PUBLISHING COMPANY
Chicago, Illinois

This publication is designed to provide accurate and authoritative information in regard to the subject matter covered. It is sold with the understanding that the publisher is not engaged in rendering legal, accounting or other professional service. If legal advice or other expert assistance is required, the services of a competent professional person should be sought.

FROM A DECLARATION OF PRINCIPLES JOINTLY ADOPTED BY A COMMITTEE OF THE AMERICAN BAR ASSOCIATION AND A COMMITTEE OF PUBLISHERS.

Library of Congress Cataloging in Publication Data Available

ISBN 0-917253-28-0

Printed in the United States of America

1 2 3 4 5 6 7 8 9 0

For Barbara

TABLE OF CONTENTS

Acknowledgements

This book would not have been possible without exceptional support from Tom Russo, Senior Partner at Cadwalader, Wickersham & Taft, who well deserves his accolades as the country's leading commodities lawyer. Special thanks also to Maurine Bartlett of Cadwalader; if I could help Maurine with trading as much as she has helped me with writing, she'd be a millionaire.

I would also like to thank a number of other people who provided valuable assistance on portions of the book: Bill Silber, Helmut Weymar, Keith Ross, Mike Ryan, David Mitchell, Gary Stumpp, Ken Coleman, Tina Ravitz, Ray Davis, Steve Trow, Ken Tatz, Broni Grala, Scott Allen, Vace Astarjian, Alan Karter, Jim Buhrmaster, and Mike Pinellas. Greg Kipnis, Laszlo Birinyi, and Nick Hanson were especially generous in sharing their exceptional knowledge of the equity markets. Any errors or shortcomings in the text are the sole responsibility of the author.

Appreciation also to John Connor, Dale Horowitz, Ken Lipper and Laszlo Birinyi for their roles in awakening my interest in the financial markets.

Also, I thank the word processors at Cadwalader, who did a marvellous job in return for one extra-bubbly New Years Eve.

Finally, to my wife, Barbara, whose support never wavered even on those occasional early trading days when it appeared as though I was reading my charts upside down.

CHAPTER 1

Introduction

It is no coincidence that stock index futures are the hottest new game in the financial world, and it is no secret that they offer unparalleled opportunities to turn stock market savvy into enormous profits. These contracts can also be used as a hedging device to protect existing profitable positions in the stock market or to lock in a set rate of return on an investment. After trading for only four years, these financial instruments produce daily dollar volume already in excess of that of the New York Stock Exchange. Stock index futures are the most actively traded contract on the Chicago Mercantile Exchange.

Market participants are a diverse and often surprisingly conservative group. In August 1982, for instance, the Westinghouse Electric Corporation pension fund invested just prior to the initial leg of the bull market and reaped a profit of more than $3 million in just one month. The Harvard University Endowment Fund was also quick to capitalize on the profit potential of stock index futures.

Skillful use of these financial instruments is spawning the financial world's newest generation of millionaires. Portfolio managers who can identify overvalued and undervalued contract prices have been able to outperform the stock market in an era when a majority of money managers have failed to do so.

Numerous other portfolio managers have recognized the importance of understanding stock index futures even if they do not intend to invest in them. This is because stock index futures have changed the rules of investing in the stock market itself by becoming the proverbial "tail that wags the dog." Stock index futures can be a critical tool in short-term and long-term market timing decisions. A portfolio manager who does not recognize certain signals they give is a bit like an offensive tackle who does not hear when the quarterback calls a new play at the line of scrimmage. Sometimes it is inconsequential, but sometimes it causes a loss.

Therefore, stock index futures ought to be understood by any serious stock market investor. These futures usually anticipate the intraday shifts in the direction of the stock market by anywhere from five to forty minutes. Because market direction and momentum often change several times a day, many investors could benefit from stock index futures simply by timing market entries and exits with reference to them. Although these futures have less value in predicting longer-term stock market trends, they are still a useful indicator of market sentiment over a longer time horizon.

A stock index futures contract is a leveraged trading vehicle that allows an investor to realize cash profits from favorable price movements of a specified portfolio or index of stocks. This trading vehicle is a standardized contract in which two parties agree, in lieu of physical delivery of stock certificates, to exchange cash in the amount of the difference between the value of a specified portfolio on the trade date and on a contractually specified expiration date in the future. A stock index futures contract is a derivative instrument because an investor's profit or loss is determined through indirect participation in the aggregate price of designated shares rather than through direct ownership of these shares.

This is not a go-go book designed to tell you how much money you would have amassed if only you had begun pyramiding stock index futures in August 1982. Rather, I hope to convey to the speculator not only a trader's sense of how and when to take calculated risks, but also the difference between calculated judgment and rash, careless action. To the hedger, I hope to convey various hedging strategies, optimal employment of each strategy and legal regulations applicable to various institutions with respect to hedging with stock index futures.

Any rational program of investment in stock index futures or stock index options must begin with an assessment of your personal (or institutional) financial situation. To be blunt, you should risk no more trading capital than you can comfortably afford to lose. You must also remember that futures trading losses can substantially exceed the amount you initially deposit with your broker. You should be mindful too, that futures trading is, in a narrow sense, a zero sum game that produces a loser for every winner.

That said, there is no better way to demonstrate the potential speculative use of stock index futures than with one go-go example. Let's make Friday, August 13, 1982 our lucky day. Assume that you, too, had sniffed the coming bull market and had $10,500 to invest on that day. You had a strong enough feeling about the market that you were willing to risk half of your investment before deciding you were wrong and liquidating. You were considering four alternatives.

Your first choice would have been to buy stock in IBM. Shares of IBM could have been purchased that day for a price of 62 7/8. If you were somewhat aggressive and chose to buy on margin, you could have purchased approximately 330 shares of IBM with your $10,500. If you held the stock until year end you would have done well—on Monday, December 27 you could have sold it at 96 3/8 for a pre-tax gain of $11,055.

Your second choice was to play a low-priced but strong company in the consumer electronics field because you felt any recovery would be led by consumers. You picked Sony because the Japanese can't seem to do anything wrong lately. With your $10,500 you could have bought approximately 1,800 shares of Sony on margin at approximately 11 3/4. On December 27, you could have sold that stock at a price of 15. Sure, you'd be up $5,850, but the rest of the bulls would have left you in their dust. This illustrates that an investment decision that seemed eminently logical at the time can leave one extremely disappointed. It also underscores one of the primary advantages of the use of stock index futures: if you are right about the general direction of the market, you won't be left high and dry by the whimsical and often unpredictable performance of a particular stock.

If you were among the savviest of stock pickers and a keen predictor of market turns, your third alternative would have been to take your $10,500 and purchase 3,000 shares of Chrysler on margin at a price of 7. On December 27, you could have sold that stock at 18, giving you a whopping $33,000 gain. Not bad in any circumstance, but remember that during those dark days, very few investors were brave enough to risk money on Chrysler.

Your fourth alternative was to invest in stock index futures. On our fateful Friday the 13th, you could have purchased 3 December futures contracts on the New York Stock Exchange Composite Index for a price of 60.70. On December 27, you could have sold contracts for a price of 82.15, realizing a profit of $32,175.

But, you say, a Chrysler investor appears to be $825 ahead of the person who played stock index futures. While this is true before tax, it highlights another major advantage of stock index futures. Our Chrysler investor, who is in a 50 percent tax bracket, has a short-term capital gain that leaves him with an after-tax profit of only $16,500. Our stock index futures player will have an after-tax profit of $21,880 because profits on these contracts are presently taxed at a maximum rate of 32 percent. Even the person whose wallet is fat because a stock pick outperformed the 1982 bull market should thus consider stock index futures the next time he or she has strong feelings about another bull (or bear) market.

The following chart illustrates the results of each of these four investment alternatives:

Investment	Aug. 13	Dec. 27	Pre-Tax Gain	After-Tax Gain (Assumes Maximum Rate)
Sony	11 3/4	15	$ 5,850	$ 2,925
IBM	62 7/8	96 3/8	11,055	5,528
Chrysler	7	18	33,000	16,500
NYSE Future	60.70	82.15	$32,175	$21,879

As we will see later, this example can be fine-tuned in several ways. Dividends would have accrued to stock players during the 4 1/2 month holding period, but not to stock index players. But the stock player who put down only 50 percent of the value of the stock purchased would have paid the broker approximately $275 in interest on a margin loan of $5,250. On the other hand, the stock index player would have deposited only a bit more than 10 percent of the value of the index futures contracts purchased.

Further, because no security is purchased at that point, a stock index player would pay no interest on margin debt. In fact, many stock index players earn interest while holding either a long or short futures position because they are permitted to make their margin deposit with a Treasury bill on which they can generally retain the interest. On the other hand, when a customer pays cash to a stock broker, the customer earns no interest on that money.

Finally, commission costs would have been far higher for the stock transactions.

A simple calculation reveals that our stock index futures investment produced an annualized return on capital of over 2,000 percent! But before it seems altogether too easy, remember that there is downside risk commensurate with the upside potential. Also remember that on that Friday the 13th, many Cassandras said that the next stop on the Dow would be 690. As we shall see, there are ways to guard against downside risk. In our example, you could have instructed your broker to liquidate your position in the event that half of your $10,500 had been lost. Such an instruction would have seemed particularly prudent on Monday, August 16, when the NYSE futures did in fact retreat one last time, trading as low as 58.30 (not quite low enough to trigger liquidation). So even though the market bottom was four percent away from your entry point, your earnings amounted to six times what you had at risk. Not a bad calculus.

Although our August 13th example illustrates the tremendous potential of stock index futures, one cannot overlook that $1,200 per contract was at risk and could have been lost. Every trade involves focusing on the potential losses as well as the potential gains. My intent is to discuss sophisticated and prudent trading strategies that will assist the reader in refining and improving the risk-reward calculation.

Stock index options play a part in some of these strategies. These options were not introduced until 1983. However, had stock index options been available on that Friday the 13th, an investor could have turned an investment of a few hundred dollars into huge gains, while risking no more than the purchase price of the option. Because so many possibilities exist for speculating in and hedging with options, certain unique characteristics of stock index options are discussed separately in an appendix to this book.

Although substantial profits are indeed possible from investment in stock index futures, they are hardly automatic. There are people who have consistently invested successfully in these instruments. This is because they have studied the market and become familiar with its basic movements, patterns and idiosyncrasies. While there is always more to learn about the stock index market, this book is designed to be a giant step toward the level of sophistication that could put you in the class of consistent money-makers.

An encouraging aspect of the stock index futures market is that nobody is too far ahead of you because this market is only four years old. Thus, while gold traders may have ten or twenty years of experience and expertise in that market, nobody has more than a four-year edge on you in the stock index game.

Nor is every successful stock index futures trader a genius. In fact, most traders will tell you that the key elements to success are discipline, a basic understanding of fundamental economic influences on the market, and an understanding of market nuances and patterns.

We have noted that stock index futures offer the advantages of leverage and reduced taxes on gains. As will be shown in detail later, they also offer substantially lower transactions costs than trading in stocks themselves. Moreover, in certain ways, trading in stock index futures is safer than trading directly in particular stocks. Trading in individual stocks requires access to a phenomenal amount of information. Even if information about earnings or developments affecting a company are published, that doesn't mean you will be the first person to receive and to act upon it. In many cases, the price of a particular stock may be heavily influenced by the actions of one or two large individual or institutional shareholders whose decisions are affected by considerations other than fundamental company news. No comparable disadvantages exist with respect to stock index futures.

So far we have talked primarily about the bulls. Stock index futures may be even more advantageous to someone who is bearish. It can be difficult and expensive to take a short position in a common stock. After selling a stock short, you are still obligated to deliver a stock certificate to your broker for redelivery to the purchaser, usually within seven business days. If you don't have a certificate to deliver, you must borrow one until such time as you do purchase the stock. The lender of that certificate will charge you interest.

With stock index futures, it costs no more to be short than it does to be long. After selling a stock index future short, you need not deliver anything except sufficient margin to your broker. Your broker's clearing department will credit or debit your account depending on whether your position moves for or against you. You pay no interest charges for maintaining a short position.

If stock index futures are for you, there is a lot to learn. What did that "price" of 60.70 for NYSE December stock index future represent and how was it determined? How does this price relate to the stock index itself? Once all this makes sense, how do you go about buying one of these contracts? The following pages will review not only the mechanics of trading in stock index futures, but also some of the methods used by traders to attempt to predict movements in these futures prices.

Just as the price movements of any other commodity future relate to prices of an underlying hard commodity, stock index futures relate to the level of the underlying soft or intangible commodity. If the price of gold for delivery in six months jumps too far ahead of the current or spot price of gold, speculators or arbitrageurs will take advantage of what they perceive as an aberration in the normal price relationship between the spot and futures prices by buying the spot month and selling the futures contract. Although the arbitrage is more complicated in the case of stock index futures and the underlying stocks comprising an index, that arbitrage is still possible. Hence the price of a stock index futures contract will always bear a reasonable, but not constant, relationship to the level of its corresponding index. That being so, a discussion of the movement of futures prices would proceed in something of a vacuum without some understanding of what indexes are.

CHAPTER 2

The Underlying Indexes

Stock indexes have existed for many years. Each represents an attempt to gauge performance of the stock market. Practically speaking, however, there is more than one stock market in today's world. There is, of course, the venerable (some would say antiquated) New York Stock Exchange (NYSE), but not all companies can be, or want to be, listed on the NYSE. Then there is the American Stock Exchange (Amex), which is heavily weighted toward companies in the high-tech, energy, and natural resource sectors of the economy.

The National Association of Securities Dealers sponsors what is known as the NASDAQ System, which is a group of stocks that are traded over-the-counter (i.e., over the telephone) rather than on any exchange floor. Some well-known companies, such as MCI, People Express, Apple Computer, Genentech, and Intel are included in this group. A broader over-the-counter market contains numerous small companies, which are very often new and which may also be highly speculative investments.

Although there are mathematical differences in the calculation of various indexes measuring the performance of these and other ''stock markets,'' each such index measures changes in the cumulative value of shares of stock in the companies comprising that index over a selected period of time.

Thanks to computers, indexes are continually updated during the trading day, and changes are flashed on quote screens throughout the country each minute. The flash of a new level of an index does not necessarily affect the price of a stock index futures contract. In fact, futures prices may often be moving in the opposite direction of the underlying index! This is because the futures market has already anticipated current movements in the underlying index and is reacting to perceptions of movements likely to occur a half hour or so away. Thus, although stock index traders may appear to ignore such minute-to-minute changes in an index, they are in fact keenly aware of those movements.

THE DOW JONES INDUSTRIAL AVERAGE

The most widely followed index is the Dow Jones Industrial Average (DJIA). The Dow was first tabulated in 1884 as an average of eleven issues. By 1928, it had evolved to an average of the prices of thirty industrial companies, fifteen of which are still Dow components. However, even since 1976, the Dow has been transformed by a change of six component stocks, as American Express, IBM, McDonald's, Merck & Co., Minnesota Mining & Manufacturing, and Philip Morris were added at various times to replace American Brands, Anaconda, Chrysler, Esmark, General Foods, and Johns Manville. In order to prevent the Dow from suddenly jumping or falling ten points due to changes in its components or because of certain corporate events, the sum of the share prices is divided by a divisor that is designed to neutralize such events. For example, the divisor was changed from 1.230 to 1.194 in January 1984 to reflect the substitution of new AT&T shares for the old AT&T shares, and it has been changed more recently to below 1.00. The divisor would also be changed after stock splits or after stock dividends that exceed 5 percent of outstanding stock. The current divisor is regularly printed in *The Wall Street Journal* and in *Barron's*. The Dow Jones Industrial Average can be accessed on most stock quotation machines by typing in "INDU" or "DJIA."

The Dow, which was below 500 as late as 1958, does not always reflect movements in the stock market as a whole. During the 1970s, the Dow went up 5 percent (from 800 to 838), while the NYSE Composite Index increased 20 percent (from 51.53 to 61.95). Studies involving shorter time periods show only a .90 correlation between monthly movements in those two indexes. This is not surprising in that the Dow is disproportionately weighted toward smokestack industries. Moreover, many traders believe that 30 companies is simply too small a statistical sample to be particularly reliable in measuring the performance of the market as a whole. Nevertheless, the 30 stocks in the Dow account for nearly one quarter of the capitalization of all stocks listed on the New York Stock Exchange.

The Dow is a price-weighted average, which means that the dollar movement of each of its stocks is weighed equally (i.e., without regard to the total value of the outstanding shares of a component stock). In other words, price-weighting is premised upon a portfolio of an equal number of shares of each stock in the index, even though the value of each such stock is likely to be different. Thus, if a $10 stock rises by $1 and a $100 stock also rises by $1, they will have the same impact on the Dow average even though they have experienced radically different moves in percentage terms. Conversely, suppose both stocks go up 5 percent. The $10 stock moves 1/2 point higher, and the $100 stock goes up 5 points. In that case, the change in the $100 stock would have a ten times greater impact on the Dow. This may be viewed as distorting, particularly when a lower priced stock has a higher capitalization (share price times shares outstanding).

Another complicating factor involves presentation of Dow bar charts. Have you ever noticed how often bar charts in newspapers make it appear as though the Dow has fluctuated in a 30- or 40-point range in one trading day? Was it really up 20 and then down 20 all in one day? Well, not usually. Instead of depicting the actual high at any particular time or day, the high on a Dow bar chart published by Dow Jones & Co. represents the aggregate high of all Dow stocks, regardless of the time of day each respective high was achieved. If those highs occurred at different times, the Dow would not have fluctuated over the entire range shown.

Nevertheless, the Dow can move rather suddenly. If each Dow stock were to uptick an eighth in the same minute, the Dow would move nearly four points higher (30/8 divided by approximately 1).

Similarly, when Union Carbide opened six points lower after the Bhopal tragedy, the Dow suddenly flashed minus six points when it had been down only a point in the preceding minute.

The Dow has a psychological impact on traders, particularly when it approaches multiples of 100 and, to a lesser extent, when it nears certain multiples of 20. The market doesn't necessarily stop on a dime when it hits one of these old reliable support or resistance levels. For example, consider the six months between late July 1984 and early April 1985 depicted in Figure 2-1. I have marked eight points that illustrate the usefulness and limitations of support and resistance levels. The chart indicates that while these levels can be valuable reference points, they are often imprecise and thus not always useful for minute-to-minute trading decisions. In other words, it is more the exception than the rule to have the market stop on a dime because one of these familiar Dow levels is reached. The points selected focus on 1160 and 1200 as support levels and 1240 and 1300 as resistance levels.

After the explosive rally of August 1984, the Dow had great difficulty in penetrating the so-called 1240 resistance level, as shown at points 1, 3, and 5 and on later dates. It found support especially at the 1200 level (points 2 and 4) and at the 1160 level (points 6 and 7). Once it finally broke out of the 1240 resistance, it rocketed 20 points in little more than an hour to register a one-day gain of 36 points. The next major resistance level was 1300 (including point 8). Let us look at the exact levels at which the Dow stopped when it hit a support or resistance level. These levels reflect real-time trading rather than the composite daily high or low of the Dow stocks that *The Wall Street Journal* graphs depict.

Point	Level	Actual
1	1240	1247.35
2	1200	1198.65
3	1240	1247.13
4	1200	1196.22
5	1240	1244.37
6	1160	1160.78
7	1160	1158.02
8	1300	1306.10

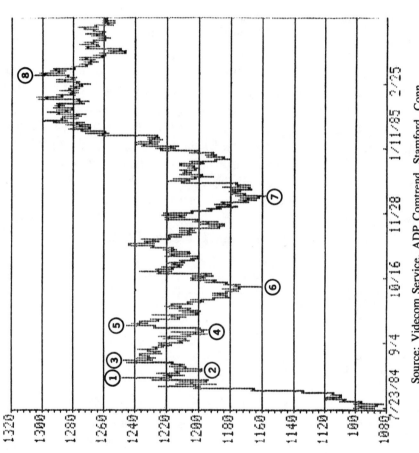

Source: Videocom Service, ADP Comtrend, Stamford, Conn.

FIGURE 2-1. DOW SUPPORT AND RESISTANCE LEVELS

What does this unscientific study suggest about Dow-based support and resistance levels? It is good to be cognizant of them but unwise to bet the ranch on the exact dollar level at which the market will reverse direction. In fact, trading volume often gets very active at these levels, which suggests that many people are betting on whether the market will penetrate a particular level. However, the bulk of this activity is attributable to large players who can get out of the market in seconds if they are wrong. Traders being traders, they love to play games of chicken at these levels.

There are no stock index futures contracts traded in the United States based directly on the Dow average. Dow Jones & Company successfully litigated to prevent The Chicago Board of Trade from using that average as an underlying index for a futures contract. Also, threats of litigation led the Toronto Stock Exchange to halt the development of a Dow-based stock index futures contract. The diehards who insist on betting the Dow must go all the way to Ladbroke's, the London bookmaker. (At this writing, the Ladbroke spread is eight points. Thus, if the Dow is at 1800, you can "buy" an interest at 1804 and "sell" an interest at 1796. No commission is added. The minimum stake is five British pounds for each full point.)

Since the Dow has only an indirect application to stock index futures trading, it's time to become familiar with the actual indexes underlying the futures contracts.

THE S&P 500 INDEX

Standard & Poor's 500 Index, known as the S&P 500, is a widely recognized barometer of the stock market as a whole. It is the benchmark against which the performance of most portfolio managers is measured. It is also used by the United States Commerce Department as one of the components of the Index of Leading Indicators. The S&P 500 Index serves as the underlying index for the most widely traded stock index futures, those traded on the Chicago Mercantile Exchange.

The S&P 500 Index is based on the stock prices of 500 different companies—400 industrials, 40 utilities, 20 transportation companies, and 40 financial institutions. Approximately 475 of the S&P firms are presently listed on the NYSE. Although the market value of those 500 firms is equal to approximately 80 percent of the value of all stocks listed on the New York Stock Exchange, the list of companies does not match the Fortune 500 list of the country's largest firms. This is due in part to an effort to reflect a cross-section of industry groups. For that reason, the components of this index are also altered on occasion. For instance, after the breakup of AT&T, several utility companies were dropped to make room for the new regional telephone companies. While old AT&T comprised almost 5 percent of the S&P 500 index, the shares of new AT&T alone have a weighting of only about 1.5 percent.

Unlike the Dow, the S&P 500 is a capitalization-weighted[1] index, so that changes in the price of a particular stock will influence the index in proportion to the total market value of the outstanding common stock of that particular company. In other words, the appropriate weight for a particular stock is determined by multiplying the number of its outstanding shares by its market price per share. For example, IBM accounts for approximately 5.8 percent of the S&P 500 Index, and General Motors accounts for approximately 1.8 percent of the Index. At the other end of the scale, the 60 smallest companies included in the S&P 500 index together account for only 1 percent of the index.

The S&P 500 Index is calculated using the base years 1941–1943 = 10. A base period of a few years is used in an effort to avoid distortions that might result from the use of a single day as the base level of an index. When that index is at 200, total share prices of S&P 500 companies are 20 times what they were in the period 1941–1943. It is worth remembering that these numbers reflect no adjustment for inflation.

Most stock or commodity quotation machines will give you the most current reading of the S&P 500 if you enter the symbol "SPX" or "INX."

[1]Capitalization refers to market capitilization, i.e., share price times shares outstanding.

THE NEW YORK STOCK EXCHANGE COMPOSITE INDEX

The New York Stock Exchange (NYSE) Composite Index is the underlying index for another widely traded futures contract, that is traded on the New York Futures Exchange. The index is calculated in a manner similar to the S&P 500 and its movements correlate very closely with those of the S&P 500. The NYSE Index is composed of the approximately 1,500 stocks listed on the New York Stock Exchange. As with the S&P 500, it is an arithmetic average that weights stocks by capitalization. IBM comprises approximately 4 percent of this index and thus may affect movements of the index as much as all of the 75 smallest companies listed on the NYSE taken together. The effect of IBM on the index is most appreciated when IBM opens a point higher and the index, which usually flashes a change of .01 or .02 each minute, suddenly moves by .07 or .08. For instance, on August 3, 1984, IBM did not trade until 10:45 a.m., when it opened up 2 3/8. The NYSE Composite Index, which had begun to cool off after an exceptionally sharp upward swing in the first half hour, jumped from 92.48 (or 17 cents) in that minute.

The NYSE Composite Index was first calculated at the end of 1965 and was arbitrarily set at 50 on December 31, 1965. As with other indexes, its divisor removes aberrations that would have occurred due to events such as new listings, delistings, stock splits, stock dividends, and reorganizations. When this index reached the 100 level in early 1985, shares on the New York Stock Exchange were valued at twice their 1965 level, before adjusting for inflation. This yields an interesting comparison with the Dow average, which was flirting with the 1300 level at the same time, thus making it only 34 percent higher than it was at the end of 1965.

Traders generally view a one point change in the NYSE Composite Index as the approximate equivalent of a change of 12.50 points in the Dow. However, this is only a general rule of thumb. For example, when the Dow hit its old record of 1287 in November 1983, the NYSE Composite Index never cracked 100, but when the Dow reached the same level in early 1985, the NYSE Index topped 105. Similarly, there are plenty of days when the Dow rises twelve points and the NYSE

Composite Index advances very little. On other days, the "broad market," for which the NYSE Composite Index can be considered a proxy, may be strong, but the Dow may advance only one or two points. When a market report says that the average share of stock is up a quarter or 25 cents, the NYSE Composite Index will generally be up approximately .75 (i.e., 75 cents).

Most stock or commodity quotation machines will give you the up-to-the-minute reading of this index if you punch in the symbol "NYQ" or "NYA."

THE VALUE LINE INDEX

The Value Line Index is the broadest index on which a futures contract is based. It underlies futures traded on the Kansas City Board of Trade. As of late 1985, this index encompassed 1,694 stocks, which collectively accounted for over 96 percent of the total dollar volume of equity trades in the United States. Therefore, even though 75 percent of the Value Line stocks are traded on the New York Stock Exchange, this average is considered to reflect the movement of so-called "second-tier" stocks. The bias in favor of the second-tier stocks is increased by an equal weighting procedure.

This index gives equal weight to the percentage changes in the prices of each of its component stocks, regardless of their absolute price levels or aggregate market values. An equally weighted index assumes that an equal dollar amount (rather than an equal number of shares as in a price-weighted index) is invested in each constituent stock.

Unlike the other indexes, the Value Line Index is a geometric average rather than an arithmetic average. An arithmetic mean is found by dividing the sum of a series of numbers by the number of tabulations (n); a geometric mean is reached by finding the nth root of the product of the tabulations. In this process, the percentage change in the price of each stock is averaged so that a one percent change in a $10 stock would be given the same weight as a one percent change in a $100 stock. Another quirk of a geometric average is that it has a built-in downward bias, as indicated by the following table of four stocks:

	Opening Price	Closing Price	Net Change	Percent Change
	4.00	6.00	+2.00	+50%
	8.00	10.00	+2.00	+25
	4.00	2.00	−2.00	−50
	8.00	6.00	−2.00	−25
Total	24.00	24.00		
Arithmetic				0
Geometric				−8.4%

The effect of different methods of computing an index can be illustrated by an example assuming that the Dow Average and the S&P, NYSE, and Value Line Indexes are all composed of the same two stocks. Company A has 100 shares outstanding, and Company B has 200 shares. Both stocks are at $100 on Day 1, so each index is at 100. On Day 2, A falls to $90, and B rises to $110. Let us see how each index would reflect those fluctuations:

$$\text{Dow} = \frac{90 + 110}{2} = 100$$

$$\text{S\&P, NYSE} = \frac{(100 \cdot 90) + (200 \cdot 110)}{(100 \cdot 100) + (200 \cdot 100)} = 103.33$$

$$\text{Value Line} = \sqrt{90 \cdot 110} = 99.50$$

The Value Line Index was set at 100 on June 30, 1961. Its ticker symbol is "XVL" or "VL" followed by the code letter for the current month.

MAJOR MARKET INDEX

In response to the perceived desirability of trading an index of a few leading companies akin to the Dow, the American Stock Exchange in 1983 developed its Major Market Index. This index is comprised of only 20 stocks. It correlates closely with movements in the Dow Jones Industrial Average and is computed in essentially the same manner as the Dow. It is computed by adding up the prices of each of the 20 stocks and dividing by a divisor that was originally set at 5. The divisor has changed as stock splits, stock dividends, and other changes (such as reorganizations) require. The Amex has reported a .97 correlation between this index and the Dow. However, this correlation was not very useful following the tragedy in Bhopal when Union Carbide dragged the Dow down, while the Major Market Index rallied.

The similarity in the component companies of the Dow and the Major Market Index is most easily observed in table form:

Dow (30)	MMI (20)
Allied Corp.	
Aluminum Co. (Alcoa)	
American Can	
American Express	American Express
AT&T	AT&T
Bethlehem Steel	
Chevron	Chevron
	Coca-Cola
	Dow Chemical
Dupont	Dupont
Eastman Kodak	Eastman Kodak
Exxon	Exxon
General Electric	General Electric
General Motors	General Motors
Goodyear	
Inco	
IBM	IBM
International Paper	International Paper
	Johnson & Johnson
McDonald's	
Merck & Co.	Merck & Co.
Minnesota M&M	Minnesota M&M
	Mobil
Navistar	
Owens Illinois	
Philip Morris	Philip Morris
Procter & Gamble	Procter & Gamble
Sears, Roebuck	Sears, Roebuck
Texaco	
Union Carbide	
U.S. Steel	U.S. Steel
United Technologies	
Westinghouse Electric	
Woolworth	

The representation of certain economic sectors in these indexes is quite similar as well. Perhaps the major difference is that the MMI is a bit more heavily influenced by oil stocks. Also, the Dow has two stocks in the packaging/container industry while the MMI has none.

At the end of 1983, only options were traded on the Major Market Index. However, futures contracts were introduced by the Chicago Board of Trade in July 1984 with great success. Although this index was invented by the American Stock Exchange, the Amex had no commodity exchange subsidiary and was thus unable to trade futures contracts on indexes it had developed. Concomitantly, the Chicago Board of Trade was eager to launch a stock index product after its unsuccessful court battle regarding futures on the Dow. Thus, the two exchanges entered into an agreement under which options on the MMI would trade in New York and MMI futures would trade in Chicago.

The ticker symbol for the Major Market Index itself is "XMI." However, the futures contracts on this index use the ticker symbols "MX" for the original contract and "BC" for the newer "big contract," followed by the appropriate expiration month code. Thus, when your broker tells you the "missiles are taking off," it is no cause for alarm—unless, of course, you are short.

OVER-THE-COUNTER INDEXES

In an effort to develop stock index business stemming from the phenomenal growth of the over-the-counter market, exchanges have developed indexes that reflect its performance. The OTC equity market in the United States is one of the largest equity securities markets in the world. On the basis of dollar value, the over-the-counter market in securities quoted on the National Association of Securities Dealers Automated Quotation system (NASDAQ) is the second largest equity market in the United States and the third largest in the world, behind only the New York and Tokyo Stock Exchanges. NASDAQ is growing at a time when the NYSE and Amex have been experiencing net decreases in listings. NASDAQ's 1984 share volume of over 15 billion shares was over two-thirds of the share volume of the NYSE in 1984 and constituted an increase of approximately 1,000 percent in share volume in ten years. A total of 4,097 companies were traded on NASDAQ at the end of 1984.

The Philadelphia Stock Exchange was first off the mark by listing futures and options on its National Over-the-Counter Index of the 100 largest OTC stocks. This XOC index is capitalization-weighted, but no stock accounts for more than 6.5 percent and no industry group accounts for more than 20 percent of its value. The index was set equal to 150 on September 28, 1984.

Similarly, the National Association of Securities Dealers (NASD) has developed its own index, called the NASDAQ 100. The NASD worked in cooperation with the Chicago Board of Trade to facilitate trading in futures on that exchange and to initiate trading in options on the index using the NASDAQ over-the-counter market system. The NASDAQ 100 Index is a capitalization-weighted index of the 100 largest nonfinancial OTC stocks. It was set at 250 on February 1, 1985.

The CME's entry in the OTC futures arena is the SPOC 250, a new S&P index of 250 OTC issues. Its initial value was set at 150 on December 31, 1984. The SPOC index is price-weighted, as is the Dow Jones Average. Thus, the index will not be disproportionately influenced by a small number of OTC companies that have a large number of high-priced shares outstanding. It is presently the only index based on the mean of the bid and offer for each stock, rather than on the last sale. The ticker symbol for the SPOC 250 is "OCX."

It was thought that the race for dominance of OTC futures would probably be settled by the end of 1986. But after the first few months of trading, OTC futures appear to be facing a struggle for survival rather than a race for dominance.

UNTRADED INDEXES

Although several other indexes provide various measures of market performance, they offer no trading opportunities. For instance, the Wilshire Associates 5000 Equity Index represents the market value of 5,000 NYSE, Amex, and over-the-counter issues tabulated as a dollar figure. At the end of 1984, this figure was $1.7 trillion.

The American Stock Exchange also tabulates a Market Value Index that measures the aggregate market value of the more than 800 Amex stocks, ADRs, and warrants. The Amex has delisted its options on this index.

SUB-INDEXES

Sub-indexes, also known as industry indexes, have developed for two reasons. One is simply that the exchanges are looking for more ways to increase market share in the stock index field. A more legitimate reason for the proliferation of sub-indexes is that portfolio managers are looking for alternatives that produce more precise hedging vehicles. For example, if a mutual fund or portfolio is heavily invested in computer stocks, trading based on an index tracking only computer stocks would be expected to produce a more precise hedge than would an offsetting position based on movements in the market as a whole. This is because an industry group as a whole can, for some period of time, diverge from movements of the broad market.

Under criteria agreed to by the SEC and the CFTC, a sub- index would have to (1) include 25 or more stocks, (2) have a total capitalization of at least $75 billion and be maintained at over $50 billion, and (3) have no single stock that constitutes more than 25 percent of the weighted value of the index and no three stocks that together constitute more than 45 percent of the index value. The two agencies may review and modify these standards from time to time.

Experimentation with futures contracts based on such sub-indexes has not been successful. At the end of 1985, no futures contracts based on any sub-indexes were trading. The New York Futures Exchange introduced a Financial Index based on prices of shares in Big-Board financial services companies, which are particularly sensitive to changes in interest rates. The contract, which was intended to serve primarily as a tool for hedging against interest-rate changes, never traded very actively and soon became dormant. But because better interest-rate hedges are available with Treasury bill, Eurodollar, or Treasury bond futures contracts, the experience of the New York Futures Exchange does not necessarily spell the end of futures contracts on other sub-indexes.

Option contracts based on other sub-indexes have not fared much better. In fact, of numerous sub-index options introduced to date, the only moderately successful products have been options traded on the Computer Technology Index (Amex), Technology Index (Pacific), Oil Index (Amex), and Gold/Silver Index (Philadelphia).

THE OEX

The greatest coup in the development of new indexes by exchanges was scored by The Chicago Board Options Exchange (CBOE). It developed a broad-based index of 100 leading stocks for the purpose of trading options. The index was initially called the "CBOE 100" and is now known as the "S&P 100," or simply the "OEX." The success of that index is perhaps unparalleled by any financial product introduced in the 1980s. Open interest in OEX options is well in excess of 1,000,000 contracts, and daily volume usually ranges between 250,000 and 500,000 options.

As of November 1985, five companies accounted for nearly one-third of the S&P 100 Index, and IBM alone composed 13.6 percent of this index, as shown:

IBM	13.6%
Exxon	6.9
GE	4.5
GM	3.7
AT&T	3.6
	32.3%

The top-heavy nature of this index has led to some charges that it is too susceptible to manipulation by professional traders. In fact, there have been charges of manipulation in the minutes preceding the expiration of the option, particularly in April 1984 and March 1985. To date, however, regulators have been satisfied that the sometimes dramatic price swings in the minutes preceding expiration of these options are a function of complex but legitimate arbitrage operations. The regulators, concerned as they are about public confidence in the market, seem to have been vindicated by the explosive volume in these OEX options. These options are discussed in greater detail in Appendix A.

FOREIGN INDEXES

The next major horizon for trading in stock indexes may well be international. Given the unprecedented flows of investment capital across international boundaries, there should be demand for such trading opportunities. A recent linkage between the Chicago Mercantile Exchange (CME) and the Singapore International Monetary Exchange (Simex) designed to expand trading opportunities in gold and/or foreign currencies has already spawned an agreement to expand trading opportunities in foreign equity indexes. Table 2-1 lists the major stock markets, or "bourses" as they are sometimes known, and gives an indication of the great variation in performance of equities in different parts of the globe at any particular point in time. The essential terms of each foreign futures contract and the nature of each underlying index are discussed in Chapter 3.

Investors may sense a strengthening in the economy of one of the countries listed in Table 2-1, but even reasonably sophisticated investors might have little basis for making investment decisions regarding particular equities without undue expense. Both language barriers and relatively lax disclosure laws often make it difficult to obtain fundamental information about many overseas companies. Thus, futures and options on foreign indexes may accelerate the flow of capital into foreign markets.

The Chicago Board of Trade is exploring the possibility of becoming the first domestic exchange to trade contracts based on foreign stock indexes on its own floor. It is moving ahead with plans to introduce futures contracts based on the London and Canadian markets.

The CME has received exclusive licensing rights to develop a futures contract on the Nikkei Average (formerly called the "Nikkei

TABLE 2-1

Country	Index	1985 H	1985 L	July 7-9, 1986
*Australia	All-Ordinaries	1052.5	715.3	1125
*Canada	TSE 300	2900.6	2348.5	2997
France	CAC General	265.8	180.9	366
Germany	FAZ General	649.1	382.4	606
*Hong Kong	Hang Seng	1762.5	1220.7	1752
Italy	Milan Banco Comm. ltd.	460.0	228.6	703
†Japan	Nikkei	13128	11545	17734
†Singapore	Straits Times	852.7	596.2	733
Switzerland	Swiss Bank Corp. Index	587.9	388.7	545
*U.K	FTSE-100	1702.9	1206.1	1614
*U.S.	S&P 500	212.02	163.68	242

*Stock index futures contracts presently offered.
†Stock index futures contracts expected in 1986.

Dow Jones Average''), which is a composite of 225 stocks traded on the Tokyo Stock Exchange. It is the most widely recognized barometer of the Japanese stock market. The index is derived with the same method used to calculate the Dow Jones Average. The CME plans to sub-license these rights to the Singapore International Monetary Exchange and to introduce the contract first in Singapore. The CME's trading link with Simex would facilitate the eventual trading of the Japanese contract on both the Simex and the CME.

Despite the continuing development of the stock index market, there are politically powerful critics of stock index futures who would prefer that foreign stock index futures be the only stock index futures. Rep. John Dingell, chairman of the House Energy and Commerce Committee, has been a particularly vociferous critic.

Due in part to such criticism, Congress directed the SEC, CFTC, and Federal Reserve to conduct a joint study of the stock index and other financial futures markets. A primary congressional concern was whether the stock index futures and options markets diverted capital from the equity market itself. The study, completed at the end of 1984, concluded that "these markets can be found to have no discernible influence on capital formation in either a positive or negative way."[2] The study also noted that:

> Financial futures and options markets appear to have no measurable negative implications for the formation of capital. The new markets for financial futures and options appear to have enhanced liquidity in some of the underlying cash markets on which they are based and do not appear to have reduced the liquidity of any of these markets.[3]

A related issue addressed by that study was whether speculative activity in the futures had any destabilizing effects on the stock market itself. The study was inconclusive and considered the issue of price stability only in terms of intraday price fluctuation.

An editorial in a September 1985 issue of *Business Week* entitled "The Odds against the Casino Society" considered the capital formation issue and took a longer-term view of the price stability issue (referring not only to stock index futures, but rather to financial leverage in general):

> The case can be made that the casino society channels far too much talent and energy into financial shell games rather than into producing real goods and services and that it is a significant drain on economic growth.
>
> Beyond that, the casino society has the potential of engineering a serious financial collapse....[4]

Although the abolition of stock index futures seems quite a remote possibility, changes in tax laws or other disincentives to their use are indeed a possibility.

---

[2]Board of Governors of the Federal Reserve System, Commodity Futures Trading Commission, and Securities and Exchange Commission, A Study of the Effects on the Economy of Trading in Futures and Options (December 1984), p. I-17.

[3]Ibid., p. I-2.

[4]"The Odds against the Casino Society," *Business Week,* Sept. 1985, p. 144.

CHAPTER 3

Basics of Index Futures

FUTURES CONTRACTS IN GENERAL

A futures contract is a standardized contract made on a commodity exchange that provides for the future delivery of a specified quantity of a particular commodity on a specified delivery date, leaving the price as the only term to be established by the buyer and seller. A trader who initiates a futures contract position by agreeing to purchase the underlying commodity at a future date is said to be "long" in the futures market (i.e., has purchased a futures contract), while a trader who initiates a position by agreeing to sell the underlying commodity at a future date is "short" (i.e., has sold a futures contract). The obligation represented by a futures contract generally may be satisfied either by taking or making delivery of the underlying commodity, depending upon whether one has a long or short position, or by making an offsetting sale or purchase of an equivalent but opposite futures contract on the same exchange before the conclusion of trading in that delivery month. Over 95 percent of all futures contracts do not result in an actual delivery because most parties to futures contracts "cash out" through offsetting trades.

Unlike the purchaser of a stock or corporate bond, the purchaser of a stock index futures contract does not acquire an equity or debt interest in a company or even in a group of companies. Rather, a stock index futures contract is a derivative instrument because an investor's profit or loss is determined through indirect participation in the aggregate price of designated shares rather than through direct ownership of those shares.

CASH SETTLEMENT

Stock index futures contracts differ from traditional futures contracts in that settlement at maturity can be made only in cash—no such contract provides for physical delivery of any of the securities comprising the underlying indexes. Cash settlement is employed because the alternative would be physical delivery of a large stack of stock certificates for full or fractional shares in all stocks composing the index. Fractional shares would have to be delivered in order to perfectly mirror the index, a very cumbersome procedure to say the least. Thus the two parties to a stock index futures contract agree, in lieu of physical delivery of stock certificates, to exchange cash in the amount of the difference between the value of those stock certificates on the trade date and their value on the contractually specified future expiration date. In other words, the amount of cash that is delivered is a function of the fluctuation in the portfolio of stocks whose value is reflected by the particular stock index underlying the futures contract in question.

As noted, for practical purposes most commodity futures contracts are offset by liquidation, which involves a transfer of cash, rather than by physical delivery of the actual underlying commodity. Stock index futures contracts simply implement cash settlement in the case of the five percent of contracts that might not otherwise be settled in cash.

Cash settlement virtually eliminates the possibility of "squeezes", an infamous practice in which traders with long positions in a particular commodity either create or take advantage of temporary shortages of the deliverable grade of that commodity, thus forcing the shorts, who have delivery obligations, to bid prices even higher. For example, potato futures contracts became cash-settled in 1983, in part in response to a highly controversial squeeze.

Stock index futures contracts were not the first contracts to implement cash settlement. Futures contracts on three-month Eurodollar time deposits, inaugurated on the CME in 1981, have always settled in cash because actually delivering part of somebody's savings account sitting somewhere outside of the United States would be about as much fun as delivering a pile of stock certificates and scrip for fractional shares.

DEVELOPMENT OF THE MARKET

Cash settlement removed a roadblock from long-standing efforts to develop a more efficient way to "buy the market." Stock index futures are not the first method developed which allows investors to buy the market. Some mutual funds today, known as index funds, hold a portfolio that closely mirrors the S&P 500 or some other index. But those funds offer neither the leverage, liquidity, nor inexpensive transaction costs available with stock index futures.

Although stock index futures had been on the drawing board for a number of years, they did not begin trading until February 1982. Following approval of such trading by the Commodity Futures Trading Commission (CFTC), the Kansas City Board of Trade initiated trading on Value Line Index futures on February 24, 1982, with a volume of 1,758 contracts and open interest of 613 contracts.

Even though Kansas City deserves much of the credit for pioneering stock index futures, it did not maintain its monopoly for long. The Chicago Mercantile Exchange began trading the S&P 500 futures on April 21, 1982. Even on day one, this contract was the dominant stock index futures contract, with first-day volume of 3,694 contracts.

The NYSE, which is often criticized for its inability to respond to investor needs in the rapidly changing equity arena, began trading NYSE Index futures on May 6, 1982 on its wholly-owned subsidiary, the New York Futures Exchange or NYFE (pronounced "knife"). First-day volume exceeded 6,000 contracts.

The Chicago Board of Trade did not begin trading the Major Market Index futures until July 1984.

STRUCTURE OF THE MAJOR CONTRACTS

Presently the four contracts mentioned above are the major stock index futures contracts. Each of the three original stock index futures contracts has a dollar value of $500 times its currently quoted price. This arbitrary $500 figure is known as the "index multiplier." The Major Market Index maxi contract differs in that it has an index multiplier of $250.

An S&P contract quoted at 200.00 has a value of $100,000. The minimum price fluctuation or tick for each S&P futures contract is $25, represented by a minimum fluctuation or tick in the contract price of .05. If an S&P contract were to advance a full point from 200 to 201, a person holding a long position would have a $500 gain while a person holding a short position would incur a corresponding $500 loss. If an S&P contract were to drop one tick from 200.00 to 199.95, each long would have a $25 loss, and each short would have a corresponding $25 gain.

Similarly, an NYSE future quoted at 120.00 has a value of $60,000 and moves in minimum ticks of .05 or $25. Because the NYSE Composite Index has a lower dollar value, it tends to have a narrower daily trading range than does an S&P contract, even though their percentage changes tend to be much the same.

Why the $500 index multiplier? In one sense, it is an arbitrary number. But in order for any futures contract to be a viable commercial product, it must have standardized terms that are acceptable to a broad range of market participants. For example, speculators and hedgers in the gold market have agreed that a contract size of 100 ounces of gold is most closely suited to their respective needs. The $500 index multiplier was selected in much the same fashion. It results in a contract large enough to facilitate institutional hedging of portfolios, but not so large as to discourage participation by speculators who provide liquidity in the market.

All of the original contracts are presently traded on a quarterly delivery-month cycle of March, June, September, and December. The expiration date of each contract is the third Friday of the delivery month.

The MMI futures contract has several unique features. The MMI maxi contract has a dollar value of $250 times its quoted price and trades in increments of .05, worth $12.50. At a level of 300, the maxi contract would have a value of $75,000. There are MMI contracts expiring in each of the three nearest months as well as in the normal March, June, September, and December rotation.

Trading in MMI futures begins 15 minutes before the New York Stock Exchange opens. Thus, MMI futures are presently the only stock index futures contracts to open ahead of the NYSE. There has been no statistically significant evidence of the ability of the MMI contract to foreshadow the direction of the stock market each day.

The CBT initially introduced an older version of the MMI contract that differs from its newer sibling primarily in that it has a $100 index multiplier. Its trading volume declined markedly upon the introduction of the maxi contract. Presumably, the CBT concluded that the $250 multiplier would reduce transactions costs for hedgers and still attract sufficient interest from speculators.

MINOR CONTRACTS

While the four contracts discussed above are the most prominent stock index futures contracts, there are other contracts. The Chicago Board of Trade offers a contract on the NASDAQ 100 Index, and the Chicago Mercantile Exchange lists a contract on the SPOC 250 Index. The essential difference in the terms of these two contracts is the index multiplier, which is $250 ($12.50 per minimum tick of .05) for the NASDAQ 100 versus $500 ($25 per minimum tick of .05) for the SPOC 250.

Other thinly traded contracts, although illiquid, may be of interest to smaller investors. The CME lists a futures contract on the S&P 100 Index (or OEX) that has a $200 multiplier, and the Kansas City Board of Trade (KCBT) lists a mini Value Line contract that has a $100 multiplier. A contract based on the price-weighted Financial News Composite Index of 30 U.S. stocks is listed on INTEX, a Bermuda exchange. The Philadelphia Board of Trade lists a contract based on its National OTC Index that has a $500 multiplier. As noted, the original MMI

TABLE 3-1. SUMMARY OF LEADING CONTACTS

	S & P 500	NYSE Composite	Value Line	Major Market	SPOC-250	NASDAQ-100
Exchange	CME	NYFE	KCBT	CBT	CME	CBT
Ticker Symbol*	SP	YX	KV	BC	OT	ND
Cash Index Symbol	SPX, INX	NYA, NYQ	VL, XVL	XMI	OCX	IXD
Index Multiplier	$500	$500	$500	$250	$500	$250
Quotation	.05 = $25.00	.05 = $25.00	.05 = $25.00	.05 = $12.50	.05 = $500	.05 = $12.50
Contract Value at Dec. 31, 1985	212.45 $106,225	122.40 $ 61,200	218.40 $109,200	294.60 $ 73,650	196.50 $ 98,250	270.00 $ 67,500
Type of Weighting	Capitalization	Capitalization	Equal	Price	Price	Capitalization
Type of Average	Arithmetic	Arithmetic	Geometric	Arithmetic	Arithmetic	Arithmetic
Number of Stocks	500	Approx. 1,500	1,685	20	250	100
Contract Months	March June Sept. Dec.	March June Sept. Dec.	March June Sept. Dec.	Same, plus nearest 3 months	March June Sept. Dec.	March June Sept. Dec.
Approximate Daily Volume	75,000	11,000	4,000	6,500	Under 100	Under 100

*Followed by month symbols: H (March), M (June), U (September), Z (December) contract with the $100 multiplier has been relegated to minor league status.

THE MARK-TO-MARKET SYSTEM

The cash settlement system for stock index futures does not simply involve a lump-sum payment to those with gains upon either expiration or liquidation of a particular contract. Instead, cash payments are transferred on a daily basis using what is known as a "mark-to-market" system. Under this system, the exchange clearinghouse transfers funds to and from the accounts of clearing members, which in turn credit or debit the accounts of market participants on a daily basis in accordance with net gains or losses occurring on that day.

A final netting out procedure occurs when positions outstanding upon expiration of a particular contract are similarly settled by transfer of funds. Settlement on the expiration date is based on the difference between the settlement price on the next to last trading day and the value (to the nearest .01) of the underlying index at the close of trading on the last day. Cash settlement for new positions established on the last day of trading and held to the close of business that day is based on the difference between the transaction price of a new position and value of the underlying index at expiration. Settlement at expiration therefore does not involve the transfer of the full value of the futures contract.

MARGIN

Daily cash transfers are possible even when new participants enter the stock index futures market because commodity exchanges require that funds be already on deposit or immediately forthcoming from a customer in order for a trade to be executed. In contrast, participants in the securities market generally have seven business days in which to make margin payments.

Commodity margin and securities margin are similar insofar as margin payments provide brokers with protection against possible trading losses. However, commodity margin functions as a good-faith payment or performance bond on an unfulfilled contractual obligation that is yet to be either performed by delivery or negated by an offsetting futures transaction. In contrast, securities margin is a down payment for property that has already changed ownership.

Margin on securities is presently regulated by the Federal Reserve, the SEC, and the appropriate stock exchange while regulation of commodity futures margin is the exclusive province of the commodity exchanges. Whether the Federal Reserve or the CFTC will at some point seek to impose margin requirements on stock index futures is an open question. In 1984, the Fed considered imposing its own margin requirements on stock index futures. On the other hand, in 1985, the Fed began considering getting out of the business of margin regulation altogether.

Upon deposit of initial margin, the futures trader in general, and the stock index trader in particular, enjoy one advantage not shared by participants in either the equity or options markets. The profit or loss in commodity accounts is calculated and the money credited to a trader's account on a daily basis. Thus, if your futures contract moves a full point in your favor, you have a profit of $500. That $500 profit may be withdrawn from your account and reinvested at any time before liquidation of the contract. A $500 paper profit in a stock or an option can't be touched until the stock or option is sold.

However, should you incur a loss, your broker will immediately debit your account in the amount of that loss and will ask you to deposit more money immediately if the funds on deposit are reduced to a stated minimum. Thus, while stock index futures trading offers the advantage of substantial leverage and minimal initial margin requirements, these advantages can quickly become disadvantages to the undisciplined and unsophisticated trader.

There are several practical effects of the differences in commodities and securities margin. Commodities margin regulations offer somewhat more flexibility as to what constitutes acceptable collateral. While Federal Reserve regulations permit a stock broker to accept only cash, exempt securities, and marginable securities (at a discounted value) as margin for stock transactions, most commodity exchanges allow a commodity broker to accept letters of credit and physical commodities in addition to the collateral which is acceptable in the securities industry.

Moreover, a customer who deposits cash into a commodities account is generally unable to keep the interest on those funds, whereas customers with securities accounts are frequently paid interest on cash balances. Several lawsuits are pending on the issue of whether customers with commodity account cash balances are entitled to receive interest. Unless those suits are decided in favor of the customer, commodity traders will continue to have an incentive to keep Treasury bills rather than cash in their accounts so that their money earns interest. Many commodity brokers charge a quarterly rollover fee each time the bill matures.

The more significant difference to a speculator between securities and commodities margin is the degree of leverage afforded by each. In the securities world, one must put up at least 50 percent of the value of any stock purchased as an initial margin deposit. In the commodities world, however, one may often put up less than 10 percent of the value of the underlying commodity as initial margin. This substantial leverage allows an investor to take advantage of a favorable market move by holding a large position with very little money down. However, leverage is a two-edged sword. When the market moves adversely, your losses may not always be limited to the amount of your initial margin deposit.

Due to the small size of initial margin deposits and the volatility of stock index futures, a broker will reserve the right to require immediate deposit of an additional sum, known as "maintenance margin," in the event of an adverse market move. A maintenance margin call is generally issued when your initial margin is depleted to the point where it reaches the maintenance margin requirement. For example, the initial margin requirement for an S&P 500 contract is $6,000, and the maintenance margin requirement is $2,500. Assume you buy an S&P contract at 190.00. If it goes to 185.00, you are down $2,500. Since you are still left with $3,500 to meet your $2,500 maintenance margin requirement, no maintenance margin call will be issued. But when the contract reaches 182.95, your $3,525 loss will leave less than

$2,500 of your initial $6,000 margin still in place. Once you dip below that $2,500 maintenance margin level, you must restore the balance in your account to the $6,000 initial margin level by depositing an additional $3,525 with your brokerage firm.

If those additional funds do not reach your broker promptly, the broker could conceivably liquidate your position. Virtually all commodity brokers reserve the right in the customer agreement you sign when you open an account to undertake such liquidation without prior notice to you, though they almost never exercise this right. Nevertheless, interpretations of the relevant CFTC regulations have specified that margin rules are designed to protect the broker rather than the customer, and thus the broker is not liable for a failure to promptly notify a customer of the need for maintenance margin before liquidating a position. Forced liquidation can be prevented by depositing sufficient extra initial margin to cover your position to whatever market level you select as your maximum loss, should this amount exceed the required sum. Better yet, unless you are a hedger, get out of the market before you lose your initial margin.

The initial margin and maintenance margin requirements as of early 1986 for speculators were as follows:

	Initial	Maintenance
S&P 500	$6,000	$2,500
NYSE Composite	3,500	1,500
KC Value Line	6,500	2,000
Major Market	1,750	500
Major Market Maxi	3,500	1,250
SPOC 250	6,000	1,500
NASDAQ 100	3,500	1,250

Margin requirements are established by each commodity exchange as an absolute dollar amount rather than a percentage of purchase price, as in the case of stock margin requirements. The value of a futures contract may rise or fall substantially before the initial margin requirement is altered. Except for a reduction from $2,300 to $1,750 in the MMI requirement, these requirements have not been changed since the contracts began trading. In any event, your commodity broker is free to impose stiffer margin requirements than those imposed by each exchange.

While all stock index futures contracts offer great leverage, the degree of leverage does vary among the contracts. One can easily calculate a leverage factor for each contract. First, find the margin requirement in percentage terms by dividing the dollar margin requirement by the value of the futures contract. The leverage factor is the reciprocal of the percentage margin requirement. While the leverage factors change, they were, based upon margin requirements and futures prices in early July, 1986:

	Percent Margin	Leverage Factor
S&P 500	4.7%	21.26
NYSE Composite	4.8	20.97
Value Line	5.2	19.25
Major Market	4.8	20.96
Major Market Maxi	3.8	26.20
SPOC 250	4.9	20.27

These contracts offer more leverage than was available in the stock market in the late 1920s.

The CBT permitted even greater leverage on the NASDAQ 100 futures until their contract became dormant as of this writing.

CLEARINGHOUSE

Every trade on an exchange must be cleared through a member of the clearinghouse. The first part of clearing a trade is the comparison process. This process involves matching up trading cards at the end of the day so that when X's card says that he sold ten contracts to Y, a clerk for one of the various clearing members ensures that there is a corresponding trading card from Y indicating that he bought ten contracts from X. Exchange members who are not clearing members pay a small per-contract charge to a clearing member to have their trades reconciled in this manner. If the CME reports open interest of 80,000 stock index futures contracts, the books of its clearinghouse will show 80,000 long positions and 80,000 short positions.

Once trades are reconciled, the clearinghouse substitutes itself as the opposite party to every person who has an open position. In other words, generally speaking, the clearinghouse functions as "the seller to every buyer and the buyer to every seller."[1] In effect, a clearinghouse facilitates the financial integrity of the market by guaranteeing to each clearing member that other clearing members can make good on their obligations.

The clearinghouse provides futures traders with substantial protection against defaults on futures contracts, but not complete protection. As discussed in detail in Chapter 10, the guarantee of the clearinghouse is limited to assuring each clearing member of the performance of other clearing members. The clearinghouse makes no guarantee directly to customers, be they customers of a clearing member or of any other broker.

Nevertheless, the intermediary function of the clearinghouse removes the need to deal with one's original counterpart when liquidating a transaction. This distinguishes a futures contract from a forward contract or other over-the-counter transaction, which can only be unwound with one's original counterpart. The intermediary function facilitates liquidity in the marketplace because a trader need not rely on the good faith of any particular opposite party to get out of a position.

FOREIGN CONTRACTS

The London International Financial Futures Exchange (LIFFE, pronounced "life") introduced a futures contract in 1984 based on the Financial Times Stock Exchange 100 Index (FTSE-100 or "Footsie") and the London Stock Exchange lists options on that index. The

---

[1]"A Party to Every Trade," brochure published by Board of Trade Clearing Corp.

FTSE-100 Index is a capitalization-weighted index of most of the largest 100 companies listed on the London Stock Exchange. This index, which was under 500 as recently as 1979, had tripled in value by late 1985. Figure 3–1 depicts the sharp rise in the Footsie futures between mid-1984 and late 1985.

Since the FTSE-100 Index is well over 1000, a futures quotation reflects a FTSE-100 Index value divided by 10. The value of a full index point is £250. The minimum price fluctuation is .05 (5 basis points) worth £12.50. As with domestic contracts, the delivery months are March, June, September, and December. Average daily volume was about 500 contracts and open interest approximately 3,000 contracts in late 1985.

The Hong Kong Futures Exchange began trading futures based on the Hang Seng index in early 1986. Although that index was first published in 1969, its base value of 100 is measured as of July 31, 1964. This index is exceptionally volatile and has swung between 747 and 1692 between January 1984 and July 1985.

The Hang Seng Index is a capitalization-weighted arithmetic average of 33 stocks in four sectors. Once dominated by property companies, the industry groups in the Hang Seng Index now break down as follows: commerce and industry, fourteen stocks (29 percent weight); finance, four stocks (28 percent); utilities, six stocks (22 percent); and property companies, nine stocks (21 percent). The Hong Kong and Shanghai Bank alone composes 17 percent of the index. Other major stocks are the Hang Seng Bank, Hutchinson Whampoa, China Light & Power, Hong Kong Electric Holdings, Hong Kong Land, and Swire Pacific.

The contract is similar to American contracts in that it expires quarterly in March, June, September, and December. The index multiplier is HK$50 times the level of the indexes. Thus, a contract traded at 1500 is worth HK$75,000 (or $10,000 at an exchange rate of 7.5 Hong Kong dollars to one U.S. dollar). The contract has been designed to trade at minimum ticks of a full point on the Hang Seng Index.

There has been some preliminary inquiry to the HKFE about trading NYSE Composite Index futures in Hong Kong.

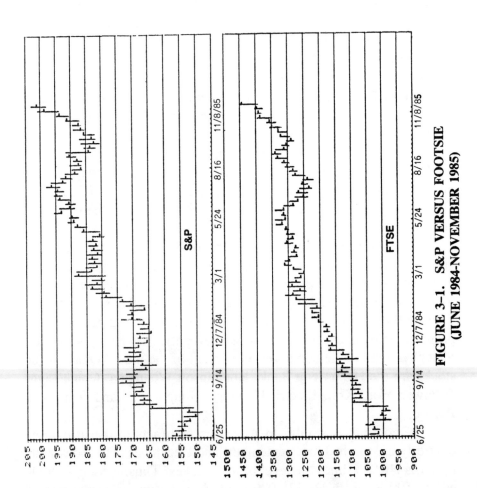

FIGURE 3–1. S&P VERSUS FOOTSIE
(JUNE 1984-NOVEMBER 1985)

In February 1983, the Sydney Futures Exchange introduced a futures contract based on the Australian All-Ordinaries Index. Futures volume currently runs about 2,000 contracts per day. The All-Ordinaries Index is a capitalization-weighted arithmetic average of all shares listed on Australian stock exchanges. It is estimated that one firm, Broken Hill Proprietary (BHP), accounts for approximately 10–12 percent of the value of this index and about a dozen companies account for 50 percent of its value. These companies are primarily natural resource, energy, and banking firms.

This futures contract is valued at A$100 times the value of the index. Thus, when the futures contract pierced the 1000 barrier, it had a value of A$100,000 (or approximately U.S. $70,000 at an exchange rate of 1.42 Australian dollars per U.S. dollar).

Both the Sydney Futures Exchange and the Sydney Stock Exchange list options relating to the All-Ordinaries Index.

The Toronto Futures Exchange has introduced a futures contract on the TSE 300 Composite Index, an arithmetic capitalization-weighted index that reflects 14 different Canadian industry groups. The futures contract is valued at C$10 times the level of the index. At a recent level of 2600, the contract was worth C$26,000 (or U.S. $19,500 at an exchange rate of C$1 = U.S. $.75). The contract has yet to experience much trading volume. Toronto has had somewhat more success with a unique product in which an investor can buy a contract on a spot index that expires daily.

The futures exchange in Singapore has also announced plans to develop a futures contract based upon a local index.

CHAPTER 4

Opening an Individual Account

Now that you have a basic idea of what stock index futures contracts are and how they work, you need to understand the practicalities of how to select a broker and place an order. But before you focus too heavily on market subtleties, it is critical that you know yourself.

DISCIPLINE—A PREREQUISITE

People who lack discipline in their personal financial affairs are inviting disaster in playing the futures markets. If you are someone who always accepts a double-or-nothing bet or who must always change just one more $100 bill in a casino, I would recommend that you not speculate in stock index futures, no matter what your broker says.

When I visit a casino, I view it as $10 worth of entertainment. I know the odds are against me, and I do not expect to win. When my $10 is gone, I am gone. If you decide you get $200 worth of entertainment out of a casino, fine, but if you are the sort who winds up spending $500 when you planned to spend $200, stay away from stock index futures contracts. If you know that you have a tendency to overspend, but just cannot stay away from the market, buy options instead.

Discipline is a beguiling notion, but most professional traders rate it as the single most important attribute of a trader. The most significant aspect of discipline is a willingness to get out of losing positions, that is, to acknowledge that you are $100 or $1,000 poorer and to take your lumps without hesitation when need be.

A second aspect of discipline involves keeping the size of your position well within what is affordable. I have watched people be right about the market for five days in a row. On the following Monday they got too confident and bought ten contracts instead of just one. The first day they are wrong is the last day they play. With stock index futures, you can bat over .800 and still be bounced from the big leagues overnight. Conversely, a disciplined trader can bat under .500 and still reap handsome profits by cutting losses quickly and capitalizing on proportionately large gains.

FINDING A BROKER

Just as bad pitching can hurt a team with good batting, a bad broker can make you wish you never stepped up to the plate. Finding a stock index broker is not quite as simple as finding a stock broker because the pool of legally qualified futures brokers is smaller than the pool of stock brokers.

In searching for a broker, you might begin by asking your stock broker if the firm can handle your stock index futures orders. If not, your broker may be able to recommend a commodity broker. Alternatively, you can respond to brokers' advertisements on the commodities page of a newspaper until you find the right one.

A broker must be registered with the CFTC as a futures commission merchant (FCM) or an introducing broker in order to do business with customers in stock index futures. An FCM is the commodity world's version of a stock broker who executes customer orders, carries customer accounts, and handles customer money. An introducing broker is generally an individual or small firm qualified to handle customer orders, but not qualified to handle any customer money or carry customer accounts. Thus, an introducing broker has an arrangement with an FCM under which the FCM does most of the paperwork on the account. Doing business with an introducing broker puts your assets in no added danger because he or she can hold none of your funds.

Since transaction costs can play a huge role in your ultimate success as a stock index trader, a basic consideration is whether to choose a discount broker or a full-service broker. Remember that, in some respects, you are dealing with a zero-sum game before commissions. Costs do vary substantially among stock index brokers.

Discount brokers generally charge between $15 and $35 per round turn while full-service brokers may charge anywhere from $50 to $100. "Round turn" refers to the cost of getting into and out of the market. The norm in the commodities world is to charge one commission for both sides of a trade. That commission is generally payable upon the closing or expiration of a position, but some firms do charge a half-turn commission when a position is established. The practice in the securities industry is to charge separate commissions for buying and selling stock.

There are certain disadvantages to using a discount broker. Few discount brokers provide market information or research material. A discount broker generally will not give you recommendations or color on market movements on a particular day. Moreover, because some discount brokerage firms have lean staffs, you might be placed on hold for a few seconds when you are anxious to place an order. Moreover, you might not deal with the same person each time you call a discount brokerage firm. Finally, some discount brokers may employ personnel who are not experienced and who may be less likely to execute your orders at favorable prices.

As the stock index futures brokerage business becomes more competitive, however, some discount brokerage firms are beginning to provide certain services associated with full-service firms. Thus, careful shopping may produce a broker who can save you money while providing adequate service.

TRANSACTION COSTS

Whatever broker you select, you will pay much lower transactions costs than you would with stocks themselves. A retail customer who uses a full-service broker to buy 2,000 shares of stock priced at

$40, and thus worth $80,000, will pay a commission of approximately 20 cents per share, or $400. If you want to sell that stock two weeks later, you will pay your broker another $400. In contrast, a full-service commodity broker would charge you a total of $100 or less to cover both the purchase and subsequent sale of a stock index futures contract worth $80,000 (e.g., one S&P contract priced at 160.00).

Many brokerage firms charge the same commission regardless or which stock index futures contract you buy. Thus, you will pay the same commission whether you buy an S&P contract worth $120,000, or a NYFE contract worth $70,000. Presumably, one reason many traders prefer to use the S&P contract rather than the similar NYFE contract is that they get more bang for their buck. In other words, if they are right on the market, they can recoup their commission costs in just a few minutes, whereas the smaller NYFE contract tends not to fluctuate quite so rapidly.

OPENING AN ACCOUNT

There is nothing complicated about opening an account, but you should take at least a minute to review the customer agreement and the forms attached to it. A customer agreement gives a broker the right to liquidate your open positions if you do not meet your margin calls promptly. In the world of futures trading, "promptly" does not means "the check is in the mail." It generally means wire transfer or a check transmitted by messenger. Thus, you should be aware that if the market is moving rapidly against you, and your funds do not arrive with your broker within a few hours after a margin call is made, a position that you wanted to keep open might be closed out.

Another portion of the customer agreement that you should scrutinize is the section specifying the time period within which you must protest and seek to correct any error in your customer statement. Typically, the customer agreement will provide that you must notify your broker of a possible error in just a few days, or your statement will be deemed conclusive. Whether that sort of provision will hold up in court or arbitration is another matter, but even if you prevail, it may be a long time before you get your money back.

You should also be aware of so-called "minimum balance" requirements. Some brokers will offer cheap commissions if you keep a minimum balance of several thousand dollars on deposit. If this figure is $5,000, the broker will be earning approximately $350–$500 in interest on your money in a year. I recall a situation in which a broker explained to me that his firm really did not make any money on a $5,000 minimum balance because most of the funds were posted to the clearinghouse to cover its margin requirements. Convincing as that may sound, it is not always true because most firms have customers with offsetting positions and need to post margin with the clearinghouse only to the extent that their own customer positions are not offsetting. When I suggested that the firm would, in fact, be earning $500 in interest on my money because most exchanges use such a net clearing system, the salesman let loose an abusive tirade and abruptly hung up. Not the type of fellow I'd want helping me out in the event of a clerical error on my account statement.

Once all of the preliminaries are taken care of, it is time to look over enough market data to decide on an initial strategy. Access to such data requires either a computer, a broker who uses a computer, or a willingness to tabulate information available in major newspapers.

Much information is available both in tables and in graphic form in many leading newspapers. Reprinted in Figure 4–1 are sample stock index quotes as they would appear in a newspaper, with explanations of how to read the table.

But a cautionary note. I have been surprised by the number of inaccuracies in data appearing in newspapers. I remember a day in January 1984 when the Dow was down 20 points, but rebounded in the final hour to close with a small gain. Although the NYSE Composite Index also rebounded, a newspaper graph depicted a closing at the day's low, thereby creating the misleading impression of a continued downtrend.

Similar numerical errors sometimes appear in the stock index price tables. Fortunately, much erroneous data looks suspicious to a trained eye. For instance, when the closing price is lower than the day's low, you can safely bet that the newspaper transposed two columns. But not all errors are that easy to spot. The safest approach is simply to confirm all data with a broker or on a computer.

	A	B	C	D	E	F	G	H	
S&P 500 INDEX (CME) 500 times index									
J ⌠ Sept	240.20	240.20	234.00	234.85	—	6.05	255.20	187.00	103,413	
⌊ Dec	241.60	241.85	235.60	236.50	—	6.10	257.25	209.50	5,766	
K ── Est vol 81,762;		vol Fri; 51,508;			open int 109,239,				−747.	
The index: High 240.25;		Low 235.23;			Close 236.01				−4.22	L
NYSE COMPOSITE INDEX (NYFE) 500 times index									
Sept	138.25	138.30	134.75	135.20	—	3.50	146.80	108.10	9,944	
Dec	139.05	139.20	135.70	136.10	—	3.60	148.00	121.10	1,181	
Mar87	140.05	140.05	136.70	137.05	—	3.65	148.95	136.50	421	
Est vol 11,260;		vol Fri 7,397			open int 11,593, +44.					M
The index: High 138.45		Low 135.82			Close 136.11				−2.30	
KC VALUE LINE INDEX (KC) 500 times index									
Sept	228.50	228.60	222.70	223.15	—	6.05	250.35	199.45	7,327	
Dec	229.40	229.40	224.00	224.10	—	6.00	250.10	224.00	350	
Mar87	225.00	225.60	225.00	225.20	—	6.00	231.20	225.00	107	
Est vol. 3,400;		vol Fri 2,047;			open int 7,784, +193.					
The index: High 230.58;		Low 227.23;			Close 227.38				−3.12	
MAJOR MKT INDEX (CBT) $250 times index									
Aug	344.80	345.50	337.70	338.95	—	7.05	366.20	333.75	3,079	
Sept	345.00	345.90	338.20	339.55	—	7.20	366.90	331.00	4,395	
Est vol 6,000;		vol Fri 4,090;			open int 7,479 +263.					
The index: High 346.19;		Low 337.66;			Close 338.67				−7.52	

A Opening price on previous day
B High price on previous day
C Low price on previous day
D Closing price on previous day
E Change from previous closing price
F High price over life of the contract
G Low price over life of the contract
H Open interest for each contract delivery month. Each unit represents one long
  position and one short position.
J Contract delivery months that are currently traded
K The number of contracts traded in the previous two trading sessions
L The index multiplier
M Total open interest and change from previous day

FIGURE 4–1. NEWSPAPER STOCK INDEX FUTURES TABLE

After you have formulated an initial strategy, you are ready to place your first order. At this point it is helpful to be familiar with the different types of orders that can be entered and the advantages and disadvantages of each.

MARKET ORDER

The most common type of order is a market order. With a market order, you simply tell your broker to immediately buy or sell a stated amount of futures contracts at the most advantageous price obtainable at the time the order is capable of execution. Just as in the case of stock, there is always a bid and an offer for a commodity futures contract, including a stock index future. If you call your broker to buy IBM stock, he might tell you that the last sale was 120 1/8 and that the market is now 120 bid, 120 1/4 offered.

If you are very eager to buy IBM and think there is a danger that you will miss the market if you do not act quickly, you should place a market order. Upon receiving such an order, a broker will go into the IBM trading crowd and make it known to a specialist that he has an order to buy. He may bid 120 1/8 for a while, but if it looks like the offer at 120 1/4 might soon vanish, he will probably buy IBM for your account at 120 1/4.

Execution of a market order in a futures trading ring differs only in that the broker informs the trading crowd in general, rather than a particular specialist, of the order. The broker does so by repeatedly shouting a particular price while standing in the trading ring, hoping that someone will respond and agree to be the opposite party in the transaction. For instance, if an S&P contract at the time is 180.00 bid and offered at 180.05, the broker will enter the trading ring and shout "even bid" (i.e., 180.00 bid) for a stated number of contracts. He may repeat himself three or four times in an effort to buy the contracts at your side of the market. However, if the broker senses that no one is willing to sell to him at the bid side of the market, he will "reach" and buy from someone who is selling for 180.05.

You should assume that when you give a market order to sell, it will be executed, or filled, at the bid side of the market. Sometimes a commodity broker will, in fact, get trades executed on your side of the market, but that should not be your expectation when you place a market order.

The advantage of a market order is clear—you are guaranteed that you will buy or sell at or near the time that you place your order. One cautionary note, however, is that prices can change, and change very quickly, so if your broker quotes the market over the telephone at "180.00 bid offered at .05," there is simply no guarantee that you will buy the contract for the price of 180.05 or better (i.e., cheaper). If the report comes back that you bought a contract for 180.10, that is not necessarily the broker's fault. In a sharp run-up, it is possible that the broker in fact did a very good job for you.

The disadvantage of a market order is equally apparent. You lose the competitive edge if you give a tick to the other player every time you come in or out of the market. In a zero-sum game, this puts you at a small initial disadvantage, which can be quickly overcome even with the smallest favorable price movement.

With that said, the issue is when and when not to use a market order. A market order is best used when you have a particularly strong feeling that the market may suddenly move and you do not want to miss out. It does not take long to sense that such moves occur with greater frequency at particular times of the day or after certain fundamental or technical developments. Increased familiarity with some of the intraday trading patterns discussed in Chapter 6 can help you decide when to place a market order. Of course, the disadvantage in opting not to use a market order arises when you suspect that there will be a three o'clock rally, but you instruct your broker to buy an S&P contract at a price not to exceed 179.95. Thereafter, the contract trades no lower than 180.00 before rallying, leaving your order unfilled. This can be a source of great frustration.

As I have learned the hard way, it can be even more frustrating to miss the market when you are trying to get out of a position. I've called my broker and been told the market is "75 bid, at 80," to which I've responded, "Okay, sell one at 75." A minute later, I'm told that I have no "confirm" (i.e., report of execution) and that the market is "65 bid, at 70." Finally I say in exasperation, "Just get me out at the market." If you've got a profit and you want to get out, then get out.

Remember that the quotes on your broker's screen may not be absolutely current. Usually, it doesn't matter, but in a fast market, it does. In such cases, a market order at least guarantees that you will get in or out.

Floor brokers estimate that more than 40 percent of the customer orders they receive are market orders.

LIMIT ORDER

A limit order is an order to buy or sell a stated amount of futures contracts at a specified price, or at a better price, if obtainable. The main function of a limit order is either to transact at a set target price or to preserve the edge in your favor, in other words, to increase your chances of buying on the bid side of the market or selling at the offered side of the market. An advantage of a limit order is that you may not be giving away ticks when you enter or exit the market. A disadvantage is that you may never get in or out of the market at the level you anticipated.

It is difficult to enter a limit order during periods when the market appears to be moving quickly in one direction. However, if you observe that the S&Ps have been trading in a narrow range of, for example, 220.20 to 220.60 during the previous hour or so, it might not hurt to put in a limit order to buy contracts at 220.25 or sell contracts at 220.55. If you see no reason for the market to break out of that trading range for a while, there is no sense in having your broker sell contracts when they get to the .30 level or to buy them when they have climbed to .50. Again, the risk is that if you place a limit order to buy at 220.25, the market may not trade at that level again before going to the moon.

Part of the calculus in determining whether or when to use limit orders depends upon the skill of your broker in getting executions at his side of the market. This tends to be a rather subjective evaluation.

Even so, some commodity trading firms use different brokers and attempt, through the use of computers, to quantify each broker's success in achieving favorable executions. After you gain some trading experience, it is also possible to evaluate how skilled your broker is at accurately sensing when the market is about to tick up or down.

STOP ORDER

Perhaps the single most important type of order is the stop order. A stop order is an order that becomes a market order when a transaction occurs at a price equal to (or less favorable than) the price you specify when you leave your order. A stop order is often called a "stop-loss order" because its function is to prevent you from being blindsided by an adverse market move that occurs before you have time to react. A stop order can thus be viewed as automatic trading discipline because it serves to liquidate an unprofitable position before losses mount to an unacceptable level. Whenever I buy or sell a contract and leave the trading floor, I always enter a stop order—without fail!

Figure 4–2 demonstrates both the protections and frustrations associated with stop orders. The chart depicts two trading channels in the S&P 500 March 1985 future during the week between February 5 and February 11. In this case, the trading channels were established by drawing in two sets of parallel lines—no magic to that. Three different stop orders have been entered at critical levels. In each case, the order was entered four ticks below a support line (i.e., a sell stop protecting a long position) or above a resistance line (i.e., a buy stop protecting a short position). This protects you against a single freak trade that may occur through that line, but is, of course, more expensive in two senses. First, and most obvious, you give up an additional $25 per tick as the market moves against you. Second, when the market pierces a strong support level, it may drop with a vengeance.

When a sudden drop occurs, there is no guarantee that your broker will be able to execute your order at the price you specified. Remember that a stop order becomes a market order and that if everybody

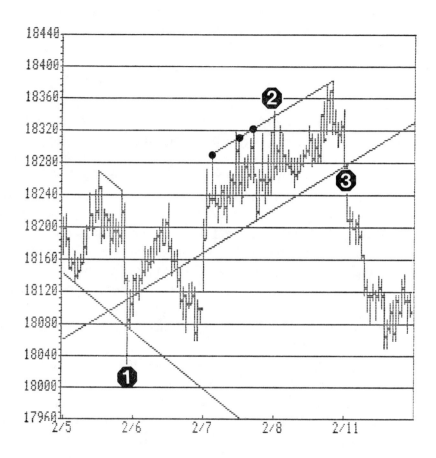

Source: Videcom Service, ADP Comtrend, Stamford, Conn.

FIGURE 4–2. PLACEMENT OF STOP-LOSS ORDERS

is panicking and trying to sell at once, your broker may be forced to liquidate your position at a price several ticks away from your stop-loss price. This happens because many traders with long positions place their orders right below so-called "support lines" and, correspondingly, many traders with short positions place their orders just above so-called "resistance lines." (These lines are discussed in Chapter 5.) A large number of stop orders can thus be triggered at once, and the market may move quickly when it reaches such a cluster of orders.

If you wish to assess your broker's skill in executing your stop order, you can request a time and sales report from the exchange involved. This report will list in sequence all trades that occurred at the time of day in question, showing how many trades were executed ahead of yours once the market reached the price on your stop order.

Order number 1 in Figure 4-2 is enough to make well-intentioned traders swear off stop orders. It depicts the classic whipsaw. The stop was set at 180.60, providing four ticks of protection. In this case, the market traded down to 180.30 in a matter of minutes, and then about-faced just as quickly. It traded as high as 182.30 (a $1,000 move) the next day before coming off again.

Professional traders realize that there are times when a brief selling panic can be induced by a few large stop orders, with no substantial change in the condition of the market. Thus, sometimes pit traders will wait for stop orders to cause the market to drop four or five ticks and then buy back into it at what they consider to be bargain prices. This so-called "running of stops" occurred with greater frequency in the early days of stock index futures trading.

Of course, you will feel the same frustration that I have felt when I have missed a good move because I was "stopped out." It is indeed possible to be whipsawed by stop orders, but if you suffer an occasional opportunity loss because you are left out of a market rally, this is better than the substantial real losses that could result from not using stop orders. Also, opportunity losses can be minimized by a broker promptly confirming execution of stop orders to you by telephone. This way you can get back into the market if you are still convinced that it will rise. Thus, even in the worst-case scenario depicted by order 1 in Figure 4-2, you could have re-entered the market once it climbed above 180.80.

Order 2 indicates that four ticks of protection isn't such a bad idea after all. In that instance the market moved two ticks outside of the trading channel, which was formed by connecting the three heavily marked points and ignoring the one fluke. Order 2 depicts a buy stop, which is used by someone who has a short position and wishes to be protected against an upside breakout. In this case, a trader who sold short at 183.20 could have made a $300 profit later in the day (by covering at 182.60), while risking only $200. Not a great trade, but not bad either. Alternatively, that trader could have kept re-entering his stop so that it would remain four ticks above that trading channel. Had he done so, he could have eventually covered the short position below 181.00 for a profit of over $1,000 per contract. As the end of Figure 4–2 shows, there was ample opportunity to cover in that area.

The importance of entering stop orders is illustrated by order 3. Remember, there is nothing hypothetical about this example. The market is not a charity, and it can punish those who do not enter stop orders.

In this example, someone holding a long position could have placed a stop at 182.60, and that is allowing for a reasonably ''wide'' trading channel, as the figure shows. That trader would have saved $1,000 per contract in the course of just two hours. He would have paid for this book 30 times over just by heeding this paragraph!

Given my warnings about a stop order becoming a market order when the stop is activated, let us analyze the market a bit more closely to see where the order would have been filled in a market that was dropping very quickly. The stop order placed at 182.60 on February 6 would have been triggered at 10:16 a.m., which was the first time the market traded 182.60. The market remained 60 bid through four trades in the next minutes, so you would have sold at 60 (or possibly even 65, which also traded at 10:17 a.m.). Within 15 minutes, the market was already down to 182.00. That is why stops are helpful.

When the market moves in your favor, it is fine to be euphoric, but do not leave it at that or the euphoria might be short-lived. Most traders would advise you to move your stop orders, raising them as the market trades higher when you are long and lowering them as the market trades lower when you are short. Do not let gains slip away.

For instance, in Figure 4–2, the trading channel that gave rise to order 3 had already formed at the opening of the prior trading day. A stop order four ticks below the same trading channel a day earlier would have been at approximately 181.95. Thus, by moving the stop higher, an additional $300 would have been saved.

Just so that there is absolutely no misunderstanding, I always tell my broker my position when I enter a stop order. That minimizes the chances that my order for a sell-stop will be improperly recorded as a buy-stop (or vice-versa).

A broker will properly assume that you intend any order, including a stop order, to be valid only for the day on which it is placed and null thereafter. So if you plan to keep a position on and want the continued protection of a stop order, you must specify that the order is "GTC" (good till canceled).

The stop orders in the above example are all geared to very short-term trading. Longer-term traders will often use wider stops. I know some very successful traders of S&P futures whose stops vary from approximately $2,000 to $6,000 per contract, i.e., four or eight or twelve full points. Many traders, myself included, have been whip-sawed out of good positions by stops that were too tight.

What happens if you enter your stop order, and the broker manages to forget to fill it? Under general principles of agency law, your broker would be legally obligated to make good any losses you incurred because of that omission. Disputes over unfilled stop orders generally revolve around questions of fact rather than questions of law. This is one reason that increasing numbers of commodity brokers tape record all incoming phone conversations.

The more difficult problem occurs when your stop order, or any order for that matter, is filled at a somewhat suspicious price. This question is addressed in some detail in Chapter 10.

OTHER TYPES OF ORDERS

Although market, limit, and stop orders are the most frequently placed, there are other types of orders.

When I cannot watch the market all day, but expect it to trade in a particular range, I will often enter an OCO order. That stands for "one cancels other." To take a simple hypothetical, if I expect an S&P contract to be locked in a trading range of 260 to 262, I might wait for the opportunity to buy two contracts at 260.10 and then instruct my broker as follows: "sell two 259.90 stop, sell two 261.90 MIT, OCO." This is not as strange as it sounds. I've told the broker to dump the contracts at whichever level occurs first. By specifying OCO, my broker understands that he should tear up the second order slip when the first order is executed. Such an order is useful when you feel that the market is likely to bounce back and forth within that trading range.

The reference to "MIT" in the OCO order illustrated above stands for "market if touched." Such an order is essentially the converse of a stop order. In the example, a market-if-touched order to sell was left because the market was expected to go no higher than 262. Such an order ensures that profits are taken when the market reaches what appears to be the most profitable point within a trading range. By contrast, a stop order to sell at 261.90 would typically be placed by a trader who is long at a higher price and who wishes to minimize losses rather than to maximize profits. An MIT order can also be used to initiate a position, but this is a risky approach unless your broker simultaneously takes a stop order to protect you from loss on any position which is initiated pursuant to an MIT order.

An MIT order to buy becomes a market order once the contract trades at or below a certain level. An MIT order to sell becomes a market order once the contract trades at or above a certain level. You would place an MIT order to buy when you expect the market to test a particular support line before rallying. In the above example, had you been short at 262, an MIT order to buy at 260.10 might be a prudent way to take a profit.

At the other end of the spectrum from a GTC order is a fill-or-kill order, also called an "immediate or cancel" order. A fill-or-kill order can be a market or limit order that is to be executed in whole or in part as soon as it is transmitted to the trading floor. It is possible to enter a fill-or-kill order to "buy five 160.10 limit" and wind up buying less than all five contracts. Any portion of a fill-or-kill order not immediately filled is treated as canceled.

Since the trading practices associated with the open outcry system used in a futures ring permit a counterpart to take only a portion of the contracts which you bid for or offer, an all-or-none order is not recognized in the commodity world.

Some traders use "at-the-open" or "at-the-close" orders. An at-the-open order can be either a market or limit order and is to be executed during the opening call, generally within the first minute of trading, or not at all. I personally feel that a customer who places a market order (or sometimes even a limit order) during the opening minute can be at a substantial disadvantage because openings can be wild and woolly at times. It can be tough to get a favorable execution until the dust settles.

An at-the-close order can only be a market order. It is to be executed at, or as near as practicable to, the close. The acceptance of an at-the-close order by a floor member does not make him responsible for an execution at the closing price. It is advisable to check with your broker to see if there is any time beyond which an order will not be accepted.

Certain other orders merit brief attention. A scale order is an order to buy or sell a fixed number of contracts gradually as the market moves in your favor. "Scaling in" refers to the practice of buying (or selling) several contracts and then waiting for the market to confirm your view before committing the balance of your capital. Using the example of an S&P contract locked in a trading range of 260 to 262, one might enter a scale order as follows: "Buy three at 260.10, buy two at 260.20, buy one at 260.30." On the sell side, you might instruct your broker to "sell three at 261.90, sell two at 261.80, sell one at 261.70."

The NYFE rulebook recognizes a stop limit order, which, as the name suggests, trigger a buy or sell order once trading take place at or through a given level, but imposes a limit on the price you are willing to pay to get out of the market. Such orders are not prudent in stock index futures trading because a rapidly fluctuating market may never return to the specified limit price.

Finally, one can enter a spread order to purchase a futures contract in one delivery month and to sell a contract in a different delivery month. Such a spread order will ensure simultaneous execution of both legs and may result in your broker getting a slightly better bid-ask spread on the transaction.

CHAPTER 5

Market Feel and Trading Psychology

Much ado has been made about traders going from rags to riches due to some uncanny "market feel." Market feel is not a type of ESP that some people are endowed with at birth. Some of Wall Street's most respected traders started out by losing sizable sums of money. Market feel comes from study of markets and trading. Just as a batter learns to take advantage of a pitcher's curve balls by stepping up and swinging until he is familiar with the pitcher's tricks, a trader learns to take advantage of the market's curve balls by stepping up and swinging until the market's tricks become familiar rather than intimidating. In either game, if you strike out too often, you try another sport.

Part of understanding the psychology of stock index futures is understanding the mindset of those who populate the trading pits and those who are major institutional or individual traders. Although stock index futures cannot be discussed in a vacuum excluding the stock market itself, my purpose here is not to summarize the vast accumulation of literature on stock market psychology into a few pithy sentences. Rather, it is to focus on key aspects of the psychology of the stock index futures market, and to note critical differences between stock market and futures market psychology.

It is important to be aware of certain contrasts between the psychology of the stock market and that of the stock index futures market. Remember that many of the players on the stock side are different people with different investment goals than those in the stock index futures market. On the whole, futures players have a shorter time horizon than do stock players—open interest for stock index futures contracts with less than six months to expiration amounts to over 97 percent of the total.

This difference in time horizon may be attributed to a variety of factors. For one, stock transaction costs are substantially higher, so a stock investor can't afford to change his mind several times in a day or week as a futures trader can. If a stockbroker encouraged the frequency of trading that is common in the futures market, he'd be in trouble for churning. Also, a tax incentive presently encourages holding stocks for at least six months. No comparable incentive affects futures trading.

Further, many stock investors are motivated by the desire to buy "value" in the form of underpriced stocks that are bound to provide a sound return, even if it takes time. In contrast, not all stock index futures traders care about value in the form of underpriced contracts. In fact, many speculators prefer to buy overpriced contracts believing that buying by smart money raises the prices and that there is little downside risk in buying overvalued contracts when it takes only seconds to get out of the market.

Strange, isn't it? One can argue that stock buyers and stock index futures buyers are purchasing essentially the same assets, and yet they often have diametrically opposite outlooks on intrinsic value.

Just as stock traders and futures traders can differ in their outlook, futures traders differ among themselves. In fact, I believe that most floor or "pit" traders have a substantially different approach to the market than position traders, who are attempting to capitalize on market trends of varying duration. Let us discuss each outlook in turn.

PIT TRADING PSYCHOLOGY

Most people are puzzled when I explain that many successful pit traders do not necessarily have any opinion on which direction the market is going. Others seem puzzled by the fact that a trader could be bidding a quarter one minute and offering at a half a minute later. Is it possible to quantify what makes these people operate the way they do?

Understanding the time horizon of someone in a commodity ring is one key to the psychology of pit trading. People who trade on the floor of an exchange tend to have an even shorter-term outlook than futures traders in general. A pit trader generally believes that it it not easy to predict what the market might be doing in two days or two weeks, but predicting what the market is likely to do in the next two *minutes* is less difficult. To make profits in the trading ring, that is essentially all one must do. For example, two ticks on the S&P futures contract can be loosely equated to a move of approximately 75 cents on the Dow. Thus, a trader who buys ten contracts and is right about that 75-cent move in the Dow can often pocket two ticks times ten contracts. That twenty-tick profit amounts to $500 in the bank for just a few minutes of work. The faster one can get in and out of a contract, the less time left for anxiety.

Better yet, a pit trader can make profits even without much ability to predict minute-to-minute fluctuations in the market. A pit trader is happiest when doing what is affectionately known as "scalping." Remember that in any market, there is always a bid and an ask price. For instance, if IBM's last trade was at 125, the stock might be 124 7/8 bid, offered at 125 1/8. Scalpers make money simply by buying contracts at the bid side of the market and selling them as quickly as possible at the offered side of the market (or selling first and quickly covering). For example, if one can buy ten NYFE contracts at 125.00 and sell them a minute later for a price of 125.05, one will make a profit of $250 for a minimal risk.

In the best of all worlds, both sides of the transaction will occur before the bid-ask fluctuates at all. Even on days when the Dow has climbed more than 30 points, I have made money by selling short and then covering quickly. Since such activity is such a desirable way to make money, it is not always easy to buy at the bid side or sell at the offered side, even in the trading ring.

There are a number of pit traders who usually have no strong conviction about the overall direction of the market. Such a trader knows that the percentages favor him over time if he manages to buy on the bid side of the market and sell at the offered side. Most people who trade in this manner are content to make a one or two tick profit on each contract. This gives some indication as to why a number of people are generally willing to sell even when the market is rising.

I am aware of only one academic study of market-makers in stock index futures.[1] In it, Silber concluded that scalper earnings are positively related to the size of the bid-asked spread and negatively related to the length of time a position is held. He found that the two successful scalpers studied tended to lose money on trades held open for longer than three minutes. He also found that these two scalpers held trading positions open for an average time of less than two minutes.

Nevertheless, many pit traders do have opinions on the market, at least over a very short time span. Such traders may be very sensitive to retail order flow, to developments in other markets or in key stocks, or to how many buyers step up as the market reaches an important technical support line. These pit traders also often surmise what a major institution or trader is doing just by watching the broker that usually handles those orders. Some pit traders act on their sense of the degree to which other traders in the pit are net long or net short, much as a card counter surmises who holds what at a blackjack table. Thus, many people in the trading crowd not only have opinions on the market, but these opinions are often based upon their perception of what others are doing.

POSITION TRADING PSYCHOLOGY

Even the shrewdest position traders know that they are not always right and that the market can confound. People on one of the finest block-trading desks in the world, at Salomon Brothers, used to drill into my mind the phrase, "You can't outguess the market."

Examples abound in which some economic news changes the fundamental outlook for the market, but the market moves in precisely the opposite direction to what a rational observer would expect. IBM

[1]W. Silber, "Market-Maker Behavior in an Auction Market: An Analysis of Scalpers in Futures Markets," *The Journal of Finance* XXXIX, no. 4 (September 1984).

releases lower first-quarter earnings for 1985, and the stock climbs over a point. The consumer price index for March 1985 suggests a possible resurgence in inflation, and the Dow climbs 12 points. On March 19, 1985, gold soars $35, and the dollar tumbles, suggesting shaken confidence in our financial system, but the Dow soars 21 points. On April 11, 1985, it was announced that March retail sales dropped by the largest monthly amount in seven years. Still, the Dow rose eight points in the first fifteen minutes of trading and closed up 3.75. Of course, everybody has an explanation in retrospect. But if we dissect these examples, we may be able to discern a few axioms about how traders react.

A first axiom is that traders have a tendency to focus on the short-term impact of economic news, even if the same news might have opposite effects over time. Consider a weakening dollar. Over the long haul, a weakening dollar should be inflationary. But in the short-term, it means higher profits for blue-chip stocks with a high volume of international sales.

Or consider the announcement that retail sales for March 1985 were off by a surprising 1.9 percent. I bet most traders couldn't have told you if that 1.9 percent drop was relative to February 1985 or March 1984. But no matter—they knew it was a bad number, a possible harbinger of a weakening economy. So do stocks go down? Perversely, they go up. In this instance, the likely explanation is that the prospect of a weaker economy suggested a possible reduction in demand for credit, spurring a bond rally. On that day, lower interest rates were the short-term effect while a weakened economy was a more distant concern.

A second axiom is that traders often think more in relative than rational terms. This "relative" outlook on the assessment of market developments occurs in two steps: (1) measuring the divergence between a piece of actual news relative to expected news ("news divergence") and (2) assessing the initial reaction of the market relative to its expected reaction given a particular degree of news divergence (or "news surprise" in the event of a completely unexpected bulletin). This relative way of thinking is perhaps best conveyed by illustration.

Consider April 23, 1985. Inflation had been under control at about
4 percent per year. The March CPI number, due out before the opening, was expected by most forecasters to be up .3 or .4 percent. The
actual number was up .5 percent (5.8 percent annualized), a bad number in both absolute and relative terms. So a trader would expect the
market to open lower, which in fact it did. But how much lower? Is
the market acting more or less resiliently than it has on other occasions when digesting other bad news of similar importance? Traders
are very sensitive to the market's initial reaction as compared to what
that reaction might have been.

On April 23, the Dow was down only about two points in the early minutes. (See Figure 5–1.) The S&P and NYSE futures traded down
to their support lines on a ninety-day bar chart but did not penetrate
those lines, so the market did not open as low as it might have in the
circumstances. This makes any trader, and especially one with a short
position, think that if a knockout punch couldn't push the market more
than two points lower, nothing would. The market now feels strong.
Time for short sellers to cover their positions or place pretty tight stop-
loss orders. It is also a good opportunity for traders with no position
to "buy low." The Dow gradually climbed throughout the morning.
In early afternoon, General Motors announced earnings 34 percent
below last year's and also below the estimates of Wall Street analysts.
More bad news, both in an absolute and a relative sense. The Dow
went down. But more significantly, it only backed up four points and
did not reach the morning's lows.

So what does a trader think? If this bearish news doesn't make
the market go down, nothing will—at least today. A trader who has
no position is unlikely to sell into a market that, rationally or not, refuses
to go down. The trader realizes that he or she is too small to fight
the trend single-handedly. Perhaps more important, traders with short
positions begin to worry and to cover their positions at small losses.
That kind of thinking was probably responsible for a big part of the
final-hour surge. Although I was not especially optimistic about the
upside prospects for the market that day, I was one of the buyers just
to cover my short position and prevent any significant losses. Once
those panics get going, there is no telling whether the Dow might move

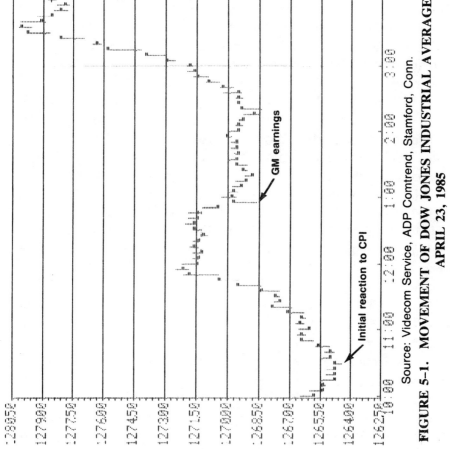

FIGURE 5-1. MOVEMENT OF DOW JONES INDUSTRIAL AVERAGE APRIL 23, 1985

Source: Videcom Service, ADP Comtrend, Stamford, Conn.

ten, twenty, or thirty points in final-hour trading. On that day, it closed twelve points higher, seven of which were added in the final hour.

Why is the notion of relativity so important? Investors react to information as it develops, using any clue or estimate that might give them an edge. Those reactions move prices. If the actual news varies from the consensus expectation already built into prices, the market reaction can seem puzzling to an observer who just sees news that is bad in absolute terms, rather than news that is not as bad as expected. Perhaps this psychology gave rise to the old market adage, "Buy the rumor, sell the news."

The same psychology is illustrated by the movement of IBM stock when IBM released lower first-quarter earnings for 1985. The stock climbed over a point, but IBM shares had fallen several points earlier in the week because investors had expected the worst. The old adage worked in reverse for bad news: "Sell the rumor and buy the news."

Having established the "why" of relativity, let us turn to the next logical question—the "how" of relativity. How is relativity measured? Relative to what? To answer this question, we must elaborate on the previously mentioned support lines and their counterparts, resistance lines.

A support line is a threshold level formed by a line, which can be horizontal or diagonal, connecting several market bottoms. That line is expected to support the market in its next downtrend. If the market falls below the line, technically oriented traders view it as a sign of weakness. In the ensuing loss of confidence, many traders will sell short, or at least postpone any buying.

Conversely, a resistance line is a threshold level formed by a line connecting several market tops. It is expected to restrain the market the next time it uptrends and approaches that line. If the market goes above the line, traders view this penetration as a sign of strength. Analysis of the market's ability or inability to hold or pierce various support and resistance lines is part of what is generally called "technical analysis."

The general idea behind technical analysis is that the consensus reaction to all fundamental factors is reflected in the movement of share prices and the index as a whole, and, consequently, in the patterns formed by those movements. Thus, a look at the patterns on an index price chart will provide a view of the market's reaction to general economic conditions and fundamental news developments in the context of certain benchmarks.

People seek benchmarks in any field of endeavor. As in physics, everything is relative in the stock market. People need some measuring rod to quantify information and to compare actual results to expectations. People seek patterns in order to find some rhyme or reason and predictive value in quantified information. For instance, if Racehorse A has run four consecutive miles in 1:40 and 3/5, 2/5, 1/5, and 1:40, one might bet on it in a race against a horse that has consistently run 1:40. Or, if a presidential candidate gets 10, 15, and 20 percent of the vote in the first three primaries, he or she will experience a substantial increase in contributions and press coverage as pundits become bullish on his or her prospects. That game of searching for patterns is essentially the same in the stock market.

Technical analysis is rooted in the human desire to find threshold levels to serve as yardsticks of sufficient or insufficient progress in some endeavor. For instance, a salesperson who sells $1 million worth of widgets wins a prize vacation in the Caribbean for the strong performance, while the colleague who sold $999,000 is deemed weak and stays home because he did not surpass the threshold. Judging by retailers' pricing strategies, consumers must look very differently at items marked $10.00 and $9.95. So it is in the market. A close on the Dow of 1000 may be judged as strong, while 995 may be considered weak. In absolute terms, there is very little difference between the two levels. But in psychological terms, there may be a world of difference.

Use of support and resistance lines as thresholds is by no means foolproof. But if the market has bounced off a well-defined support line twice before, enough technically oriented traders are likely to decide that it is a good bet to do so again. It is a good bet for two reasons.

The first reason is that if a pronounced bull or bear trend emerges from a particular market pattern often enough, certain traders will anticipate that same trend whenever they see that particular market pattern and buy or sell accordingly. Perhaps there is a Pavlovian aspect to such responses.

Pavlov demonstrated that when it garners a reward for responding in a certain manner to a pattern, even the simplest brain is likely to continue to respond in the same manner whenever the same pattern is presented. Stretching Pavlov's work just a bit, one could hypothesize that if a trader is rewarded frequently enough for responding in a certain manner to a technical pattern that resembles something he has seen before, he is likely to continue responding in the same manner. Thus if a trader has profited 75 percent of the time he bought at a triple bottom, he is likely to buy the next time such a formation presents itself.

I still remember—clear as a bell—the technical patterns that preceded my biggest wins. Those patterns almost get imprinted on one's mind. And I know what I'm going to do the next time I see one of those patterns.

The second reason thresholds are good bets is that support and resistance lines permit a position trader to refine his risk-reward calculus to provide substantial profits if the guess is correct and minimal losses if it is wrong. In other words, if he buys on a support line and the market continues to decline, he takes a small loss by selling as soon as, or shortly after, that support line is cracked. If he is right and captures a new trend, he can let his profits run. A successful trader, knowing that he has an opportunity to make an appreciable profit before a pattern runs its course, will maintain his position until the price reverses by a predetermined amount, causing a sell alarm to go off.

Consider this proposition. Pick a coin of your choice. Now suppose I offer you a game in which you pay me a $25 commission each time you flip the coin. In return, I will pay you $25 every time the coin comes up heads if you will pay me $25 for every time the coin lands on tails. Hopefully, you would decide that this is not a very good game.

But suppose I offer you $100 for every heads if you will pay me $25 (plus a $25 commission) for every tails. Suddenly this is not a bad proposition. Similarly, technical analysis may give you only slightly better than fifty-fifty odds of determining whether the next market move will be up or down. But if you buy on a technical support line and the market disappoints you by going down, you get out as soon as that support line is pierced, thus minimizing your loss. But if you are right, you may have caught a new short-term trend and can make a profit that exceeds the amount of the expected loss should the market move adversely.

I try to outguess the short-term market when a good risk-reward situation presents itself. For instance, if the market is near a technical support line and stocks look cheap relative to bonds, I'll buy. But when I make a bet that I have a fifty-fifty chance of winning, I try to make the expected payoff higher than the expected loss. That's why I use technical analysis. If the market trades in a range from 1240 to 1300 and I buy at 1241, my upside is as much as 60 points and my downside risk is only about five points to the point at which my stop gets hit. Once in a while, the upside is far greater than that 60 points because the market breaks out from its trading range.

Many people use support and resistance levels not only to try to ascertain market direction, but also to establish good odds on each trade. As with anything else in the market, support and resistance levels are not foolproof, and even the most skilled traders are sometimes whipsawed.

Even so, most successful traders are cognizant of the value of technical analysis. But, you may say, technical analysis is nothing more than Wall Street's answer to voodoo. That may well be true, but it is also true that many well-capitalized market participants rely heavily on technical analysis. In fact, since so many traders from the commodity markets, where technical analysis has long been an integral part of trading, have been joining the ranks of stock index futures traders, technical analysis is likely to become even more influential in the stock index futures market. Moreover, because so much capital is committed on the basis of technical analysis, the self-fulfilling prophecy aspect of technical analysis, in and of itself, makes it worthwhile to be aware of the technical indicators. Indeed, in today's market, there are computers programmed to buy or sell in response to technical signals.

The more cynical may wish to consider the trader who one day referred to technical analysis as a lot of hocus-pocus. After a time, he revised his view to, "Still a lot of hocus-pocus, but a darn good way to make money." As another highly successful trader put it, "The difference between a fundamentalist and a technician is about three years and three million dollars."

Most traders do not rely on technical analysis in a vacuum. Many employ fundamental analysis on both a macro scale (e.g., fiscal and monetary policy, reaction to government economic statistics, etc.) and on a micro scale (e.g., corporate profits and other indicators of the health of individual companies). Surely, a fundamental news development can move the prices of stock index futures. But on many occasions, prices will move quickly to the nearest salient technical support or resistance line. Then, the focus shifts to the notion of relativity as traders conduct a tug-of-war over whether the news is sufficiently important to move prices through that technical level.

TRENDS AND THE HERD INSTINCT

Few traders will volunteer to be the first to attempt to buck an established market trend. Usually, the goal among speculators is to let someone else be the guinea pig—but to be the first follower once it looks like the pig is getting fat. Out of such motives arises what is fondly known as the herd instinct. Traders recognize the potency of the herd instinct. In fact, in addition to their trading badges, many floor traders wear another badge with the saying, "The trend is your friend."

If all of these traders are just followers, who are the leaders? What precipitates a new trend? Part of the answer is that the leaders are the ones that play with big money. Someone who buys 500 contracts will move the market. If I buy ten, I won't move the market. Since I can't be a leader, my goal is to be a good follower.

But there are a lot of well-capitalized investors. What makes the leaders act rather than react? A news development might do it. The enormous rally in the autumn of 1985 began the day after the Group of Five agreed on joint efforts to reduce the value of the dollar. Drops in the dollar have often led traders to buy stocks on the theory that U.S.-based multinationals will increase their foreign-source incomes and that U.S. firms will find it easier to export. Developments in another market might do it. Stocks might rise when bond prices rise because stocks offer a relatively more attractive return whenever bond yields fall. Since both the dollar and bonds open for trading in the United States before the stock market does, it pays to know how these markets have opened.

Some market leaders act out of a conviction that a trend has gone too far and that the market is overpriced or underpriced by an amount sufficient to induce them to establish a new long-term position. In fact, such ''value-oriented'' investors may begin to accumulate a position before the trend is moving their way on the theory that they cannot predict tops or bottoms and that they can ''ride out'' a short-term movement given the prospects for sizable long-term rewards.

But most market leaders also remain acutely aware of technically important levels in the market. Their trading is often based on the same risk-reward strategy discussed earlier. For instance, in early April 1985, the 180.00 level was recognized as a key technical support line on the S&P 500 June contract. On April 8, the market acted poorly all day and for the final half-hour, danced around above and below that number, closing just above it. The market tested that level one more time the next day and stopped four ticks above the previous day's low. That was enough to convince traders that the market was feeling stronger.

The mood changed and the market headed north, with the S&P contract closing at 182.75 for the week. A trader who bought at 180.00 made slightly over $1,300 per contract. Had that trader been wrong, he probably would have been out at about 179.65 (as Figure 5–2 indicates, a tick below the low on April 8) for a loss of $175 per contract. This example is not to suggest that one should rely on technical analysis in a vacuum. This mood change was undoubtedly encouraged by a two-point rally in the bond market during the same period. Nevertheless, the technicals presented a risk-reward scenario that was good in the short-term and even better over the next few weeks as the market climbed sharply in April and May.

Trading psychology is such that if the contract had fallen under the 180 level, briefly pierced it again without being able to maintain it, and traded one to three ticks lower in the final fifteen minutes, some traders would have gone home short and been prepared to cover at perhaps 180.20. The difference between 179.90 and 180.10 in terms

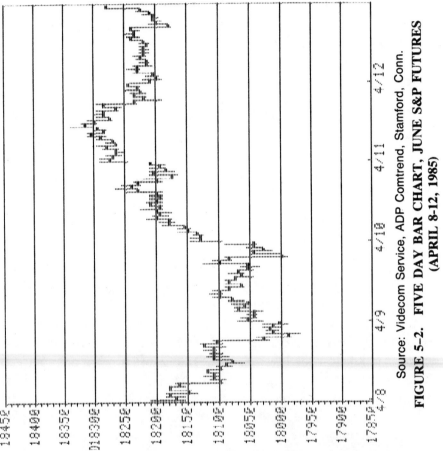

Source: Videcom Service, ADP Comtrend, Stamford, Conn.

FIGURE 5-2. FIVE DAY BAR CHART, JUNE S&P FUTURES (APRIL 8-12, 1985)

of movement of the Dow is minuscule, about 1.50 points, but to a trader it could be the difference between the market acting weak or providing some encouragement.

Well-capitalized traders are not always prepared to lead. They too can be followers who just exacerbate herd tendencies. In fact, the role of trend-setter may shift among well-capitalized traders from one major move to the next.

If investors who buy on technical signals or major news developments are often the initial trend-setters, who are the first players to get on the bandwagon? It appears that fear can be a stronger emotion than greed. Often the early stages of a new trend are spurred by liquidation of positions rather than net new commitments. A Salomon Brothers study of the start of the bull market in 1982 concluded that:

> The price stampede was probably most influenced by traders who were buying stock to cover short sales.... There was also a great deal of short covering in the futures market.... The number of contracts available for trading was reduced by 13.9 percent in the first four weeks of the rally. This probably resulted from short traders covering their contracts, thus causing the number of contracts available to shrink, as contracts were canceled. From this, two results ensued: first, the buying drove prices up; and second, fewer contracts were available for subsequent trading.[2]

As Table 5–1 indicates, open interest experienced its sharpest drop of the month during the week between August 13 and 20, when the rally began.

TABLE 5–1.

Week	Value Line	S&P 500	NYSE	Total	Percent Change from Previous
August 6, 1982	5,740	15,861	6,466	28,067	
August 13, 1982	5,753	15,413	5,886	27,052	– 3.6
August 20, 1982	6,388	14,169	4,531	25,088	– 7.3
August 27, 1982	5,520	13,749	4,883	24,152	– 3.7
September 3, 1982	6,059	14,359	5,333	25,751	+ 6.6

[2]Laszlo Birinyi, Jr. and Susan L. Field, *Rally on Wall Street—An Anatomy of the Stock Market Performance August 13–October 11, 1982* (New York: Salomon Brothers Inc, November 1982).

RECORD YOUR MARKET OBSERVATIONS

An appreciation of past market performance under similar conditions can be developed and refined by keeping a trading diary. A trading diary should serve two functions. One is to review actual trades and to write down what you did right and, more importantly, what you did wrong and do not care to repeat. The other is to record your thoughts as to what the market is likely to do in the near term. A month or so later, flip back and read your thoughts and begin to develop a sense of what you anticipated well and what you overlooked. Keeping such a diary is not necessarily an exercise for idlers. Some of those with legendary market feel have kept diaries. The great Jesse Livermore spent an hour each morning recording his thoughts in writing before trading began.[3]

Let me share one entry from my market diary with you. I selected this passage before I had any idea whether my prognostication would prove right or wrong because it relates to an interesting juncture in the market. I was particularly interested in two very long-term charts which are reproduced in Figure 5-3.

> January 11, 1985. Good time to sell. Who knows when breakout from this triangle will occur but I say it's down. Economic fundamentals are lousy. Budget woes will resurface after State of Union—traders will say Reagan proposals are not enough. Bank woes, farmers' troubles will also cause selling at major resistance levels. Declining commodity prices make me uneasy. The smart money already fears a crash. A reversal in the dollar would be inflationary, would drain money from our capital markets, and would be terrible psychologically on investor confidence. High premiums on futures contracts tell me there isn't enough pessimism to fuel major advance. There is no follow-through whenever we have a sharp advance in a day. Lower high every time. Individual stocks are getting badly punished if earnings don't meet expectations—sign of latent nervousness. Market is paying a high multiple for

[3]Livermore, one of the greatest speculators of all time, provided superb trading insights in a book written using a pseudonym. See Edwin L. LeFevre, *Reminiscences of a Stock Operator* (Fraser Publishing, 1980 reprint).

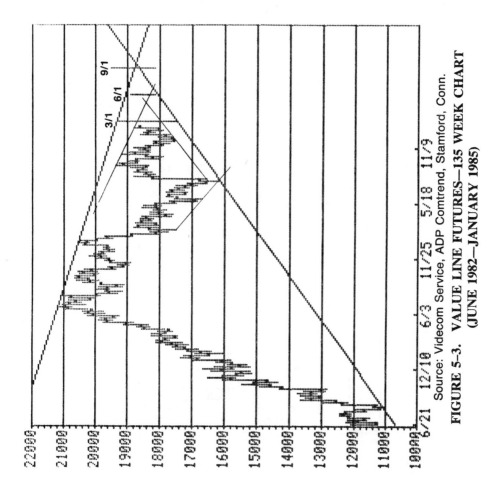

Source: Videcom Service, ADP Comtrend, Stamford, Conn.

FIGURE 5–3. VALUE LINE FUTURES—135 WEEK CHART (JUNE 1982—JANUARY 1985)

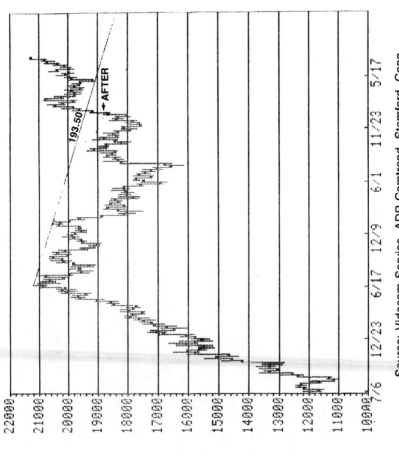

Source: Videcom Service, ADP Comtrend, Stamford, Conn.

FIGURE 5–3. (Continued) VALUE LINE FUTURES—THE AFTERMATH

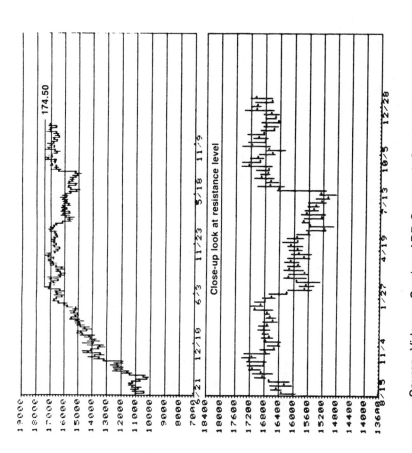

Source: Videcom Service, ADP Comtrend, Stamford, Conn.

FIGURE 5–3. (Concluded) 135 WEEK CHART OF S&P 500 FUTURES SHOWING MAJOR RESISTANCE LEVEL

earnings when net present valued at these rates, just like 1929. Stocks are already strong relative to bonds, so a push from that market is unlikely. Bond futures can't maintain 72.00 anyway. Pretty soon too much money growth will be considered inflationary and too little will be recessionary. If AFC team wins Super Bowl, would make a great short. Traders would freak, just like last year. Otherwise, just sell the resistance level. Cover if S&P finally breaks above 174.50 or Value Line tops 193.50; start appreciating "countervailing influences."

Of course, every entry in a trading diary need not be quite this exhaustive, but it is good to organize your thoughts. Part of organizing your thoughts involves consideration of appropriate action in the event that your analysis is wrong, or just plain untimely.

Since the market was at such an interesting juncture when that diary entry was written, I put aside my legal work for the three days following the Super Bowl in order to trade full time. When I walked in Monday morning, one of the brokers remarked to me that I had picked a bad day to trade because it was a bank holiday. It turned out to be an expensive holiday for the banks, and could have been an expensive day for me as well had I not been mindful of a critical attribute of a trader—flexibility. Even though I was dead wrong on which way the market would go when the Value Line future reached 193.50 and the S&P future reached 174.50, I watched my net worth go up one percent a day for the next three days. I started appreciating "countervailing influences" as soon as the S&P traded through 174.50 and the Value Line traded through 193.50. At that point, I decided that my fundamental analysis could wait and that it was time to adhere to a more basic principle: "Don't spit in the wind."

The Dow went up 36 points (or 3 percent) to 1264 that Monday and didn't stop until it flirted with 1300. The newspapers reported that the market rose because investors became more optimistic on the general economic outlook. Three percent more optimistic in just one day, I presume. As one superb trader said to me, "News is a lagging indicator."

Consider this as an alternative hypothesis. Traders, who can be superstitious, were not about to sell short immediately following an

NFC victory in the Super Bowl, because of a spurious correlation between wins by teams from the original NFL and bull markets for the ensuing year. In fact, enough traders were outright buyers to push the market through the triangle-shaped technical pattern that had formed during the previous 135 weeks (see Figure 5-3). Once that breakout had occurred, the buying just fed on itself as traders became bullish simply because this crucial resistance level had been pierced.

A trading diary is a good way to crystallize an opinion, and to develop an early warning signal to recognize when you are wrong. A trading diary is also a good place to record your own observations about market psychology and your personal trading rules.

A HEAD START—HEED OTHERS' TRADING RULES

Elementary as it may seem, successful traders heed certain market axioms and develop certain trading rules that they have disciplined themselves to follow regardless of ephemeral countervailing emotions. A trading diary is a good place to record your own observations and rules as you develop them. For instance, one of my early observations was that, rational or not, there seems to be a natural human tendency to want to buy and a natural desire to hope that the price goes up. Similarly, the uninitiated often tend to be reluctant to sell something they don't own.

In contrast, an old axiom is that in extreme market conditions, the stock market is capable of dropping more rapidly than it will rise. Many veterans observe that there will always be an offer in a trading crowd, but there will not always be a bid. There seems to be a somewhat irrational tendency to be more afraid of being caught long in a market crash than being caught short in a rally—even though the ground is a lot closer than the sky.

A digression on a few other axioms and rules, some of which are more widely accepted than others, will, I hope, enhance your understanding of the psychology of the trading ring and hence of the dynamics of stock index futures trading.

The notion that the "trend is your friend" suggests that momentum tends to push a market in one direction, in both the short and long term, with some backing and filling along the way. As was discussed above, very few successful traders will maintain large positions that go against momentum.

Be Flexible

Particularly if you intend to be a day trader, try not to be habitually bullish or bearish. In other words, don't be a one-way trader. Be flexible. When I was brand new at the stock index game, I was perhaps too habitually bullish. It worked in the practice trading sessions. True enough, we were in the midst of one of the great bull markets, but my second and third weeks of trading happened to be a time when there was a pause in the bull market and in fact a slight retreat from recent highs. I learned rather quickly not to be habitually bullish.

When you have capital to spend on a number of contracts and you wish to establish a position, it often makes sense to buy in at different levels, all the while watching to ensure that the market is confirming your instincts. If the market is not confirming, do not add to a losing position. Add only to good trades. This is just another way of avoiding the mistake of thinking the market eventually has to start moving in your favor. What seems low can always go lower—examples of that axiom would fill another book. It makes sense to withhold any buy orders until downward momentum has stopped.

Cut Your Losses

Some traders maintain that one should never let a profit become a loss. However, I believe that a more sensible approach is to set a firm loss limit when you are initiating a trade and don't start hoping against hope that the market will come back if it reaches your loss limit. Some people lose money simply because they freeze. Others lose because they have some idea in the back of their mind that one particular news factor will move the market in their direction. But other forces they're not yet aware of may in fact be having a more powerful impact.

If there are to be such surprises in the market, they're always more welcome when they don't cost you any money.

Some investors are reluctant to take a small loss in the stock market because doing so means paying a big commission. One advantage of trading in futures is that commissions are generally low relative to stock market commissions and will be paid anyway, upon either the liquidation or expiration of the contract. Thus, commissions should not even be a factor in a decision to take a small loss.

Let Your Profits Run

Cutting losses has always been easy for me, maybe because I'm fairly disciplined, maybe because I get scared easily, or maybe because I've had lots of practice. For me, the tougher maxim has been, "Let your profits run." It has a beguiling ring to it. If you just remember that rule, you get rich. The problem is that it's terribly easy to become giddy, especially when you've had three losing trades in a row and will do anything for a little bit of positive reinforcement.

In my mind, there are two keys to letting your profits run. Rule number one is to avoid deciding to sell based simply upon your percentage return. A classic error is made by people who dump a position any time their profits reach some magic number like $1,000 or double what they put down, even when there is only good news in the market and no major technical resistance level close at hand. Move your stop higher, but don't get giddy and sell for no rational reason.

Rule number two—unwind a profitable position gradually. Even if you master the art of dispassionate trading, you cannot always count on perfectly following the elusive cardinal rule to "buy low, sell high". It is twice as difficult to be absolutely right on both your buy decision and your sell decision on any single contract. Your odds can be greatly improved, however, by selling only part of a position when things seem too good to be true. In fact, that strategy helps to explain who the sellers are on days when the Dow is up 30 points. In other words, if you are long and the market begins to move in your favor, do not maintain your entire position on the assumption that this is the beginning of the Dow's move to 3000. Sell gradually. Unlike the sliding scale commissions on stock trades, your transaction costs are the same when you sell a stock index futures position in several pieces. If you are a small trader who has just scraped together the $6,000 for one S&P contract, try buying two MMI or NYFE contracts.

Conversely, *do not sell all of a profitable position, no matter how strongly you feel that the market has run its course and cannot move any further in your favor.* For instance, at the opening on November 11, 1985, I had a very profitable long position after a period in which the Dow had risen 120 points in the preceding two months. I thought the run was over and was tempted to close out my position at a good profit. As much as I had to clench my teeth to stick to the let-your-profits-run rule, I decided to sell only a quarter of my position on the opening and just leave the rest alone. The Dow closed 27 points higher that day. So much for making money on gut feel.

Do not ever trade more contracts than you can prudently handle. One nice thing about the market is that tomorrow will always bring another opportunity to make money. There is no need to bet the ranch on the strong feeling you have today. Statistically speaking, you have a 50 percent chance of being wrong. Moreover, trading beyond your financial capability is a clear invitation to panic, and panic is the surest way to lose money in the market.

You must not bet the ranch because no matter how strong your feeling is, you cannot think of everything. And if you do, the market won't. I was still in law school when the news of the Iraq-Iran war and attacks on oil supplies broke. At the time, I owned options on Mobil with a week or two to expiration. I decided to hold on because the market would conclude that war means supply interruptions, ergo higher crude prices, ergo inventory profits, ergo higher stock prices. I thought of everything. Nothing happened for three days, so I threw up my hands and sold my options. Then the market thought of everything. The episode reminded me of an adage that I have heard attributed to Joe Kennedy: "I know a lot of guys who have lost their shirt by being right too soon."

Avoid Overtrading

Another maxim is that one should not overtrade. Overtrading has several disadvantages. First, brokerage commissions are likely to eat into whatever profits you make. Second, one who is overly anxious to trade often jumps into the market too quickly, without seeking the best possible execution price. Third, overtrading is sometimes the result of panicking rather than sticking to a well-thought-out strategy where you had perceived good odds. Of course, loss of nerve can be a bad thing, but too much hope can be even worse.

Information and Conclusions

A watershed occurs when a trader is no longer spooked by the market opinions of others, particularly those of successful traders. The world's most experienced traders can be wrong just as often as you, and they may change their mind about the market thirty seconds after talking to you, anyway. I am always interested in someone else's opinion because I might have overlooked one factor or another. Accepting *information* from other people is fine because it is free of charge, but accepting *conclusions* from other people may not be free. It is an invitation to trading losses. A trader should be able to weigh and evaluate information from any source, but should be able to draw his own conclusions.

The more subtle rules of the market are not absorbed overnight, nor are they constant. Just as a magician's secret won't earn him much money once it is out, neither will a trader's secret be worth much once it is common knowledge. So when a certain pattern or rule becomes too well-known, some players decide that it is time to try to change the trick. When too many journalists start writing about the Super Bowl theory (i.e., the market finishes the year higher after a victory by a team from the original NFL), it will be time to sell short after an NFC win. So far, the whole notion seems too preposterous for a respectable news story, which is fine by me.

Nevertheless, certain technical (see Chapter 6) and seasonal (e.g., tax selling, influx of IRA money) patterns are repeated time and time again. Some professional traders do well simply by recognizing the development of recurring patterns in a market.

Regardless of how much you study stock index futures, it is inevitable that you will learn from your own mistakes. There is a difference, though, between being wrong and making a mistake. Being wrong is part of the game and a necessary cost. Mistakes are unnecessary costs. They can be minimized.

It pays (or at least saves) to practice before you play, always bearing in mind that any simulation is not quite the real thing. The first time I paper-traded, I "made" $7,000 in a week and became quite worried over how to spend my 50 years of retirement. Then I went to a trader's night at the New York Futures Exchange and "made" $700. Retirement was pushed back a bit. On my first day of actual trading, I was lucky to make $50. Suddenly, it seemed clear that retirement by age 30 was not in the works.

But there are valuable lessons in paper trading. Paper trading forces one to focus on market patterns and nuances.

One of the most important observations about the futures markets is that the first 100 trades are the hardest. No matter what you learn by reading this book or any other material, your education will not be complete until you've actually gone and done it—and yes, made a few mistakes. If a book on the stock market costs me $25, I may or may not remember a particular point. If a bad trade costs me $100, that particular type of mistake is less likely to be repeated. The learning curve can be frustrating. It took two years before I had my first $1,000 day. It took another two weeks before I had my second.

The market is influenced by an infinite number of variables. There is no magic formula, no perfect multiple regression that will unfailingly predict the market's direction. The guy with the foolpoof black box does not last, or you would have read about him by now.

Although no one has discovered El Dorado, certain people do emerge as consistent winners in the stock market or in stock index futures. They are outnumbered by the losers. Fifty years ago, those consistent winners may have been the people who had the most access to inside information. There is virtually no inside information today that will dramatically move the market as a whole. Yet, there are still consistent winners in the stock index futures market.

Can market feel really help if stock prices do indeed take a random walk? Consider a migrating goose. It may appear to be on some sort of random flight, but an ornithologist who has studied the behavior of geese in similar circumstances might feel comfortable making certain predictions about a particular bird. If it's October, that goose is flying south even if it temporarily changes direction for no apparent reason. Maybe it tends to fly at between 1,200 and 1,800 feet. It usually follows a leader. The more you study, the more you know. Even the experts won't know precisely where the thing will land. But to them, its flight does not appear quite so random.

So what is this mysterious market feel? Developing a sense of how the market has reacted to similar circumstances. Assessing what is different about this situation. Talking to people because they might have thought of something you overlooked. Assimilating new information quickly. Adhering to trading rules to keep losses small enough to minimize the amount netted out from the gains. Playing the percentages. Maybe a facility for numbers. Maybe a dash of luck.

CHAPTER 6

Movement of Index Futures Prices

Although some promotional material may suggest otherwise, there is no foolproof trading strategy. Buying low and selling high is not quite as easy as some brokers make it sound. One should be wary of schematic diagrams that do not represent actual market conditions, such as a diagram that instructs you to "scale in" as the market is climbing and to sell your position at the top, just as the market is about to descend. This would be a highly successful trading strategy if the market always traded in a pattern resembling a perfect schematic pattern, but it doesn't. That is why the diagrams in this book depict actual market conditions in stock index futures. The study of actual market patterns is the best way to begin to understand the market's ebb and flow.

Stock index traders study these market patterns through technical analysis. Although stock index futures traders employ many forms of technical analysis, the number is generally less than that used by traditional stock market analysts. Most technical analysis of futures prices is more properly termed chart analysis. Analysis of charts to find support and resistance levels is perhaps the most important aspect of technical analysis.

Stock market technicians have, however, developed numerous other tools for analyzing stock prices. For example, stock market analysts may focus on the ratio of new highs to new lows, volume figures, ratio of block trades done on upticks or downticks, advance/decline figures, and the like. Most of these forms of technical

101

analysis cannot generally be applied directly to the analysis of historical futures prices.

In fact, some of these traditional indicators have become distorted by the influence of stock index futures. Consider the ratio of specialist short positions to public short positions, long considered a useful contrarian's indicator. Today, many public shorts are in fact positions hedged with stock index futures rather than the outright short positions they appear to be. My own view is that some of the traditional tools for technical analysis of the stock market are outmoded by the pervasive influence of stock index futures.

Additionally, the pace of trading today makes many traditional technical indicators outdated by the time they are available. By the time one calculates odd-lot statistics, new highs, or the moving average of an advance/decline line, the market might have moved radically. I think of August 6, 1985, when the Dow dropped almost 23 points in a few hours. Chartists began selling immediately when an important support line was broken in mid-day. Since charts can be updated continuously, traders were able to react to them instantly. Technicians who relied on more traditional types of technical information were unable to react until the Dow had dropped a full two percent. By then, it was too late to react because the market did almost nothing for the rest of the month.

As stock index traders commit ever-increasing sums of money to the equity arena, it is probable that the chart analysis they employ will become more influential than other forms of technical analysis. As noted, chart analysis is already a pervasive aspect of trading traditional commodities and may grow in influence as more commodity traders join the ranks of stock index futures traders. In fact, if you accept my premise, which unfolds through this book, that stock index futures lead the stock market, the importance of chart analysis cannot be emphasized too strongly.

Stock index traders use numerous forms of chart analysis. Some adhere rather rigidly to one or two types of charts, and some of these traders are successful, but most successful traders know the limitations of their particular system and realize that no system is foolproof. They become familiar with as many charts as possible so that they have an idea of the most salient support and resistance levels that market participants are watching.

Chart analysis can be divided into three useful segments: intraday trading, short-term trading of a week or so, and longer-term position trading. Let us examine worthwhile ways of scrutinizing patterns for each of these periods.

DAY TRADING

The stock market tends to move in fits and starts. Even on a day when the market finishes much higher, there will be periods of retreat or at least loss of momentum during the day. One might analogize to a football game that is 60 minutes long, but in which the decisive touchdown drive in a 7–0 game might take only three minutes. Similarly, a decisive move in the stock market may take place in a single half-hour of the trading day. A basic understanding of day trading is important to the investor with a long-term time horizon because a sensitivity for intraday moves will help one to pick opportune points of market entry and exit both in index futures and in the underlying stocks themselves.

For example, on December 21, 1982, the Dow closed some 25 points above the previous day's close (Figure 6–1). Yet, at 3:00 p.m., the Dow was up only two points. The chart shows how much the market is capable of moving in just a short period of time. A stock player might have profited handsomely by timing market entry on the basis of the rally in the stock index futures.

But let us turn to a brief discussion of day-trading strategy in the futures themselves, using the NYFE contract as our example. As is often the case, the futures started ticking up several minutes before the stock market itself began to rally. While the magnitude of the rally was not predictable, a quick- thinking trader would have seen 78.85 or thereabouts as a good opportunity to buy a contract. This is true for two reasons. First, the intraday support line in Figure 6–1 provided support right at the 78.80 level. Second, one would know that the Dow had just tested and held at the psychologically important 1000 level.

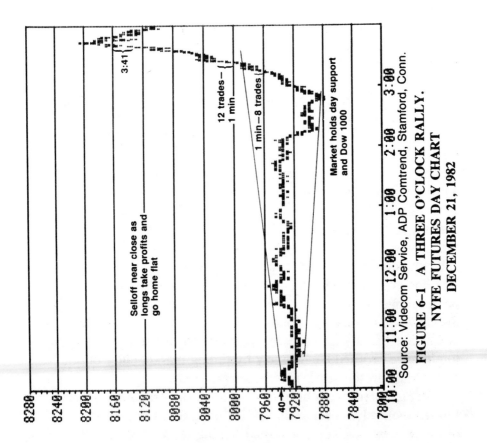

FIGURE 6-1 A THREE O'CLOCK RALLY.
NYFE FUTURES DAY CHART
DECEMBER 21, 1982

Source: Videcom Service, ADP Comtrend, Stamford, Conn.

No need to pay 85 (i.e., 78.85) for a contract while it is still on the way down. Why not wait until it has bounced off 80 and has traded 85 again? Even if we now have to pay 90 or even 95 for a contract, it now seems more likely that this support level will hold, so we buy.

Now all we have to do is hold the contract. Would we have sold it at a price of 82.00 for a profit of $1,550 for less than an hour of work? Not likely. Had we the good fortune to hold it that far, would it not have been reasonable to think that the Dow might have had another 30 point rise? Maybe so.

However, once backtracking of a predetermined amount has occurred (perhaps six ticks at these price levels), it is time to get out. The market trades as high as 82.10, and now we see it begin to backtrack rather radically from an equally sharp rise. After it has moved six ticks against us, we sell at the 81.70 level. Needless to say, we are now quite concerned that the market is particularly volatile and that this is no time for undue pause or hesitation. We just want out while we can protect a satisfactory profit and are happy to hit the first bid we see. Let's say we don't get out until 81.65. Had we purchased at the 78.90 level, this would leave us with a healthy enough profit of $1,375 per contract.

All well and good in theory, you say, but if a support line could give us such a strong buy signal why could a resistance line not offer an equally strong sell signal? The chart shows that we can draw a line indicating a possible sell at the 79.90 level. Indeed, this would not have been unreasonable at all and on the chart you notice some congestion at exactly that level. Had we bought at the 78.90 level and sold at the 79.90 level we would still have a tidy profit of $500 per contract, but that is where some traders make their first mistake. They become complacent about their profit and they're ready to take it home. Once the market has broken out of our resistance level in a convincing enough fashion, why not buy back in? This is often the thing to do as long as we are cognizant of the next resistance level.

Knowing the next resistance level is important because the Dow does not go up 25 points every day in a three o'clock rally. In fact, sometimes an afternoon rally appears to be gathering steam, only to be cut off at the half-way mark. That, too, is often explainable by a

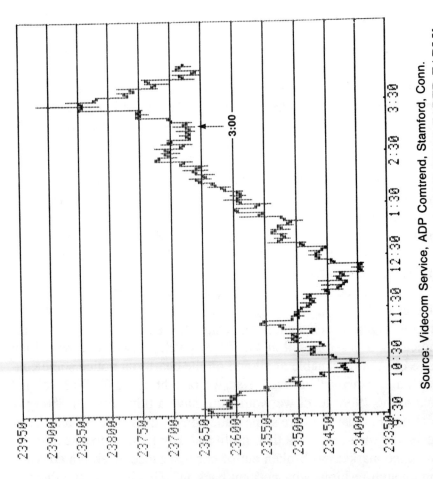

Source: Videcom Service, ADP Comtrend, Stamford, Conn.

FIGURE 6-2. A THREE O'CLOCK RALLY THAT FADED EARLY.

resistance level that many traders had in mind. Sometimes, a rally that goes too far too fast early in the day gets cut off at around 3:00 p.m. (see Figure 6.2).

You might say that in hindsight, technical analysis can explain anything and that something in the news on that December 21 must have caused the market to rally the way it did. Well, the two lead stories that day involved rejection by the United States of a proposal by Andropov on arms control and a rejection by King Hussein of a U.S. initiative on peace in the Middle East. Not exactly the sort of news that would make a market rally 25 points. Maybe there is something to this technical voodoo after all.

This is not to say that news developments are unimportant to traders during the course of the day. To be a successful trader, it is important to know what news announcements are expected during the day, but that is not enough. One must also be aware of the particular times of the day such news will be forthcoming. For instance, the government often releases key economic data early in the morning. On days when a quarterly GNP number is released at 8:30 a.m., it is a good idea to find out about it by 9:30.

Bond trading between 9:00 and 9:30 a.m. may affect the opening of the stock index futures. The time bracket from 11:30 to 12:00 is considered the Fed period. That is almost always the time of the day when the Federal Reserve System will take whatever action it intends to take on a particular day to affect interest rates. Lunchtime had been generally quiet until recently, but now seems to be a time for occasional surprise movements. The noon hour can be a major turning point if the likes of Fed Chairman Paul Volcker or Salomon Brothers chief economist Henry Kaufman makes an important luncheon speech. Many traders also look at 1:30 p.m. as a time when many portfolio managers have concluded their lunchtime discussions about the likely direction of the market and have returned to their desks to trade accordingly. Also, auctions of new Treasury securities generally take place at 1:00. A three o'clock rally often is fueled by traders who have sold stock short and rush to buy it back before the close if a market rise appears imminent. Thus, a so-called short-covering rally can have a snowball effect of sorts, a classic example of fear suddenly dominating greed. The bond futures market closes at 3:00 (Eastern Time), and many traders watch the last few minutes for any sudden moves. In sum, there are times of the day at which the market is often, but by no means always, more active and more volatile than at other times. Understanding market nuances at a particular time of day can lead to profit.

Trading on Wednesday, July 25, 1984, illustrates that point rather well, so let us digress and examine that day in some detail (see Figure 6–3). The mood was bearish. The Dow had barely managed to close above 1100 on the previous Friday. At the opening on Monday, it dropped ten points in the first half-hour and by Tuesday's close was at 1086.57. The bulls on that Wednesday were definitely the contrarians, but those few bulls were either luck or acutely conscious of the influence of the government bond market, in general, and the Federal Reserve, in particular, on stock prices.

Here is what they knew. Treasury bonds had already rallied from their lows over the course of the past three weeks and were hitting a technical resistance level. Many pundits expected bonds to retreat, but what a surprising number of investors did not realize until too late (though it was public information) was that Fed Chairman Paul Volcker was testifying that morning before the Senate Banking Committee. Any favorable pronouncement would probably push the bond futures through their resistance level. Indeed, bond futures staged a sharp rally of over a point as word of Chairman Volcker's remarks filtered out. Then, as Figure 6–3 shows, index futures retreated as the bond futures consolidated slightly. Note that the NYFE September futures contract traded as low as 86.45 at 11:20.

That price seems pretty arbitrary, but here is what the smart money was thinking. As Figure 6–3 shows, 86.40 was a rather obvious support level for the NYFE futures. Similarly, the corresponding 1080 level on the Dow was a technical triple bottom, as Figure 6–3 illustrates. Moreover, these trades at 86.45 occurred when the Fed period was only a few minutes away. Since the bond rally Volcker's testimony had produced was already very large, most market participants expected the Fed to do reverse repos (also known as matched sales). If the Fed is going to take any action, it generally does so by approximately 11:46. So how do traders divine market direction at such a juncture?

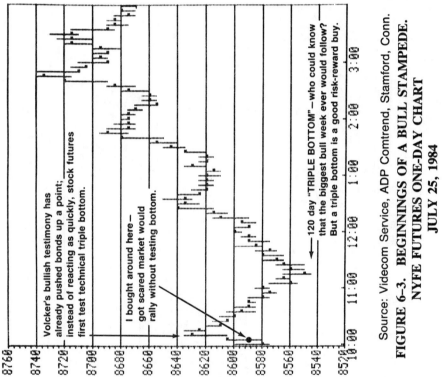

Source: Videcom Service, ADP Comtrend, Stamford, Conn.

FIGURE 6–3. BEGINNINGS OF A BULL STAMPEDE.
NYFE FUTURES ONE-DAY CHART
JULY 25, 1984

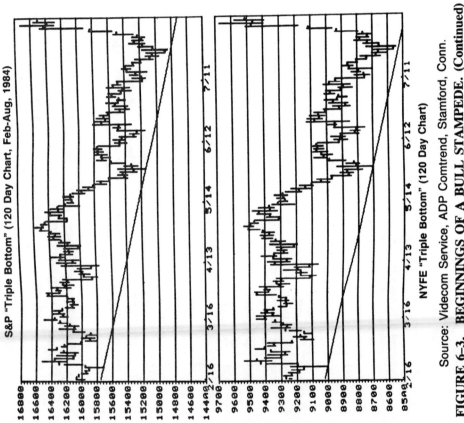

FIGURE 6–3. BEGINNINGS OF A BULL STAMPEDE. (Continued)

Source: Videcom Service, ADP Comtrend, Stamford, Conn.

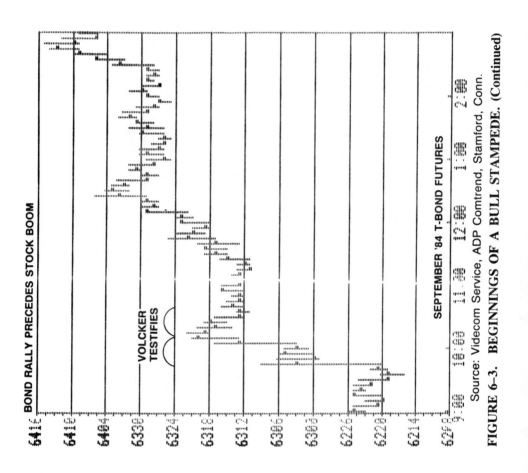

FIGURE 6–3. BEGINNINGS OF A BULL STAMPEDE. (Continued)

Source: Videcom Service, ADP Comtrend, Stamford, Conn.

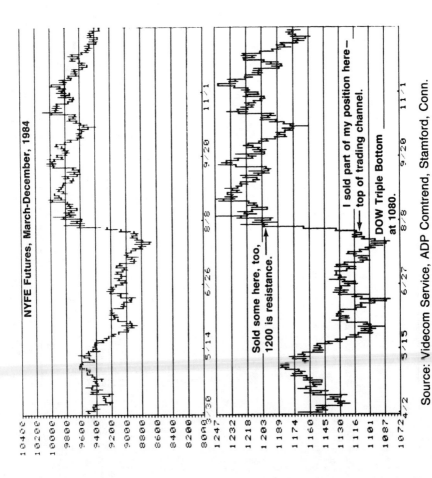

Source: Videocom Service, ADP Comtrend, Stamford, Conn.

FIGURE 6-3. BEGINNINGS OF A BULL STAMPEDE. (Concluded)

An understanding of the purpose and impact of reverse repos is helpful and worth a brief digression. The Fed can try to slow a bond market rally, maintaining market stability, by causing bond dealers to have less cash available to buy bonds. The Fed accomplishes this through a reverse repo, which involves selling securities to dealers in return for cash payment in a transaction to be unwound one day or a few days later when the dust has settled. This draining of funds from dealers will usually put a damper on their buying spree. But the market has learned to anticipate these efforts to fine-tune the market. If the Fed does not move at all when the market expects it to move or does not move aggressively enough to drain funds sufficient to cause a retreat in bond prices, the psychological reaction may push prices even higher.

Bond prices did in fact continue higher on that July 25. On that day, traders were prepared for another major price boost in bonds if by 11:46, the Fed had not announced matched sales. At 11:42, the Fed did announce matched sales. Stock index futures immediately retreated slightly and awaited the reaction from the bond market. Bonds held steady for about two minutes even though traders had expected them to fall. That sign of firmness produced another half-point rally in Treasury bond futures and a corresponding rally in the stock index futures market.

Still more bond-related news would influence the course of trading before the end of the day. At 1:30 p.m., the Treasury would auction two-year notes. Any additional rally would have to await the outcome of that auction. It did not go especially well, causing bond futures to retreat to test the 63.24 level. That line had been widely viewed as a resistance level, but became a support level once it was pierced. Once it became apparent that this level would hold, bond and stock index futures rallied to their highs of the day. Bond futures ran into a bit of profit-taking shortly before their 3:00 p.m. close. On cue, the stock index futures also retreated.

July 25 presents a good example of how readily obtainable knowledge of pending developments from the Fed and Treasury can give you an edge. A concomitant knowledge of support and resistance levels cannot guarantee profits, but it can make your edge that much sharper. That day also illustrates that there is not necessarily any magic to anticipating market movements.

Okay. Did our illustrious author do as well with foresight as with hindsight? In this case, yes. Since I spent the day in the options crowd, I bought out-of-the-money call options just after the opening and held them. Would I have lost a lot of money had the day's news been different? Not if the day's news had caused the NYFE September futures to trade below 85.20. I don't know if I would have been short, but I certainly wouldn't have stayed long. Had Volcker's pronouncements been negative, the Dow could have gone straight to 1050. The likelihood of such a drop would have increased substantially had the market penetrated a trading range that had held for five months.

While this example was intended to illustrate day-trading psychology, it comes with a noteworthy postscript. Slightly over a week later, on August 3, the Dow broke through the 1180 barrier. In just a few days, it soared to the 1270 level. My profits on the liquidation of those call options ranged from two to thirteen times my initial investment, and I blew it. They traded over twenty times what I paid for them.

That is only one example of the importance of understanding the impact of events or market nuances on a particular day's trading. There are others. For example, even after a sharp sell-off, stock indexes frequently tend to close on upticks. Is this because hope springs eternal in the human breast? Maybe, but it might also be attributed in part to the fact that by pushing up the value of their inventory, stock exchange specialists can reduce their overnight carrying costs. Understanding such nuances gives certain traders an edge.

The minutes before expiration of the December 1983 contract provide another example of such an edge. The index, which had been at 95.08 at 3:30, was dropping steadily and in fact hit 94.99 at 3:59 with expiration only a minute away. But at 3:59, savvy traders were screaming "even bid" (i.e., 95.00 bid) for the futures, banking on that end-of-the-day uptick. Sure enough, at 4:01 the index flashed 95.03. So the "fools" who bought contracts that would be "worthless" in a minute actually made a $15 per contract profit. These traders knew that the closing price of the index would not be official for a few minutes after the close because the tape generally is a bit late right at the close.

It is almost suicidal to trade without an idea of what support and resistance levels other traders are focusing on. While it is important to be disciplined enough to take a loss, an arbitrary loss allowance on a particular contract can be counterproductive. This may put you in the position of liquidating your contracts one or two ticks from a key support or resistance area that the market tests before moving in the direction you had originally anticipated. A good broker should be able to keep you abreast of critical intraday support and resistance areas.

Sometimes a particularly apparent intraday support or resistance line develops as the trading day continues. You or your broker should be aware of developments of this sort. The bar chart depicting NYFE trading on September 26, 1984 provides an example of an intraday resistance line. I entered the trading ring at 2:51 on that day. I was not aware of many readily apparent long-term support or resistance levels. The most salient pattern on this day seemed to be on the intraday chart. The Dow was up about nine points, and a lot of traders seemed bullish and already long. But as shown in Figure 6–4, each rally attempt in the afternoon was a bit weaker. Except for an occasional blip, the New York December contract had established 98.60 as an interim support level. The corresponding level in Chicago was 170.80. I said to one of my buddies, "If it trades double (meaning .55), watch out." Shortly after 3:00, trading was fairly relaxed, but we were moving toward another test of the 98.60 level after one more failure to pierce 98.85. Finally, the December S&P contract flashed 170.75 and then traded 170.70 about five seconds later. The New York market lagged Chicago by about fifteen seconds, but as soon as a 55 bid was hit, trading erupted to a frenzy. The last doubters were convinced when 98.50 traded only seconds later. By the time you could dial seven digits and endure four rings, the NYFE market was 98.35 bid (thinly) and 98.40 offered (heavily). Thus, people who were bullish but had placed stop-loss orders saved about $75 per contract as compared to bulls who did not place stop orders but sold a minute or two after the break.

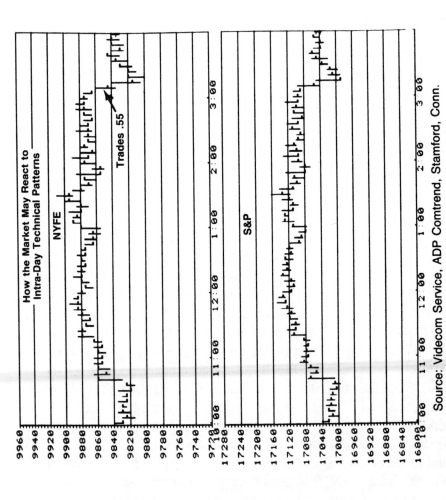

Source: Videcom Service, ADP Comtrend, Stamford, Conn.

FIGURE 6–4. INTRA-DAY PATTERNS: "IF IT TRADES DOUBLE, WATCH OUT".

INTRADAY: THE TAIL WAGS THE DOG

Several charts follow that illustrate one of the most fascinating aspects of stock index futures—that over very short time periods within a trading day, *they consistently appear to lead and predict the direction of the stock market itself.* The chart from January 12, 1983 (see Figure 6–5) is particularly instructive and is also memorable for me because it was the second week of my trading career, and it was exciting to be on the floor when the Dow went through 1100. I have marked particular times of that day as illustrative of my tail-wags-the-dog viewpoint.

At 10:15, the S&P futures reached an interim high of approximately 148.40. As the 10:15 marker on the S&P 500 Index chart shows, the index was still climbing. It took until 10:30 to reach its interim high of approximately 146.25.

The 10:42 marker shows the day's low on the futures. The cash index reached its low fifteen minutes later at 10:57. Then, the marker at 12:08 shows that another interim high on the futures occurred while the cash index was still climbing. The cash index began to level off about twelve minutes later. The next interim top at 1:04 still shows the futures leading, but also shows that the futures contract sometimes tests new levels and backs away before the cash market reacts.

The 2:28 marker identifies the day's high point for the futures. This time, the cash market moved up 20 cents (about 1 1/2 Dow points) to its high within about five minutes, by which time the futures had already retreated by approximately 80 cents (equivalent to about six points on the Dow).

The final marker, at 3:32, marks one of the more memorable of the occasional "head fakes" in the stock index futures market. The futures market made one last try at holding the 1100 level, but failed. Interestingly, the stock market itself did not follow the futures at all in that period.

The skeptic might believe that I have picked only the good example and thrown in the one exceptional head fake for credibility. On the contrary, this pattern has persisted in the ensuing years. I have also included a chart of the S&P futures and cash from November 11,

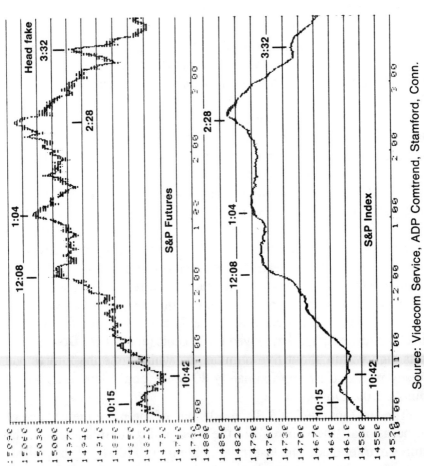

Source: Videcom Service, ADP Comtrend, Stamford, Conn.

FIGURE 6–5. TAIL WAGS DOG - I: JANUARY 12, 1983

1985 when the Dow climbed nearly 28 points (see Figure 6–6). The first marker depicts the beginning of the futures rally at about 2:40 p.m. The second marker indicates when the cash index began to climb—a full 34 minutes later. In those minutes, the futures had climbed another 1.20 points (equivalent to about 8 1/2 points on the Dow).

For a number of reasons, stock index futures do, in fact, anticipate the direction of the stock market. Some of these reasons are a bit amorphous and others quite concrete.

Let's begin with the more amorphous. Suppose you are a casual observer of football games, tuning in for perhaps an hour a week. You have a vague sense of which teams are good and which are bad, but that's about it. On the other hand, there may be a hundred odds-makers in your area that, as a group, have a pretty good record in calling games or putting down the line on a particular game. They devote more of their attention to following certain details. They know that the right tackle has a bad knee or that the fullback has a record of running poorly on muddy surfaces. They are going to pay particularly close attention when their own money is on the line.

In that sense, stock index futures traders are not much different. They, too, watch any number of factors that could affect the outcome on a particular market day. While any individual one of them might be wrong in a particular situation, as a group, professional stock index traders are a couple of hundred, or perhaps a couple of thousand, very savvy market watchers whose collective market intelligence is extremely high.

As a group, they are sensitive to a number of factors. Some of these traders watch what certain leading stocks, such as IBM or GM, are doing on the theory that these stocks may begin to move before the rest of the market follows. They watch not only changes in the last sale, but also changes in the bid-ask for a stock. Others react to a bid or offer involving a large block of stock. Certain traders are aware of when a stock trades through a previous high or low. Other traders are sensitive to market momentum. In other words, if they underlying index rises rapidly from 10:00 until 11:00 and then continues rising at a slower pace between 11:00 and noon, the futures contracts will generally stabilize and will often actually decline in price. Invariably

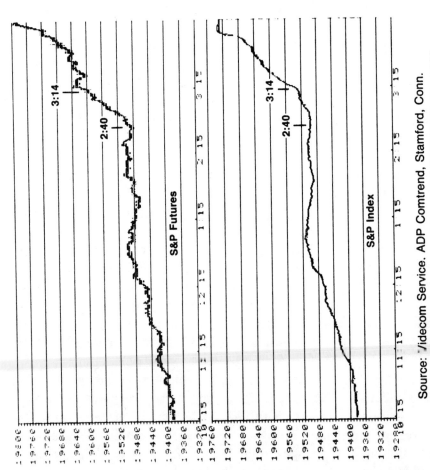

Source: Videcom Service. ADP Comtrend, Stamford, Conn.

FIGURE 6–6. TAIL WAGS DOG - II: NOVEMBER 11, 1985.

the stock market itself will follow in the same direction, but often not to the same extent.

Other traders watch for fundamental news developments and trade accordingly. Still others will be watching interest rate movements and prices in the bond market. Others will watch both the symbols on the ticker tape and the speed at which the tape moves for clues to market direction. They watch aggregate uptick and downtick indicators for evidence of an institutional buy or sell program hitting the floor. This collective expertise is one reason why stock index futures may presage movements of the stock market itself.

Another reason for this prescience is rooted in the way institutional money managers use stock index futures to alter their market exposure. Managers of large portfolios are often wary of a particular short-term fundamental or technical development and want to reduce their market exposure. Suppose a portfolio manager decided that the market was over-bought when it traded above the 1400 level. The manager has two choices to reduce equity exposure by $1 million. The obvious approach would be to sell shares of stock worth that much. A manager might have sold a block of 10,000 shares of General Motors at approximately 65, 10,000 shares of Bethelem Steel at approximately 15, and 10,000 shares of Black & Decker at approximately 20. It is, however, very expensive to sell 30,000 shares of stock, with commissions amounting to about $1,800 at an institutional rate of six cents per share.

By contrast, it is cheaper and more efficient to sell stock index futures. You can reduce your exposure by approximately the same dollar amount simply by selling 10 S&P contracts at 190 (totaling $950,000) on the Chicago Mercantile Exchange or 18 contracts at 110 (totaling $990,000) on the New York Futures Exchange. The transaction costs involved would be about 10 to 15 percent of those for the stock transaction. In this example, the round-turn charge for selling 10 S&P contracts might have been $45 per contract or $450. This works out to $225 for a half-turn (i.e., just the sale), which is 12 1/2 percent of the commission on the stock sale.

Potentially far more important is the fact that such a futures transaction could be accomplished in 30 seconds or less because a twenty-contract trade is a routine transaction in a stock index futures trading ring. In fact, it is not uncommon to see 100 or even 200 contracts, or "lots" to use the jargon, traded. In contrast, it can take at least two or three minutes to unload a block of stock at a favorable price and, as we have already seen, a market can move very suddenly. One who is in a hurry to sell cannot risk waiting to get a trade done at his price; rather, he will sell to a bidder at the latter's side of the market.

Perhaps more importantly, ten futures contracts will generally move the market a whole lot less than 10,000 shares of most stocks. That factor may substantially reduce indirect transaction costs.

Portfolio managers have also found stock index futures to be an effective way to reduce the indirect transaction costs of slippage. Slippage refers to money that is generally lost due to the bid-ask spread. The effect of slippage can be illustrated by assuming that our portfolio manager did in fact reduce his exposure by approximately $1 million as soon as the Dow slipped below 1400. Then assume, for discussion purposes, that the manager re-established the position later in the week with the market unchanged. The lower exposure could have been achieved by selling blocks of the three stocks or by selling ten December S&P futures. The actual market conditions at 10:00 a.m. on November 7, 1985 were as follows:

Item	Bid	Ask	Shares/Units Sold
GM	67 1/8	67 1/4	10,000
BS	13 5/8	13 3/4	10,000
BDK	19 5/8	19 3/4	10,000
SPZ	192.25	192.30	10

A spread of 1/8 on 30,000 shares costs $3,750 in slippage for selling those stocks at the specialist's bid price and repurchasing them at the specialist's ask price. By contrast, selling and repurchasing ten futures contracts at a one tick (or $25) market-maker's spread yields a slippage cost of only $250.

There is yet another reason why portfolio managers use futures rather than individual stocks to reduce market exposure by a given dollar amount. Suppose there is a sell-off at the 1400 level, but that selling occurs primarily in the high-tech and low-capitalization stocks. The sale of GM, BS, and BDK from a diversified portfolio would not have provided much protection against that type of sell-off. Thus, sophisticated portfolio managers recognize that stock index futures provide a qualitatively better tool for reduction of market exposure.

Finally, the manager of a portfolio that is not tax-exempt may use futures rather than stock to reduce his exposure and avoid incurring a tax liability on the sale of stock.

For all of these reasons, the first reaction to fundamental and technical market developments is reflected in the price of stock index futures; thus they generally lead the stock market itself.

Portfolio managers do in fact react more and more frequently to short-term developments in the market. Stock index futures are an efficient and increasingly utilized way to accomplish this end.

But portfolio managers are not the only market participants who contribute to the phenomenon of the futures leading the stocks themselves. A specialist on the floor of the New York Stock Exchange, as part of his duty to maintain a fair and orderly market, may wind up buying more shares of stock than he is comfortable with at a major resistance level in order to accommodate one or more sell orders. Particularly if the specialist is bearish on the market in general, he may be uncomfortable with such a large long position and unable to unwind it as rapidly as he would desire. Specialists sometimes seek to hedge their risk by offsetting on the adjacent trading floor of the New York Futures Exchange or on the floor of the Chicago Merc. In the above example, the specialist would go short with stock index futures contracts.

A specialist might also choose to rely on personal market judgment, based upon knowledge of the day's order flow, to speculate on market direction. Several specialist firms have their own trader in one of the stock index futures trading rings. A walk among the posts on the floor of the New York Stock Exchange would reveal that many specialists keep current stock index futures prices prominently displayed on their quote screens.

Sophisticated portfolio managers know that many large institutional traders with a keenly developed sense of where the market is likely to go in the next hour or two position themselves accordingly through the use of stock index futures. A portfolio manager who noticed the S&P 500 futures contract tick down by a full point over the course of twenty minutes might be more cautious about bidding aggressively for a large block of stock that he had been eyeing for some time. A decline in the price of stock index futures has an element of self-fulfilling prophecy because some portfolio managers and other investors are unwilling to buck a trend established by the smart money playing them.

Certain stocks may respond to changing market conditions more rapidly than last-sale data would indicate. If the futures decline, the bid-asked in such stocks may also decline within minutes. Even so, the futures still lead stocks, but perhaps by two or three minutes less than is apparent from the minute-by-minute dissemination of changes in a stock index.

SHORT-TERM TRENDS

Technicians use several different kinds of charts. The most familiar is the bar chart, which simply displays a trading range for a set period of time. A newspaper that prints stock market charts will generally use bar charts with one bar for each day. Many computer-generated charts use shorter time periods to indicate key trends within a day, a little "flag" marking the final price for each period.

Technical analysts establish likely trading ranges by connecting low points with subsequent low points along the line, as illustrated in the examples below. Often a pattern seems to exist on one side of a bar chart such as a parallel series of new lows, but the up side exhibits no similar pattern (or vice versa). In such cases, chartists will simply draw a parallel line to establish what they call a "channel" or "trading range." Aside from these slope lines, bar charts can be used simply to show where a contract has to trade to achieve a new high or a new low, another significant factor in the minds of many traders. Frequently some pattern will be discernible on a bar chart and, though it will not last forever, it will prove useful as a trading guideline for some time.

Moreover, sometimes a pattern will be evident on one contract or index and not on another. When the Dow exhibits a salient bar chart pattern, it should be heeded. The chart in Figure 6-7 shows 1340 to be a critical support line. Also apparent is a bearish pattern of consecutive lower highs. When the market broke below this support level on August 6, 1985,the Dow fell over twenty points in just a few hours. It then moved less in the following month than it moved in just those few hours, staying within the 1215–1235 range. The downward pressure on the overall market continued as the S&P 500 Index dropped approximately nine percent within the next six weeks.

That August 6 provides a good illustration of the importance of technical levels. Moreover, the bulk of the drop occurred in the hour in which the support line was pierced. Perhaps that was sheer coincidence. Could it be that the market was really reacting to some late-breaking bad news? The four major news stories in the next morning's paper were that the space shuttle had landed, Guyana's president died, a former *Wall Street Journal* reporter was sentenced to jail, and baseball players went on strike. I doubt that even the baseball strike did it.

One could argue that the 23 point drop was precipitated by fundamental factors such as increasing investor concern over the budget deficit, the trade deficit, or the growth in the money supply. I subscribe to the view that the fundamental analysis supplied the why of the decline. But I also believe that technical analysis explains the when of the decline. In other words, the market gradually trended toward the support line due to negative fundamentals, but broke due to technical factors.

POINT AND FIGURE CHARTS

A separate type of chart also frequently used by stock index traders is known as a point and figure chart. A point and figure chart does not show a continuum of equal time increments as a bar chart does. Rather, bars or lines on a point and figure chart reflect each change of a given magnitude in a market's direction. Such a change in direction is called a ''reversal.'' A particular line will continue in one direction

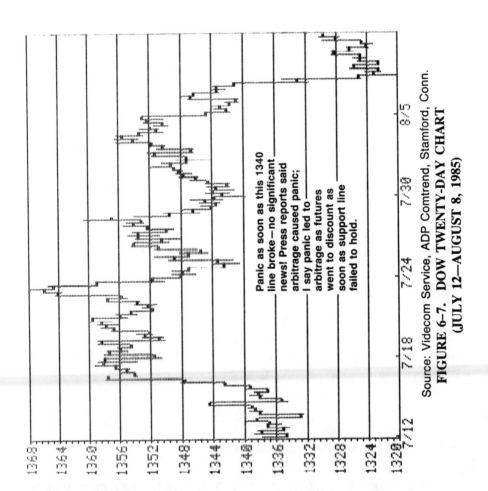

Panic as soon as this 1340
line broke—no significant
news! Press reports said
arbitrage caused panic;
I say panic led to
arbitrage as futures
went to discount as
soon as support line
failed to hold.

Source: Videcom Service, ADP Comtrend, Stamford, Conn.

**FIGURE 6-7. DOW TWENTY-DAY CHART
(JULY 12–AUGUST 8, 1985)**

until a reversal occurs. As a result, a long bar on a point and figure chart could represent only fifteen minutes of trading, while a much shorter bar could describe several hours of uneventful market activity.

The magnitude selected for a reversal is set by most traders at three times a given "increment." An increment is simply the minimum price fluctuation that will be reflected in a point and figure chart. For example, a chart commonly used for very short-term trading is called a "five by fifteen" point and figure chart. The five is the increment and, in this case, equals the minimum tick for a stock index futures contract. A movement or reversal of three times that increment, in this instance fifteen, indicates to traders a potentially significant change in market direction.

A ten by thirty point and figure chart and a twenty by sixty chart are also commonly used for stock index futures. Since a ten by thirty chart has an increment of ten, a line on such a chart would not continue in the same direction until the market moved two ticks (or ten basis points) in that direction. Thus, if the highest trade on a given day of a stock index futures contract was 99.95, the line on a ten by thirty chart might extend only as far as 99.90. On a twenty by sixty chart, the line could be as low as 99.80.

There are times when a trader frustrated by the absence of a clearly discernible pattern on a bar chart will find a pattern on a point and figure chart. Figure 6–8 is a twenty by sixty point and figure chart of the December 1985 S&P contract. It depicts the enormous rally of October and November of 1985. Although I generally do not use point and figure charts, this one was hard to ignore because a particularly salient trendline depicted 202.40 as the support line for the rally at the close of the trading in November. That line was barely broken at the close on November 29. During the next morning, the market struggled for about half an hour to get back above that line, but failed and dropped sharply in the next hour (see Figure 6–9). The Dow dropped nearly 15 points that day before resuming its huge rally.

Many day traders keep their own point and figure charts on a clipboard on graph paper, continually updating them. Instead of drawing bars, they will show an upward movement as a column of X's and a downward movement as a column of O's. Use of these charts by

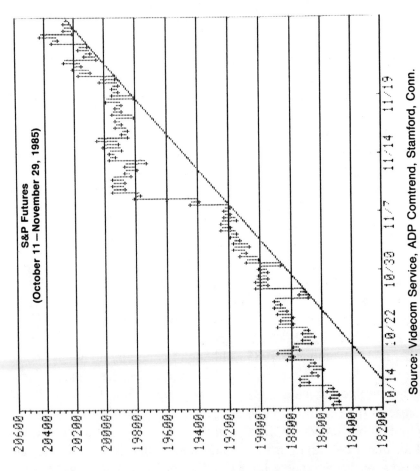

Source: Videcom Service, ADP Comtrend, Stamford, Conn.

FIGURE 6–8. POINT-AND-FIGURE SHOWING PATTERN NOT EVIDENT ON BAR CHARTS.

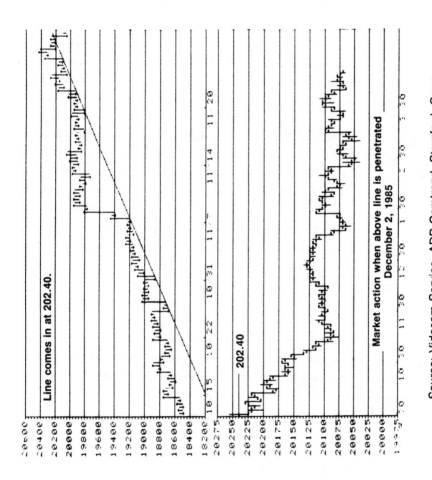

Source: Videcom Service, ADP Comtrend, Stamford, Conn.

FIGURE 6–9. S&P POINT-AND-FIGURE CHART

exchange members suggests that a substantial amount of trading is done on the basis of them, whether or not they are a particularly rational approach to investing. Some of the people who use these charts to make trading decisions have been around for some time and make a good living based primarily on this sort of trading.

However, it may not be as easy as it sounds because a support line on a point and figure chart (or any other chart) is often reached only when the market is in some sort of near-panic stage. It takes a certain disposition to be able to go out and buy in this kind of situation, minutes before most people are brave enough to join you.

Of course, in plenty of situations, the market continues right down through your supposed support line. You then sell and take a two or three tick loss. This is never pleasant, but if 50 percent of the time you lose two ticks and the other 50 percent you make five ticks, and if you can repeat this pattern three times a day, this alone would give you more than twice the national median income—before commissions, anyway.

My final caveat relates to whipsawing. On some occasions the market does penetrate a support or resistance line and then bounces right back. This can be most frustrating when you cover a position, only to have the market march off in your direction an hour later. Nevertheless, it is prudent to heed support and resistance areas in order to prevent substantial losses. On the occasions when this causes you to dump a position that turns out to be profitable, you incur an opportunity loss. This is part of the business, and not such a terrible part at that. You never owe an opportunity loss to a lender.

Figure 6–10 provides one illustration of how a trader might use a point and figure chart. It shows a series of horizontal and sloped trend lines. At certain key points on the charts a trader will judge the value of apparent patterns or trends. If what appears to be a support or resistance level on the point and figure chart coincides with a moving average level or a support or resistance level on a bar chart, it takes on added significance.

At point 1, a sloping line establishes a resistance level. That line cannot predict whether the contract will trade through 96.50, but it does suggest that if you bought at 96.25, it would make little sense

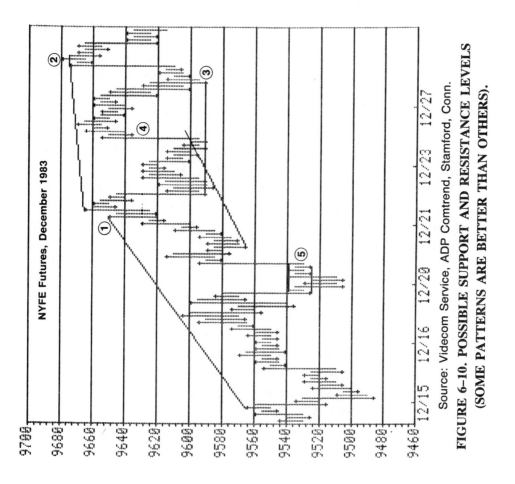

Source: Videcom Service, ADP Comtrend, Stamford, Conn.

FIGURE 6–10. POSSIBLE SUPPORT AND RESISTANCE LEVELS (SOME PATTERNS ARE BETTER THAN OTHERS).

to sell at the 96.40 or .45 level unless some other resistance level seemed clearly established. Once the contract had traded 96.50 and failed to penetrate that level, a sale would be more logical.

Penetration of a minor resistance level is exactly what happened at point 2. Although this resistance line did provide a top for the small year-end rally, the trade at 96.80 indicated that an upside breakout was possible.

Point 3 shows the use of a horizontal line to establish a buy level. Once 95.90 had held firm several times, it was established as a solid entry point. At the 96.00 level, one would have been wary and ready to sell on any weakness. After that line was cracked, it was clear sailing to 96.50. What signal would have told you to sell there? None on this chart, but you might have prudently raised your stop-loss order, perhaps to right below the line at point 4.

Similar parallel lines exist at point 5. Had you gone long at 95.25, you could have had a nice profit, but even if you had gone short at 95.40, the absence of any other resistance would have led you to cover rapidly.

Frankly, I would not have based any of my trades on any of the patterns in Figure 6-10, but these lines may be sufficient for traders who are in and out of the market more frequently than I am. I like patterns that are much more obvious. That way, enough people will see the pattern to activate the self-fulfilling prophecy syndrome.

Figure 6-11 is an example of a breakout, which in this instance is most evident on a point and figure chart. To me, the resistance line crossing at 96.00 suggested a possible spot to take a short position, but once the line was exceeded by a few ticks on the upside, it provided a clear signal to get long.

MOVING AVERAGES

Traders also look at what are known as "moving averages." At first glance, a moving average chart looks like it was prepared by a physics major who is just getting into the stock market, but its sine curves represent the average closing prices of a particular stock index

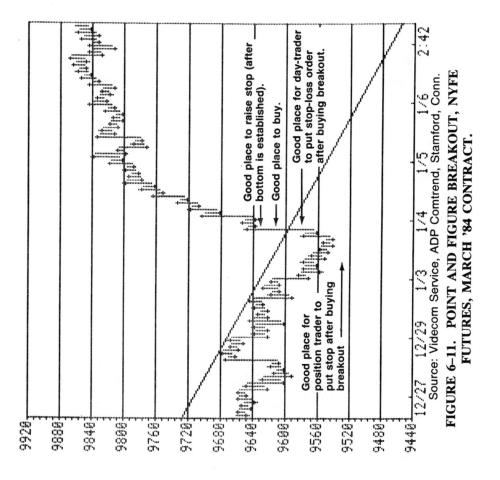

FIGURE 6–11. POINT AND FIGURE BREAKOUT, NYFE FUTURES, MARCH '84 CONTRACT.

Source: Videcom Service, ADP Comtrend, Stamford, Conn.

futures contract over a certain period of time. For example, suppose that between a Monday and a Friday a NYFE futures contract closes on successive days at 96.00, 97.00, 98.00, 99.00, and 100.00. At the close on Friday, the five-day moving average will be 98.00. At that time, the three-day moving average will be 99.00, but at the close on Wednesday, the three-day moving average would have been only 97.00. You can see that the oscillations of a short-term moving average are greater than those of a longer-term line because one price change has relatively less impact on the longer-term line. Also, at some point, the three-day moving average line must have moved above the five-day line.

A shorter-term line moving through and above a longer-term line is viewed in most quarters as a bullish sign. Similarly, a shorter-term line falling below a longer-term line is considered bearish. Also significant to many traders is the ability of the market on a given day to hold or break through a particular moving average level. Thus, a moving average line can function as a support or resistance level when standing alone, or as an indicator of market momentum when compared with other moving average lines.

Support or Resistance

Figure 6–12 shows that the five-day moving average line was at 96.30 before the opening on January 30, 1984. The futures had settled the previous Friday at 96.05. Many traders expected a strong rally because the market had been dropping steadily for two weeks, but now seemed to be buoyed by the prior evening's announcement that President Reagan would seek re-election and by unexpectedly good money supply news. Indeed, the market did open higher, trading quickly right up to 96.30, but it could not hold that level. That discouraged some technical traders and initial selling fed on itself as the Dow dropped more than ten points before closing down 8.48. No bad news came out during the day that would account for the sell-off. Traders call this a "technical reaction."

On February 24, 1984, a day on which the Dow rallied 30 points

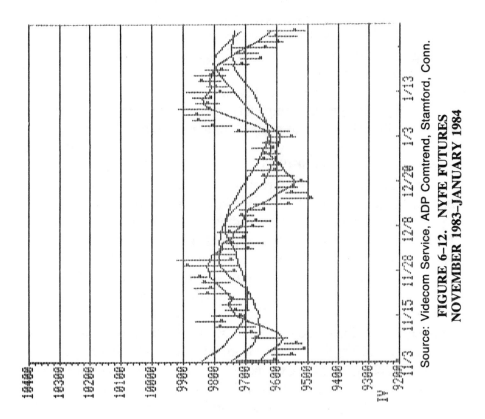

Source: Videcom Service, ADP Comtrend, Stamford, Conn.

**FIGURE 6–12. NYFE FUTURES
NOVEMBER 1983–JANUARY 1984**

to end a 160 point slide during the previous seven weeks, the NYFE March futures closed at 91.95. It could well be that this closing price was pure coincidence, but why didn't the market just keep surging? A look at Figure 6–13 shows that the twenty-day moving average line just happened to be at 91.95. It is a pretty sure bet that some technical traders were willing sellers at that price. What we don't know is how many contracts were for sale at that price. Without that knowledge, one can never be sure of how significant a particular technical line will be. As Figure 6–13 shows, the same development occurred in Chicago when the S&P 500 March futures also closed on the twenty-day moving average line.

Obviously, these charts also reveal plenty of days where the twenty-day moving average was completely irrelevant to daily market levels. In fact, critics of technical analysis might use a chart like this as an indicator that the twenty-day moving average was only coincidentally significant on just two of thirty days depicted in Figure 6–13. Fine, but common sense and the graphs displayed will tell you that when the market approaches that line, it is at least worth heeding.

Another example involves trading on September 25, 1984. The NYFE December futures contract, which had just become the most actively traded month, had been trading above the 98.20 level until the final hour. That level was the twenty-day moving average. When the futures broke that level, they dropped with a vengeance to 97.70 in a matter of just a few minutes. Once 98.20 traded, the market quickly became 98.15 bid, 98.20 offered. Then a broker on the trading floor screamed, ''100 at ten!'' That meant he wanted to sell 100 contracts at a price below the then-existing bid price, a very aggressive move. That particular broker was known to represent a major trader who, in a published interview, stated that he followed the twenty-day moving average closely. Now, there is no way to demonstrate conclusively that those 100 contracts were being offered by that particular trader because the moving average line was pierced, but it seemed to be no coincidence that the futures dropped fifty cents (equivalent to approximately six points on the Dow) as soon as the moving average line was broken.

I watched the ten-, twenty-, and thirty-day moving averages at the end of 1985. Several days after the Dow first closed above 1550,

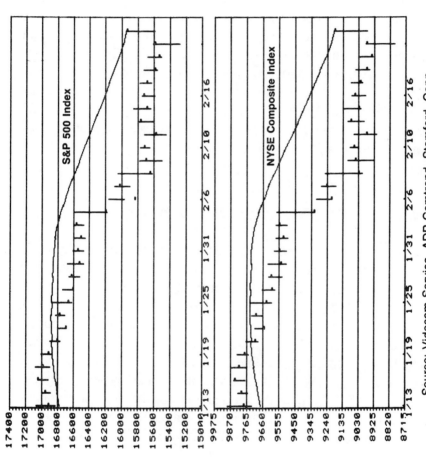

Source: Videcom Service, ADP Comtrend, Stamford, Conn.

FIGURE 6–13. TWENTY-DAY MOVING AVERAGE ENDING FEBRUARY 24, 1984 (LAST BAR).

the market consolidated and the S&P futures traded below their ten-day moving average, as Figure 6–14 shows. But after a brief dip below the twenty-day moving average, the S&P futures moved back above that line.

The market reached another interesting juncture shortly thereafter in that the futures had dipped below their twenty- and thirty-day moving averages and popped right back a few weeks later. Moreover, Figure 6–15 shows that NYFE's ten-day line had crossed below both the twenty- and thirty-day lines—a bearish indication. I based no trading on that particular chart, as I saw too much whipsaw potential in it. Moreover, I saw more salient patterns in other places during that period. The NYFE March 1986 futures had made a double top at 125 and had formed a based at 118.00. Those levels seemed more important at the time than the moving averages.

Penetration of One Moving Average Line by Another

Many traders, especially the trading managers of certain commodity funds, have developed trading systems based on the interaction of moving average lines. If a short-term line crosses below a longer-term line, that indicates weakened upward momentum and may produce a sell signal. Conversely, a short-term line crossing above a longer-term line is considered bullish. Not all reaction is instantaneous when a short-term moving average line penetrates a long-term line. Many people look at data based only on settlement prices and initiate trades the following day. Certain traders will wait for the funds to complete their buy or sell program and then trade against the funds in an effort to whipsaw them out of the market.

Calculation of Moving Averages

Anyone with a $5 pocket calculator can calculate moving averages from prices in the newspaper. Computers can calculate such averages

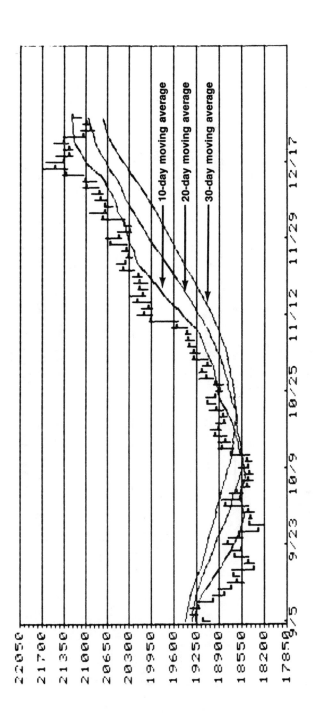

Source: Videcom Service, ADP Comtrend, Stamford, Conn.

FIGURE 6–14. S&P 500 FUTURES, YEAR END 1985:
THE TEN-DAY LINE BROKE, BUT THE TWENTY-DAY LINE HELD.

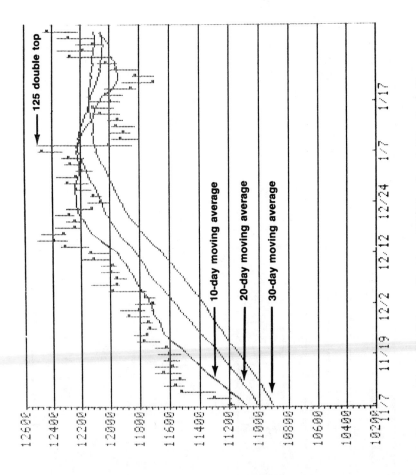

Source: Videcom Service, ADP Comtrend, Stamford, Conn.

FIGURE 6–15. NYFE FUTURES, MARCH '86 CONTRACT 60 DAY CHART ENDING FEBRUARY 3, 1986

almost instantaneously. Moving averages are generally based upon futures contract settlement prices, but the calculation can also be based upon the mean of the daily high, low, and settlement or upon various other permutations.

Of course part of the challenge is to find numbers of days that yield moving averages with predictive value. Many floor traders use twenty- and thirty-day moving averages. *Commodity Perspective* prints four-, nine-, and eighteen-day moving average lines. Figure 6–12 displayed a thirteen-day moving average in addition to the five- and twenty-day averages, but why not a three-, fourteen-, and forty-two-day moving average chart? Eventually one is bound to find something that works, at least for a limited period of time. Surprising though it may seem, major investment houses pay statisticians to develop correlations indicating exactly what moving average charts are most appropriate for a particular market. If a particular moving average works for six months before the rest of the world discovers that it's the easiest game in town, the investment house will reap a handsome return on its research investment.

Little of this research on moving average correlations has yet been completed with respect to stock index futures. To date, moving average charts seem to be more precise indicators for commodities with longer trading histories. However, as major institutions develop satisfactory correlations and commit capital accordingly, it would not be surprising to see the moving average charts gain more importance in the stock index futures market.

What do I think of moving averages? I personally have not spotted enough patterns in them to find them all that useful on a regular basis. Reliance on these charts alone can easily lead to an undesirable amount of whipsawing. Often no major trend develops as a result of either the futures penetrating a particular moving average line or one moving average line penetrating another. However, it is certainly worth keeping applicable moving average levels in the back of your mind. If such a level coincides with an important support of resistance line on a bar chart or a point and figure chart, it would take on added significance in the minds of most traders and may indeed presage a major move.

LONG-TERM ANALYSIS

Tools of long-term analysis are little different from those described above. However, some long-term trend lines are worth noting. For instance, all through the course of the 1982-1983 bull market, an eight month support line was not broken until July 29 (Figure 6–16). Many traders mark the. breaking of that line as the end of the 1982--1983 bull market.

Had you picked up the *New York Times* on the morning of July 29, you would have seen the graph akin to that shown in Figure 6–17. That chart tells me that reading the newspaper sometimes isn't enough. Compare it to the computer-generated chart in Figure 6–16, which differs in that it reaches back a few additional months and measures movement of the futures contract rather than the index itself. It is not necessary to have a computer to generate this chart. If you use graph paper to plot the high, low, and settle of the futures each day, you'll be well-equipped to trade on the basis of long-term support and resistance lines. Alternatively, long-term charts of various indexes appear in *Investor's Daily*.

Sometimes, newspaper charts do present a sufficiently comprehensive picture. The chart of the NYSE Composite Index in December 1985 revealed a clear trading channel.

A glance at the chart in Figure 6–16 shows that, despite ominous predictions of an imminent correction throughout the winter and spring of 1983, the support line held fast. This chart is particularly interesting at two points. During the months of February and March the market appeared to be forming a "head and shoulders" pattern. Technical wisdom has it that should the right shoulder dip below the so-called "neck line," the market will plunge. Many traders felt this would occur on or about April 1, 1983. Some of those traders failed to recognize that the long-term support line for the market was slightly above that neck line. When the market trended down and hit that support line, it held, setting the stage for one of the great rallies of the entire bull market.

Almost no one believed that the market could continually trade at new highs during that April, but the ones who got rich during that

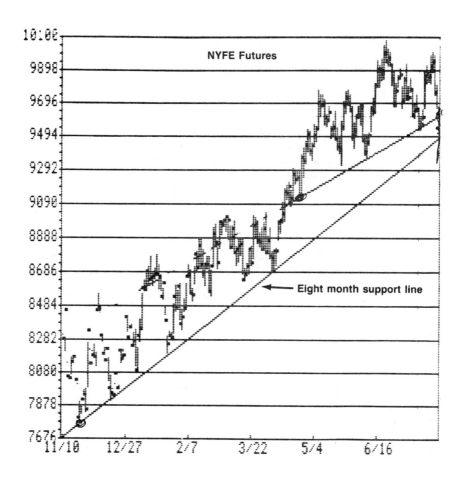

Source: Videcom Service, ADP Comtrend, Stamford, Conn.

FIGURE 6–16. END OF THE 1982–1983 LEG OF THE BULL MARKET

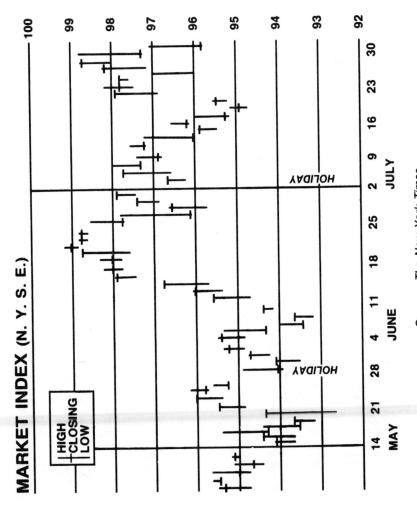

Source: *The New York Times.*

FIGURE 6–17.

rally were the ones who paid close attention to the parallel lines that established the channel in which the market traded. That phase of the bull market stopped abruptly when it hit the resistance line that formed the top end of that channel. That resistance line is formed by entering a line parallel to the long-term support line and tangential to the market high achieved at the beginning of the period shown. Perhaps, then, it should be no surprise that the same line was the top of the final bull market rally in the middle of June.

No doubt many traders, myself among them, bought stock index futures contracts again at the end of July when, after another sharp sell-off, the market reached that same long-term support line. This time, however, the market did not even put up much of a fight, and it was clear that the support line would not hold. Although I absorbed some losses once the line had been penetrated, it was apparent that the market was not coming back for a while and so it made sense to sell immediately.

I use an example of one of my own trading losses to point out what I have tried to stress several times—to achieve great gains in the stock index futures trading requires a willingness to play what you believe to be a reasonable percentage and a willingness to incur a loss if you are wrong. At the time, it certainly seemed reasonable to think that the market might bounce off that support line. Had it done so, I would have had a very profitable ride. As it was, my losses were limited and my philosophy unchanged. It is no more complicated than the example discussed earlier of someone pulling out a quarter and offering to pay me $100 every time it came up heads if I would pay them $25 when it came up tails. That is a bet I would take every time, but on one important condition: that I had $25 to lose.

Another long-term chart took shape at the end of the market's year-long retreat from the highs of July 1983. As Figure 6-18 shows, a long-term support line is formed by connecting the August 1982 low to the bottom established on July 25, 1984. Based upon this line and a similar line for the S&P 500 contract, the support level for the futures at various times will be approximately as follows:

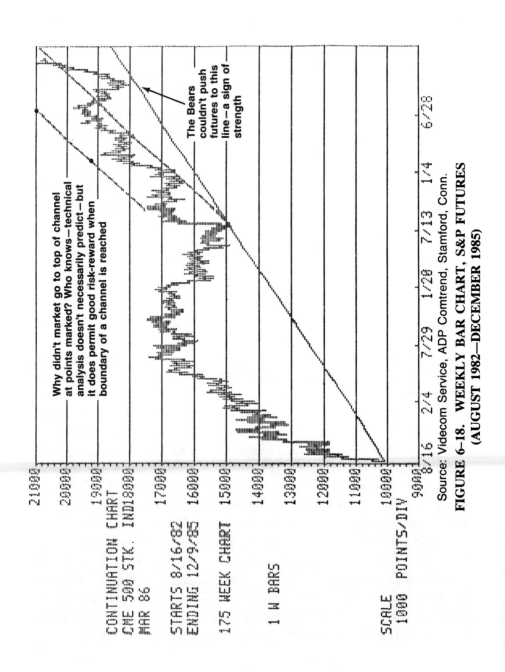

Source: Videcom Service, ADP Comtrend, Stamford, Conn.

FIGURE 6–18. WEEKLY BAR CHART, S&P FUTURES (AUGUST 1982—DECEMBER 1985)

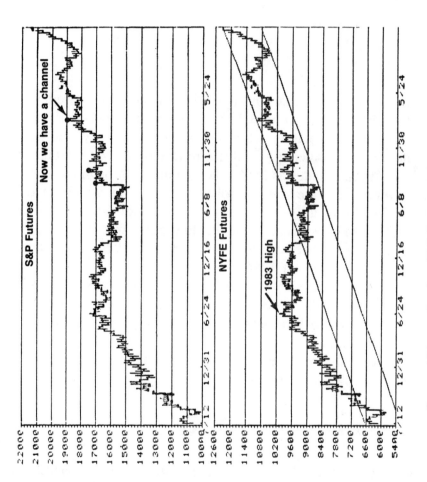

Source: Videcom Service, ADP Comtrend, Stamford, Conn.

FIGURE 6-19. FORMING A TRADING CHANNEL

Time	S&P 500	NYSE Composite
September 1985	172.5	100
January 1986	181	105
May 1986	189.5	110
September 1986	198	115
January 1987	206.5	120
May 1987	215	125

The last long-term chart in Figure 6–19 depicts resistance levels to which the market had climbed by December 13,1985—resistance that looks pretty compelling. A short position with a pretty tight stop-loss impressed me as being a good risk-reward trade. My short lasted for about fifteen minutes as the market bulldozed through those levels. However, once the market broke out of that trading channel, I concluded that it could go all the way to the top of the next trading channel, formed by yet another parallel line drawn from the market's 1983 high. Indeed, that line proved to be the next serious resistance level in the late spring of 1986.

Notice also that the Value Line contract had only recently broken out above its triple top of 212. Upon doing so, it raced all the way to the 217 level before retracing and heading higher once again. (Figure 6–20). As the market roared through formidable resistance levels with hardly a pause, I heard more than one trader with a long position smile and say, "It's like 1928 all over again."

IS THERE A TWO-MINUTE WARNING?

The major breaks through a long-term support or resistance line give rise to an inevitable question: Does one stock index futures contract regularly lead the others? If one were to regularly lead, the smart money could abandon the leading contract and simply cash in on movements in the followers. Traders have been debating this question for the four years that stock index futures have traded without establishing any inviolable rules.

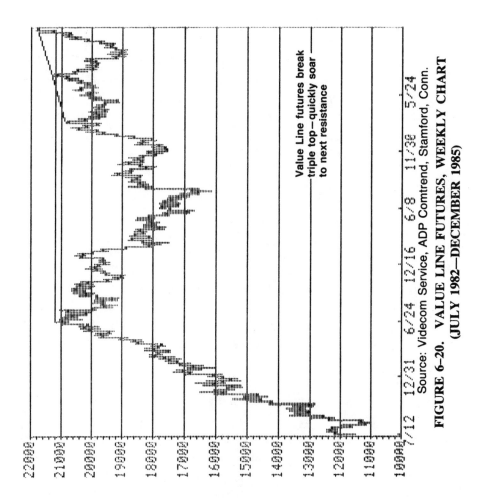

Source: Videcom Service, ADP Comtrend, Stamford, Conn.

**FIGURE 6–20. VALUE LINE FUTURES, WEEKLY CHART
(JULY 1982—DECEMBER 1985)**

But let me propose one viewpoint: it does not matter if one or the other contract *regularly* leads the others, as long as you are aware which contract is likely to lead under particular market conditions, or, better yet, which contract happens to be leading at any given point in time. This can depend on which contract is closest to its long-term support or resistance level.

In my observation, price leadership among the various stock index futures contracts varies from one major breakout to the next. Often, one contract will break through its support or resistance level ten or fifteen minutes before another contract, giving you time to get in. For example, on January 21, 1985 when the Dow rose 36 points, the resistance levels, upon which I based my trading, and the breakout times were as follows:

Contract	Resistance	Breakout
NYSE	100.80	11:01
S&P	174.50	11:09
Kansas City	193.50	11:14

When the NYSE contract penetrated its resistance line, it traded south of that line only one more time, at 11:02. Once the S&Ps broke out, they never traded below 174.50. These two contracts served as an early warning system for anyone who wanted to jump on the bandwagon in Kansas City. It is worthwhile to stay alert for other instances of early warnings.

I repeated the early warning test on Monday, December 16, 1985, the day that the three original futures contracts broke out above their respective long-term resistance levels. The various contracts had closed just a shade below their resistance levels after a strong rally on the preceding Friday. Since it is hard to pinpoint the exact level of resistance on a long-term price chart, I thought I would let the market tell me where resistance had been based on Friday's highs. My inquiry concerned which contract broke above the Friday high and held on the following Monday. As Figure 6–21 indicates, each of the futures opened strong, but fell back rather quickly before the real rally. My

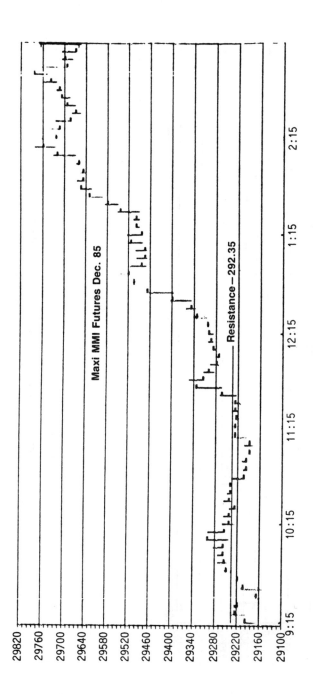

Source: Videcom Service, ADP Comtrend, Stamford, Conn.

FIGURE 6–21. USE OF SUPPORT AND RESISTANCE POINTS IS NOT ALWAYS AN EXACT SCIENCE

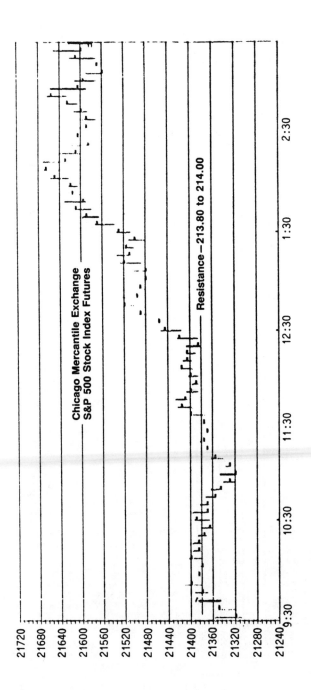

Source: Videcom Service, ADP Comtrend, Stamford, Conn.

FIGURE 6–21. (Continued)

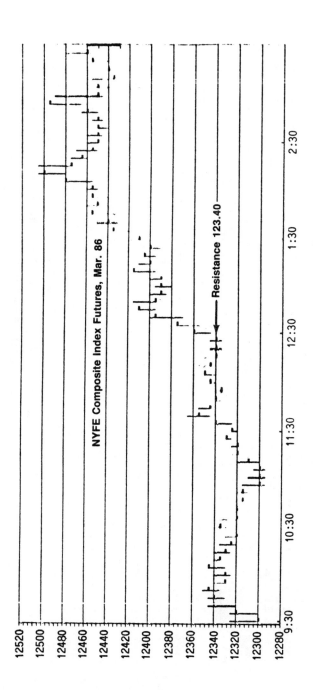

NYFE Composite Index Futures, Mar. 86

Resistance 123.40

Source: Videcom Service, ADP Comtrend, Stamford, Conn.
FIGURE 6–21. (Continued)

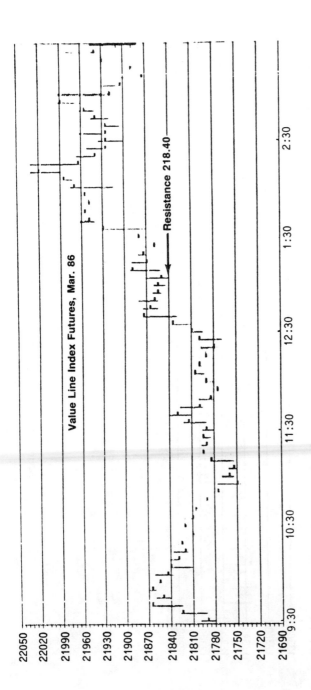

Source: Videocom Service, ADP Comtrend, Stamford, Conn.

FIGURE 6–21. (Concluded)

conclusion is the same: one contract will lead the others higher, giving an astute trader the chance to buy one of the followers. Here is a summary:

Active Contract	Estimated Resistance	Previous Day's High	Final Breakout
SPH	214.00	213.80	11:37
MXZ	—	292.35	11:37
YXH	123.50	123.40	12:29
KVH	218.00	218.40	12:42

Figure 6–21 allows you to study the price action throughout the day (and during the critical breakout period). The charts highlight how important those resistance levels were to traders. As the S&P chart indicates, prices pushed on the resistance line several times for nearly an hour while trading in a 50 cent range. Surely, if prices were always a random walk, they would have dropped below that line a few times.

As the charts indicate, the NYSE and Value Line contracts did move higher, but Value Line did not pierce its resistance level at all during that hour while the NYSE contract did so only to fall back.

Sometimes, one contract will have a clearer technical hurdle. For instance, in mid-November 1985 when the Dow surged through the 1400 mark, the Value Line futures presented what appeared to be the clearest threshold. As depicted in Figure 6–20, the market had already enjoyed quite a rally when the Value Line futures reached the barrier at 212.50. I, for one, did not expect and market to go through that level without a few days of backing and filling. When the futures penetrated that level, however, it was a sign to me that it was too soon to take profits. I got no equally clear signals from the other stock index futures contracts.

But what about the 200 days a year without major breakouts? In my observation, NYFE tends to follow the S&P 500 more often than it leads. Kansas City goes to extremes more quickly and more often, but its batting average seems no better or worse than the other contracts in predicting short-term movement.

MAJOR TECHNICAL FORMATIONS

In viewing charts, traders look for any number of patterns. Among the more important are the following:

A Flag

A flag is apparent on either a point and figure chart or a bar chart. I picked up a copy of *The Wall Street Journal* on a flight home from New Zealand. After a five-week sojourn, I had almost no idea of what was going on in the market. On the plane, I noticed the flag that I have simulated in Figure 6–22. That was all I knew, and all I needed to know.

My immediate dilemma was that if I told the customs man he was costing me more in trading profits than in customs duties by keeping me from a telephone, he'd really go through my bags! Since I had no good idea of where to put a stop-loss order on the futures, I bought call options from the public telephone outside the customs area (the Dow was already up seven) and they increased 30 percent by the time I got back to Manhattan. The Dow closed up 16 points. When I sold them a week and a half later, my profits ranged from 375 percent to 450 percent. So I like flags.

The flag is not absolutely perfect—technical formations almost never are. The bar came up a bit too high on Thursday of the week of October 18, but the pattern is still quite apparent—and it worked. In fact, the Dow was at 1460 only three weeks later.

A Head and Shoulders

A head and shoulders is formed when a moderate correction follows an intermediate top; then the market reaches new highs and falls off once again. The third rally fails to reach the old highs, peaking instead somewhere near the first intermediate top. When the market trends down again, many technical traders will sell as soon as it falls

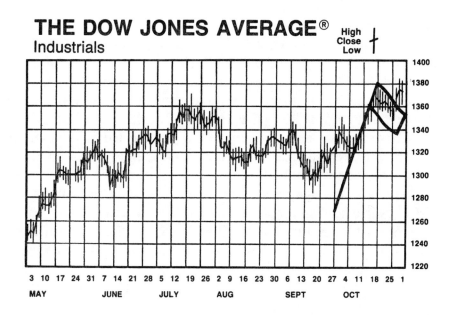

FIGURE 6–22. A SAMPLE FLAG.

below the "neckline", which is the base from which the head and right shoulder were established.

A reverse head and shoulders also appears on Figure 6–22. Again, the formation is not perfect. The right shoulder does not dip below 1310, as does the left. It's hard to pinpoint the neckline, which I have at about 1342. The market had already penetrated that level, which reconfirmed my view that the chart was bullish.

In this case, the upward breakout from the flag and the reverse head and shoulders were not especially sudden. Even an investor who just casually reads the newspaper had time to get in. The price objective after a head and shoulders breakout is the distance from the head to the neckline in the other direction.

Saucers

Another salient pattern is the saucer top or saucer bottom. A saucer top is a curved resistance line, which suggests to a technician that after a few successively weaker attempts to break through the saucer, the market will experience a downside breakout.

As this book went to press, some technicians believed that the formation that developed in the spring and summer of 1986 was a major saucer top (Figure 6–23), portending a downward movement.

Conversely, a saucer bottom would be expected to yield an upside breakout. As usual, the saucer bottom depicted by Line A in Figure 6–24 does not provide the luxury of a classically perfect shape. The market dipped through my bottom once. Thus, some technicians saw it as a reverse head and shoulders rather than a saucer. The formation gave one sufficient time to establish a long position, and sufficient reward for doing so. In two months, the S&P futures shot up by 20 points and the NYSE futures climbed 12 points.

In fact, this saucer bottom provided more time to get long than is always the case. Sometimes the market moves before the saucer is completed. In this case, the pattern would have been abundantly clear where the arrow is drawn. You still would have had to endure two days of consolidation, but once you spot a saucer, it is better to act quickly. Line B would have one acting too quickly, but it is too steep to be a saucer.

OTHER TECHNICAL MEASURES

Chart analysis is only one of many forms of technical analysis of futures prices. A thorough presentation of all of these methods requires a separate book.[1] Technical analysts review volume, open interest, large trader reports, and other data.

[1]Several books are worthwhile, notably Edwards and Magee, *Technical Analysis of Stock Trends* (John Magee, Inc., Boston, Mass.); Frost & Prechter, *Elliot Wave Principle* (New Classics Library, Gainesville, Ga.); Murphy, *Technical Analysis of the Futures Markets* (New York Institute of Finance, New York, N.Y.).

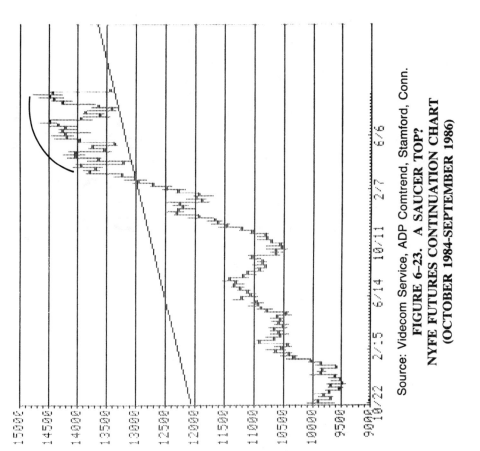

Source: Videcom Service, ADP Comtrend, Stamford, Conn.

FIGURE 6-23. A SAUCER TOP?
NYFE FUTURES CONTINUATION CHART
(OCTOBER 1984-SEPTEMBER 1986)

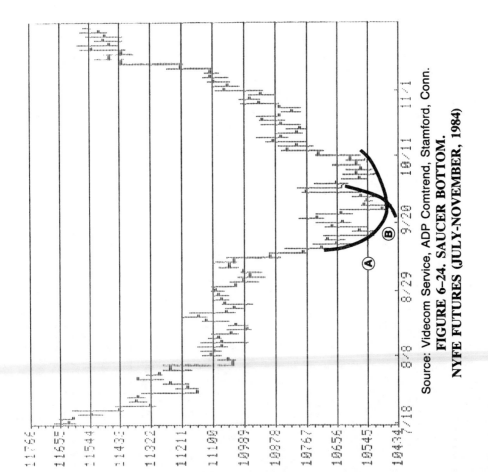

Source: Videcom Service, ADP Comtrend, Stamford, Conn.
FIGURE 6–24. SAUCER BOTTOM.
NYFE FUTURES (JULY-NOVEMBER, 1984)

Volume is supposed to give an indication of the strength of a particular movement. If a price rise is accompanied by heavy volume, the upward trend would be expected to continue. Conversely, a price rise on low volume might signal a near-term top. Similarly, if the total volume of trading increases as prices are declining, the downtrend would be expected to continue. A downtrend on light volume might be expected to end. Certain charting services include volume and open interest graphics on price charts.[2]

A similar analysis may be applied to open interest. Open interest gives an indication of who the buyers are in a rising market and who the sellers are in a declining market. When total open interest is increasing, it signifies that new positions are being established with new money flowing into the market from bulls who believe that the trend will continue. At some point during a rally, traders with short positions will start to liquidate those positions to cut their losses. Net liquidation causes open interest to decline. When open interest declines this way during a market rally, it may be attributable it to such short covering coming to dominate commitment of new money to the market. To a trader who believes that fear is a more powerful emotion than greed, short-covering accompanied by an absence of new money gives some indication that a market top may be approaching. Moreover, open interest will also decline as traders with long positions decide to stop letting their profits run and to take profits by liquidating their positions. Thus, a decline in open interest while prices are still advancing is a signal that the upward trend may be weakening.

The same analysis applies in a market downtrend. Lower prices accompanied by an increase in open interest suggest that new money is coming in to sell short. New traders believe that it is not too late to start selling even though prices have already declined somewhat. However, people holding long positions will eventually sell them at a loss during a market decline. Such liquidating sales will reduce open interest. Declining open interest signals that new sellers are no longer

[2]See *Commodity Chart Service*, published weekly by Commodity Research Bureau, Inc., 75 Montgomery Street, Jersey City, N.J.; Commodity Perspective Chart Service, 30 S. Wacker Drive, Suite 1220, Chicago, Ill.

willing to hit bids or even offer at these prices and that there will be little new selling in the market to overpower buyers. Falling in open interest also suggests that those with profitable short positions are taking profits in the belief that the market will not go much lower. This is another reason that a price downturn accompanied by lower open interest may predict the end of a downtrend.

I use open interest only as a general indication of the commitment of new capital to a rising or declining market, not as a day-to-day indicator of likely market direction. I do find open interest useful when the market nears a major long-term support or resistance level. However, open interest and volume figures can be skewed by arbitrageurs who have taken offsetting positions in the cash market, distorting the picture of commitment of speculative capital. Nevertheless, it can be worth watching open interest in conjunction with price changes, bearing in mind the rules we discussed, as summarized in the following:

Open Interest Up
- Price Up = New Buying (Technically powerful up move)
- Price Down = Hedging or Short Selling (Technically powerful down move)

Open Interest Down
- Price Up = Short Covering (Technically weak up move)
- Price down = Long Liquidation (Technically weak down move)

Some traders look at open interest in conjunction with Large Trader Reports compiled by the CFTC for indications of how the positions of the big players differ from those of the odd-lotters. Since these reports contain data that is somewhat dated, they are best used only as a general sentiment indicator rather than as a precise timing tool.

Another statistic rooted in the odd-lot theory, the ratio of call open interest to put open interest on the OEX options, is also intriguing.

As Figure 6–25 indicates, options players had the market's direction in the last quarter of 1985 all wrong. Buying of calls accelerated during the market's slide in August and early September, then put buying surged while the market soared. Notably, put buyers entered the market in droves on November 11, the day the market climbed 28 points. A problem with a chart using open interest rather than volume is that monthly expiration causes a sudden shift in the call/put ratio. Nevertheless, the chart juxtaposes one measure of market sentiment and actual market movement.

PUTTING IT ALL TOGETHER

Those who remain skeptical about technical analysis ask: "If it's so easy, why doesn't everybody do it?" I don't claim it's easy and I don't claim it's foolproof. In fact, on many occasions technical indicators seem to contradict one another. For example, December 23, 1985 shows a number of contradictions. On that day, the Dow fell over 14 points to close at 1528, some 25 points off its high of a week earlier, but some bullish signs remained. The decline was on very light volume. The premium on the futures contract was as low as it had been in a month, also a bullish sign to a contrarian investor. Finally, a flag pattern had developed over the last six trading sessions.

But many signs were not so bullish. First of all, the market had penetrated, but quickly fallen back through, a long-term resistance level. Moreover, for the first time in two months, the futures had closed below their ten-day moving average line. So what to do?

When technical indicators conflict, I will, in an admittedly subjective fashion, evaluate all of the indicators and try to differentiate what they seem to be saying from what they have said under similar circumstances in the past. For instance, light volume on a down day is normally bullish, but I discounted light volume on December 23 because it was a holiday week. Second, upon closer scrutiny, the premium was not as bullish from a contrarian viewpoint as it first appeared because even at 140, the premiums were hardly at an extreme, and were far above their lows over the past 60 days. Third, although a flag is generally

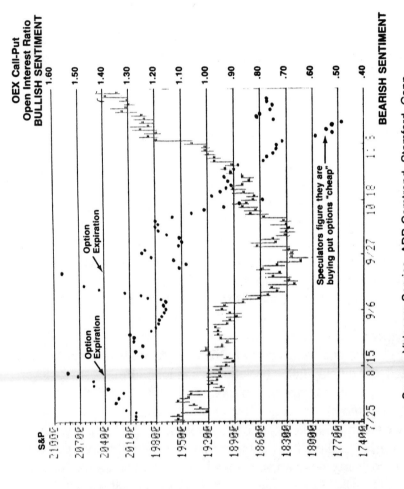

Source: Videcom Service, ADP Comtrend, Stamford, Conn.

FIGURE 6–25. 90 DAY S&P 500 VERSUS OEX CALL/PUT OPEN INTEREST (BETTING AGAINST THE CROWD CAN BE PROFITABLE).

considered a bullish formation, in this case the market closed below the bottom of the flag formation. Three normally bullish signs were not so bullish as they might have appeared at first glance. Finally, I felt that stock futures were slightly overpriced relative to bond futures, so that even a bond rally was unlikely to help stocks much. I concluded that bearish factors outweighed bullish factors on this December 23, and, accordingly maintained a short position in the market. On December 24, the Dow dropped 9.63 points, and the S&P futures closed 1.20 lower. But my postscript is equally important—assessments of this sort must be made daily, as these indicators and market conditions can change rapidly.

If you are still uncertain after such a weighing process, the best answer is to do nothing. After all, you can't get injured sitting on the sidelines. Perhaps the next day's early trading will clarify which way the market is going. Sometimes you should resist the urge to trade until certain market events unfold, i.e., when certain patterns are so dominant or so apparent as to indicate a good risk-reward trade.

CONCLUSION

You might discern two polar approaches to technical analysis. One is to develop a system of watching certain indicators that prove to be virtually foolproof over time. I have found no such El Dorado in my own search for the ultimate black-box system. Maybe a few people have found El Dorado this way, but I am suspicious of many more people who claim to have done so.

The other approach is not to swear by any particular indicator. Rather, in looking at a variety of technical formations and indicators, try to ascertain which are giving a particularly strong signal at a given point in time and to determine which chart patterns are particularly salient. There may be a good flag in October and no more flags for a year. To date, this eclectic outlook is an important part of my basic approach to trading.

Two final comments on technical analysis. Some of Wall Street's most distinguished executives have said that technical analysis is basically nonsense. I read in an old edition of *The Wall Street Journal* that a then-Chairman of Morgan Guaranty Trust stated that a month-long selling wave could not continue because the selling was all technical rather than fundamental. The newspaper was dated October 25, 1929. On the other hand, a trader who often stands near me on the floor wears a badge that reads, "Even sunken ships have charts."

CHAPTER 7

Pricing of Stock Index Futures and Their Price Relationships

An understanding of trading psychology and technical analysis is a necessary, but not sufficient, foundation for an investor who seeks an edge in the stock index futures market. This edge is increased by an understanding of fair value of a futures contract for a given level of the underlying index. This understanding will enable you to avoid paying too much to buy a contract and also to avoid selling a contract for too little. Further, in some situations, both hedgers and speculators may profit by selling overvalued contracts and buying undervalued ones.

How does one determine the fair price of a contract? What accounts for deviations from a contract's fair price? How can one profit from such deviations? Does it ever make sense to buy a contract trading for more than its fair price or to sell a contract at less than its fair price? Let us explore these questions in turn.

FAIR VALUE OF A CONTRACT

The fair value of a stock index futures contract can be established by determining the price at which, for a given level of the underlying cash index, an investor would be indifferent between owning, in proper proportion, the stocks in the index and owning the futures contract. At expiration of the futures, the price of the futures equals the price

169

of the cash index. Prior to expiration, valuation of the futures requires consideration of the cash flows associated with each alternative.

An investor who buys $1 million worth of equities would earn no interest on that $1 million but would receive dividends. One who invests the same amount in stock index futures would receive no dividends, but would earn interest, generally assumed at the current risk-free rate as measured by the yield on Treasury bills maturing when the futures expire. This is so because margin requirements leave approximately 95 percent of an investor's cash free for investment in risk-free (or other) assets. Moreover, commodity margin rules permit an investor in stock index futures to post treasury bills as margin and to keep the interest accruing on them. In contrast, the investor in equities must pay for stock by transferring funds to the seller, forfeiting any interest that could otherwise be earned on that sum.

With that knowledge, we can easily calculate the approximate intrinsic worth of a stock index futures contract, given the level of the underlying index, at a given point in time. The formula is:

Futures Price = Index Price × 1 + [(Risk-free interest rate
— Annualized Dividend Yield on stock index)
× Days Until Expiration/365)]

Let's apply the formula to a real-world example. At year-end 1983, the rate on ninety-day treasury bills was 9.25 percent. The average annual dividend yield for all component stocks of the NYSE Composite Index was 4.35 percent. The investor who opts for the futures contract gives up a revenue stream of 4.35 percent, but gains a revenue stream of 9.25 percent. One who has no opinion about market direction will be indifferent between buying equities or futures if the futures premium evaporates at the rate of 4.90 percent per annum. Since we are valuing a contract that expires in three months, that dissipation would be prorated to 1.225 percent per quarter. Therefore, since the NYSE Composite Index closed out 1983 at a level of 95.18, the intrinsic worth (also referred to as theoretical value) of the March 1984 contract would have been derived as follows:

Futures Price = 95.18 × 1 + [(.0925 − .04350) × (91/365)]
                     = 95.18 × 1 + (.049 × .25)
                     = 95.18 × 1 + .01225
                     = 95.18 × 1.01225
Futures Price = 96.35

The March 1984 contract in fact closed 1983 at a price of 96.25, a minor deviation from its intrinsic value. But on many occasions, market value deviates substantially from intrinsic value of the futures.

CAUSES OF DEVIATION FROM FAIR VALUE

Near Month

Any deviation from fair value of the futures contract closest to expiration is caused by market sentiment. Bullish sentiment will price the futures at a premium wider than that derived from the fair value calculation. Bearish sentiment will put the futures at a premium below the expected premium, or perhaps even at a discount from the cash index.[1]

A discount results from particularly bearish market sentiment, which gives rise to persistent selling pressure on the futures contracts. This selling pressure arises in large measure from people who sell futures contracts instead of stocks when their outlook becomes bearish.

It is important to distinguish between a discount, which involves just the underlying index and the futures contract closest to expiration, and a price inversion, in which each more distant delivery month's contract sells at a cheaper price. Such an inversion is not uncommon in futures trading generally. For instance, near the end of 1985, British

---

[1] For short periods of time close to expiration of the futures and when annualized dividend flows are very high, it is possible for the fair value of the futures to be at a discount to the index.

pound futures contracts had an inverted price structure in which pounds were quoted as follows:

| March 1986 | 1.4345 | September | 1.4105 |
| June | 1.4215 | December | 1.4030 |

That inversion is explained by interest rates being higher in Great Britain than in the United States, leaving an investor indifferent between owning U.S. dollars and earning approximately 8 percent or owning British pounds and earning approximately 10.5 percent, but losing that differential of approximately 2 1/2 percent to a currency hedge of the same amount. Just as with stock index futures, the prices are a function of alternative cash flows.

Distant Months

It is conceivable that more than one delivery month of stock index futures contracts could be at a discount to a particular index. It would, however, be exceedingly rare for a more distant contract to be at a discount to a contract closer to expiration as long as short-term interest rates exceed dividend yields (though this has occurred in the Australian market).

Although one can hypothesize that if the consensus among speculators is that the NYSE Composite Index will be at 150 at the end of 1987, that is the price at which the December 1987 futures contract should trade, even in 1986. In fact, this seems almost obvious. But wrong.

The price of the December 1987 contract is unlikely to be heavily affected by the relatively few open positions in it during 1986. Rather, its price depends to a large extent on short-term interest rates and the price of the nearest, and thus actively traded, month.

As a practical matter, open interest in the December 1987 contract is bound to remain small until about five months before that contract expires. This indicates that most participants in the stock index futures market have a very short-term time horizon. Index futures prices are likely to bear a strong correlation to short-term expectations about the market.

HOW TO PROFIT FROM DEVIATIONS FROM FAIR VALUE

Some traders will attempt to profit by automatically selling when the premium becomes excessive and automatically buying when the futures trade at an excessive discount. A common mistake among new traders is to jump the gun a bit and sell short when the premium reaches a trigger point (i.e., whatever maximum level has been sustained in recent weeks or months). Much to their surprise and chagrin, the underlying index often increases sharply and the futures contract shows a corresponding rise, making a short seller most uncomfortable. That is generally not a good way to profit from an excessive premium.

The more significant activity which can lock in profits (and which limits the size of the premium) is a form of arbitrage known as cash-futures arbitrage.

Arbitrage takes many forms, but all endeavor simply to profit from an aberration in price relationships. For a simple example of arbitrage, suppose IBM were trading on the New York Stock Exchange at a price of 120 and simultaneously on the Pacific Coast Exchange at 120 1/2. An arbitrager would purchase shares in New York and simultaneously sell them on the Pacific Coast, locking in a profit of half a point. Such opportunities are rare, but there any number of price aberrations that involve slightly more risk and substantially more reward.

Cash-Futures Arbitrage

How can arbitrage set parameters on the spread between futures and the underlying indexes if the futures premium gets way out of line with the index? After all, you can't sell short a futures contract and somehow buy back the underlying index as a form of arbitrage. Or can you? This is called ''cash-futures arbitrage'' and is in fact done.

An arbitrageur knows that, at expiration, the futures contract must settle at the same price as the underlying index. Thus, if short-term gyrations have produced a 4.00 point premium on an S&P contract, that is $2,000 per contract worth of premium which must evaporate by the time the contract expires. By selling the future short, an arbitrageur is assured of gaining the benefit of the evaporation of

$2,000. That sum can be "locked in" as profit if one can offset the risk of loss caused by an upward move in the underlying index and a corresponding rise in the futures contract.

So arbitrageurs have invented a way to go long the index itself. Some indexes are easier to "buy" than others. The Major Market Index is the easiest. If you sell $10 million worth of MMI futures, you simply buy the same number of shares (since the MMI is price-weighted) in each of the MMI stocks in an aggregate sum of $10 million.

A real-world example might clarify this strategy. On May 16, 1985, the June MMI future closed at 255 1/8, worth $25,512.50, when the index itself was at 253.97. An arbitrageur knows that a spread of $115.50 per contract must evaporate within the 35 days to expiration. To do an arbitrage of approximately $10 million, one would sell short 393 MMI June futures (equivalent to 157 maxi contracts) and simultaneously invest in each of the 20 MMI stocks (about 8,800 shares per stock) for a total investment of close to $10 million. The positions could be maintained until maturity of the contract.[2] In this case, the index and June futures went out at exactly 260.

Since we are hedged, we need not be particularly concerned with a breakout of profit (on the stocks) and loss (on the futures). Rather, our investor would have had the following cash flow: (1) profit from evaporation of the cash-futures spread $(255.125 - 253.97 = 1.155 \times \$100 = \$115.50 \times 393$ contracts $= \$45,391.50$ *plus* (2) dividends on the individual stocks of approximately $51,744, since the MMI had an annualized dividend yield of 5.40 percent between May 16 and June 21. Total cash flow equals $97,135.50 on $10 million over 35 days for an annualized return of 10.13 percent on a virtually risk-free transaction. Compare that 10.13 percent to the rate of 7.29 percent on treasury bills with the maturity (June 30) that most closely approximated the expiration of the futures.

---

[2]To be technically precise, one modification would have occurred due to a three-for-two split in Eastern Kodak shares which occurred on May 20. The "extra" Kodak shares would have been sold and a corresponding number of futures would have been bought back in order to maintain a properly balanced position.

Of course, transaction costs must be factored into our equation. At an institutional rate of six cents per share, commissions would have been approximately as follows:

Opening purchase of 176,000 shares of stock	$10,560
Closing sale of 176,000 shares of stock	10,560
Opening sale of 393 MMI futures	9,825
Total	$30,945

Thus, given a $97,135.50 gross profit and $30,945 in commissions, the net profit would have been $66,190.50 on $10 million over 35 days for an annualized return of 6.90 percent. In this instance, which was selected at random, arbitraging the MMI would not have been worthwhile. Often enough such an arbitrage would be profitable on the MMI, but since the MMI is so easy to buy, cash-futures arbitrage with this index is generally less profitable than such arbitrages with contracts on other indexes.

Cash-futures arbitrage with the other indexes is more cumbersome because those indexes are composed of so many more stocks. As you might expect, however, the potential returns are often significantly more attractive. Continuing with May 16 closing prices, let us consider the arbitrage available on the NYSE Composite futures. The June NYSE future closed at 108.45 when the index was at 107.50. Here, a spread of .95, or $475, must erode within 35 days. Let's do a $10 million arbitrage by selling 185 contracts on the NYFE. That's enough size to move the market, so to bring the example a bit closer to the real world, we'll assume the sales at an average price of 108.40 (perhaps sixty at 108.45, sixty at 108.40, and the balance at 108.35).

Our cash flows look like this: (1) premium erosion (108.40 − 107.50 = .90 × $500 = $450 per contract × 185 contracts = $83,250 *plus* (2) dividends on the individual NYSE stocks of approximately $38,068, since the NYSE had an annualized dividend yield of 3.97 percent between May 16 and June 21. Total cash flow = $121,318 on $10 million over 35 days for an annualized return of 12.65 percent, compared to the rate on those comparable-maturity T-bills of 7.29 percent. Subtracting commission costs of approximately $30,000 still leaves $91,318 for an annualized return of 9.52 percent, well above the T-bill rate. *Any money-market investor who is happy to do a swap to gain ten basis points ought to look closely at a strategy that can produce an annualized pickup of over 200 basis points for an investment duration under three months.*

The game gets even better. Often, shifts in market sentiment cause the premium to drop rapidly in a short period of time. In fact, a savvy investor on May 16 might have surmised that the expiration of May options the following day would exert some downward pressure on premiums, which did occur. When the premium drops sharply after an arbitrage is established, nothing says you must maintain the position until the futures expire. On May 17, the NYSE futures closed at 108.95 when the index settled at 108.48, a spread of .47. Had we unwound our arbitrage at the close, our annualized return would have been phenomenal. Our cash flow looks as follows: premium evaporation from .90 yesterday to .45 today = .45 × $500 = $225 per contract (let's make it $200, assuming we would pay 109.00, rather than the settlement price of 108.95 for the futures). $200 × 185 contracts equals $37,000, and no dividend would have accrued. We have earned $37,000, less $30,000 commissions, or $7,000 per day on $10 million for an annualized yield of 25.5 percent!

So what's the catch? Surprisingly, there isn't one. In fact, on positions held to expiration, some of the major investment banks are willing to guarantee a spread (or perhaps even a rate) to a customer so that in case of foul-ups in executing the arbitrage, the house pays.

If there is no catch, why is the game so good? Much of the answer lies in the fact that certain institutional investors face legal or internal constraints on their use of stock index futures (see Chapter 8). This reduces artificially the number of potential short sellers of high premiums. Moreover, market sentiment is a powerful force which can overwhelm the influences of existing arbitrage. Thus, the returns shown for May 16 are indeed a representative case.

However, this game is not always as simple as these examples would make it appear. It is no coincidence that the S&P, NYSE, or Value Line futures offer a return so much higher than that of the MMI futures. This is a function of the complexity of establishing arbitrages with indexes other than the MMI. An arbitrageur who buys a portfolio of an equal number of shares of each of the twenty MMI stocks succeeds in buying the index.

Consider what one must do to buy the actual S&P 500 Index. Not only must one purchase 500 stocks, but one must also buy each stock in proportion to its weighting in the index. To create a "perfect hedge," a proportional buying program in a $10 million arbitrage might include 4,750 shares of IBM, but only 390 shares of Black & Decker or 30 shares of Tonka. Obviously, at some point buying each stock in perfect proportion gets ridiculous.

With so much money to be made, arbitrageurs have overcome this obstacle. They purchase a portfolio of 200 to 400 stocks that they expect to closely track the movement of the S&P 500 Index itself. The risk of "tracking error" involved with such a strategy is minimal when arbitraging futures traded on a weighted arithmetic index such as the S&P 500 or the NYSE Composite Index.

Now that it is established that an arbitrageur can "buy an index," how can he buy it quickly enough to lock in his expected profit? In fact, an arbitrageur can and will execute the futures and cash market transactions virtually simultaneously. An NYSE member can send an order for any amount up to 2,099 shares from any of its offices directly to any specialist's post via the NYSE's automated DOT system. This may soon increase to 9,999 shares. Moreover, a member firm may also assemble a small army of "two-dollar brokers" on the NYSE floor and disperse them to different trading posts all at once. Normally, these brokers would just "lift" offers which are made either by the specialist, in the trading crowd at the specialist's post, or on the specialist's book.

Lifting orders involves an indirect transaction cost because the offers are often lifted at prices higher than the last sale. In fact, a Salomon Brothers study[3] concluded that the bid-ask spread of the S&P 500 index is usually about 0.90–1.00 in S&P 500 units, with the last

---

[3] H. Nicholas Hanson, Ph.D. and Louis I. Margolis, *Using Stock Index Futures to Create Synthetic Money Market Instruments* (New York: Salomon Brothers Inc, February 1985).

trade of the index approximately in the middle of this range. This means that taking all the offers will result in purchasing the S&P 500 at a price of about 0.50 above that reflected by last-sale data. This produces a concomitant decrease in the futures-index spread and the resulting return to the hedged portfolio (RHP).

Certain risks and costs of cash-futures arbitrage are increased when the Value Line Index is involved. First, the fact that the index is unweighted means that a drastic move in one OTC stock (e.g., a jump from 10 to 12) can move the index as much as a move of the same percentage in IBM (e.g., from 150 to 180). That is not the kind of risk that a conservative arbitrageur likes to take. Moreover, it is mathematically impossible to exactly mirror a geometric index. Additionally, illiquidity in both the Value Line futures and in many of the stocks in the Value Line index adds significantly to the cost of doing cash-futures arbitrage on that contract. Not surprisingly, then, the potential return from cash-futures arbitrage on the Value Line contract is generally higher than the return available on other stock index futures contracts. On May 16, a cash-futures arbitrage on the June Value Line contract offered an annualized return (based on last sale) of approximately 15.5 percent before commissions. This represents a large premium over the precommission rates of 12.65 percent available on the NYSE, 12.10 percent available on the S&P 500, or 10.13 percent on the MMI at the same time.

Since prices on the Value Line futures are less constrained by cash-futures arbitrage, those futures are regarded by many traders as the purest indicator of short-term market sentiment. Even so, the Value Line prices are held in line to some extent by arbitrage between it and other futures contracts.

Just as arbitrage activity limits the size of a premium, similar activity limits the amount of a discount since one can buy the future and sell the so-called mirroring portfolio. However, the players are often different when the futures trade at a discount. A classic arbitrage would involve buying the futures together with a short sale of the stocks in the mirroring portfolio. However, it is difficult to execute futures purchases and short sales simultaneously because a present NYSE rule prohibits short sales on minus ticks and zero-minus ticks.

Therefore, when the futures are at a discount, the arbitrage function is often undertaken by so-called index funds. These funds already own a portfolio designed to mirror a particular index, usually the S&P 500. When the futures are underpriced relative to the stocks, these funds will sell their stocks and buy the futures. Since the strategy involves no short sales of stock, the uptick rule (NYSE Rule 440B) does not come into play, and the stock and futures transactions can be executed simultaneously.

Arbitraging stock index futures against a closely matched portfolio is not as simple as shorting the future whenever the premium exceeds some static trigger point. This arbitrage requires fairly sophisticated calculations to determine the intrinsic worth of a contract (and thus the proper premium) at a given point in time. The intrinsic value of a futures contract depends on the time remaining until expiration as well as short-term interest streams and dividend streams that would flow from investment either in futures or the underlying equities. Interest accrues in a steady stream, but dividend payment streams vary substantially at different times of each quarter. The highest concentration of ex-dividend dates usually falls in the month prior to the quarterly expiration of stock index futures contracts. Figure 7–1 indicates how uneven dividend streams are.

One who owns stocks only during the month of March will not care about a yield of 4 percent per annum on a particular stock index if none of the stocks go ex-dividend during March. One who owns the same stocks only during the month of February might receive dividends of 1 percent during that month for an annualized rate of 12 percent.

The annualized yield is important in any cash-futures arbitrage calculation, particularly for an investor who wishes to reverse out of an arbitrage prior to the expiration of the futures contract. The annualized yield of an index cannot be perfectly forecast because neither the payment nor the amount of a particular dividend is certain until it is declared.

Now suppose that instead of holding the NYFE March 1984 contract (discussed earlier) until expiration, you plan to sell it at the end of January. The dividend payout in January is far less than the annual

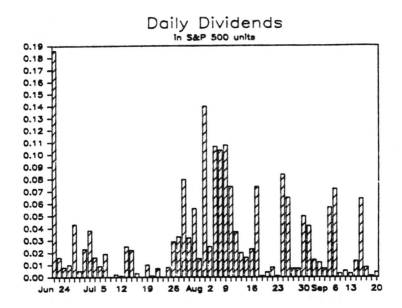

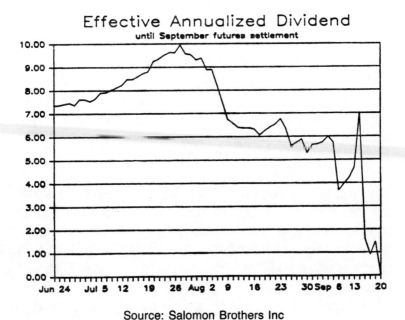

Source: Salomon Brothers Inc

FIGURE 7–1.

dividend amount divided by 12. Thus, if you still have a Treasury bill rate of 9.25 percent but a dividend rate during the futures contract holding period of only two percent annualized, you might rationally be indifferent as between owning a futures contract or a basket of actual stocks when the premium of the futures over the index is a full 7.25 percent annualized, or 1.8 percent per quarter. This translates to 96.90 based on an index of 95.18, rather than the 96.35 calculated earlier.

Some investors may use an interest rate above the risk-free rate to determine the point at which they are indifferent between owning stocks or owning futures together with short-term interest-bearing instruments. Based on the S&P 500 hedge margin requirement, an investor would have to put up approximately $300,000 worth of T-bills to buy $10 million of stock index futures. The $9.7 million that would otherwise have gone to pay for stocks can be invested at a rate above the T-bill rate. Certain investors may feel comfortable using other money-market instruments (e.g., Euro-CD's) instead of T-bills. This could make a lower premium acceptable to certain arbitrageurs selling futures, and make a higher premium tolerable to a buyer of futures.

Other factors may affect the level of premium or discount at which an investor becomes indifferent between owning stocks or futures. Certain institutions who can buy stocks on margin may finance a $10 million basket of stocks in a margin account at a cost that exceeds the risk-free interest rate. This too would make the future a relatively more attractive investment, thus potentially exerting upward pressure on the premium. Conversely, certain investors (perhaps those in institutions that cannot buy stocks on margin) may be willing to tolerate some extra premium in return for the leverage offered by stock index futures.

An investor who wishes to buy an index through either stock or futures may be willing to tolerate a larger premium since he saves on transaction costs by buying futures.

For those interested in ultimate refinement of a valuation model, one can apply present-value analysis to the dividend stream since dividend flows are uneven and because the period between the record date and payment date can vary by several weeks from stock to stock. Moreover, an investor might expect the risk-free interest rate to vary during the life of the futures contract, thus affecting his intrinsic value calculations.

Academics[4] have suggested an arbitrageur's view of the intrinsic value of the cash-futures spread might be affected by certain tax considerations, including what they have labeled a "timing option." However, empirical evidence has not shown tax considerations to exert a noticeable influence on premiums.

The cash-futures arbitrage game has any number of twists and nuances. Some institutional traders will substitute options on the underlying stocks for the stocks themselves when establishing an arbitrage against the futures. This type of arbitrage might involve the creation of a "synthetic" position in the index by using options to establish synthetic positions in each of the stocks comprising a particular index. This strategy applies particularly to the Major Market index because options are traded on each stock in it. Such as strategy would allow an arbitrageur to sidestep the NYSE uptick rule should he wish to short stocks and buy futures. Alternatively, arbitrageurs may position index options against the futures.

Another possible twist involves developing a basket of securities that correlates closely with the movement of an underlying index, but yields dividends greater than the index group as a whole. Such a strategy would require a thorough analysis of possible tracking error, since the portfolio might be influenced as much by interest-rate shifts as by movements in a particular stock index.

Some players cannot resist trying to squeeze a little bit more out of an already good arbitrage. They may begin by buying the five biggest stocks in their model portfolio, hoping that upticks caused by their purchases in those stocks will lead futures traders to further widen premiums because market leaders appear to be acting well. Futures prices will often react more quickly than the index itself to an uptick in IBM. Once the premium gets very fat, the arbitrageurs sell the futures short to the remaining bulls and rapidly cover themselves by buying the rest of their model portfolio before those stocks have a chance to rise.

---

[4] See Kenneth French and Bradford Cornell, "The Pricing of Stock Index Futures," Working Paper #43, Center for the Study of Futures Markets, Columbia Business School, October 1982.

It is important to note, however, that the initial cash outlay may not be all that is needed to lock in a profit. On the futures leg, the initial cash outlay would be required at a preferential hedge margin rate. But thereafter, even if losses on short futures positions are fully protected by corresponding upward moves in the stocks, maintenance margin will still have to be posted on a daily basis to cover the paper losses on the futures. That money must come from additional cash flow because the gains on the stocks are not yet realized, and thus cannot be posted or pledged to satisfy margin calls.

Of course, the best of all worlds for an arbitrageur would be a decline in both stock and futures prices. In a declining market, an arbitrageur who sold futures short will have daily cash flow from his futures position under the mark-to-market margining system. That cash can be used to meet maintenance margin calls on the declining stocks. Any excess cash generated can be reinvested.

Certain legal issues may arise in connection with cash-futures arbitrage programs. Among these are (1) whether customer accounts would be discretionary, (2) compliance with or exemption from speculative position limit rules, including aggregation rules, and (3) whether an FCM (futures commission merchant) that guarantees a rate can refund money if the annualized interest rate realized is below that guarantee. Moreover, regulators may look more closely at any manipulative or disruptive impact of such programs.

Arbitrage and Stock Market Gyrations

In fact, cash-futures arbitrage programs have been widely criticized as contributing to unnecessary gyrations in the stock market. This criticism has been particularly pronounced when the gyration is a downward move. It has become popular to attribute market declines strictly to arbitrage programs rather than to fundamental or technical factors that move the market.

This is a bit like blaming a Dutch boy who removes his finger for breaking a dike. The Dutch boy simply accelerated the restoration of equilibrium between too much pressure on one side of the dike and too little pressure on the other. He didn't create the pressure.

A cash-futures arbitrageur simply hastens the restoration of equilibrium between too much selling pressure on one side of an integrated market and less selling pressure on the other side. Arbitrage programs make for a convenient whipping boy, allowing ever-hopeful investors to overlook more fundamental reasons for a market decline. *The flaw in the reasoning of these critics is their failure to ask how the discount giving rise to arbitrage opportunities came about in the first instance.*

If the futures contracts did not exist, bearish investors would simply sell stocks in the first place. However, because it is easier and cheaper to sell futures than stocks, sophisticated portfolio managers will often elect to sell the futures contracts. The arbitrageurs are merely bringing the cash index back into line with futures prices. By the time that happens, the market should be viewed as having already fallen because the sellers of the futures contracts could just as easily have sold the stocks in the first instance. Instead, they elect to save on transactions costs and allow someone else who is willing to pay substantial transactions costs to profit from a temporary aberration that their selling creates.

Cash-futures arbitrage was a scapegoat for the Dow's sudden 39 point tumble on January 8, 1986. But, a look at the day's activity indicates that when the cascade began at about 2:48 (Point A on Figure 7-2), the futures premiums were actually slightly overvalued. Consequently, nobody could have been selling stocks and simultaneously buying futures when the selloff began. Rather, the sellers were portfolio managers who were worried about Volcker's comments on interest rates, the market's failure to hold the double top level of 216.50 on the S&P futures, or the day's rumors related to Libya—or just portfolio managers who got scared and sold because everybody else was selling.

Moreover, if cash-futures arbitrage pushed the stocks down, the Dow should have continued to go lower when the S&P futures reached their maximum discount of about 1.60 points at 3:48. Instead, even though 3:48 was the optimal time to sell stocks and buy futures, that is the precise time at which the Dow stocks stabilized. In fact, the Dow recovered about five points in the 12 minutes to the close.

Undoubtedly, much of this stabilization was attributable to arbitrageurs who bought futures. Even though they may have simultaneously

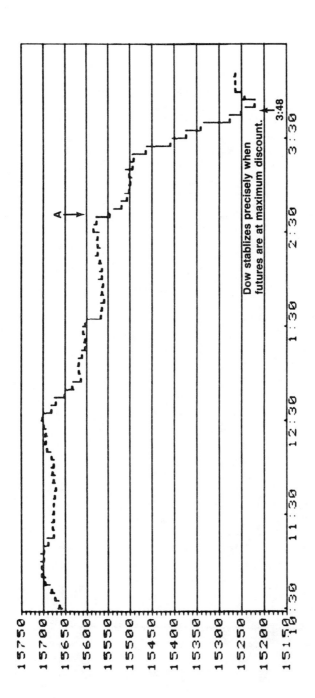

Source: Videcom Service, ADP Comtrend, Stamford, Conn.

FIGURE 7-2. DOW JONES INDUSTRIALS, JANUARY 8, 1986

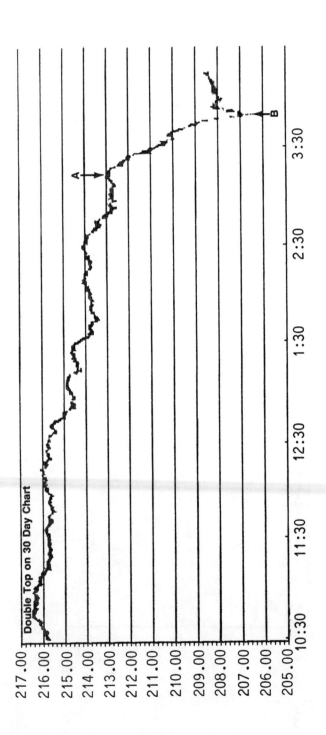

Source: Videcom Service, ADP Comtrend, Stamford, Conn.

FIGURE 7-2. MARCH S&P 500 FUTURES, JANUARY 8, 1986 (Continued)

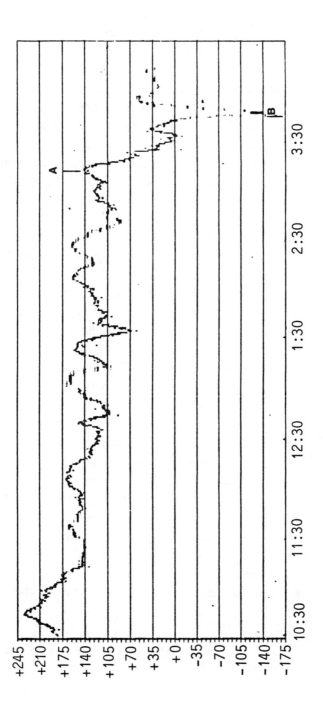

Source: Videcom Service, ADP Comtrend, Stamford, Conn.

FIGURE 7–2. SPREAD BETWEEN S&P FUTURES AND S&P INDEX, JANUARY 8, 1986 (Concluded)

sold stocks, the arbitrageurs stabilized the market by bidding up the tail that wags the dog, indicating to other market participants that the downward momentum had ceased and that it was safe to step in and buy stocks. The Dow's reversal at 3:48 speaks for itself.

As for individuals who complain that their stops were hit in stocks due to program selling, it is likely that even more stops would have been hit without the stabilizing influence of this arbitrage.

Let us review one more situation in which index-related arbitrage was widely blamed for a precipitous market decline. The Dow tumbled sharply in the week ended April 4, 1986, and the media again made index-related arbitrage the culprit—as if nothing else could have caused the market to go down.

My view is that other factors were indeed responsible for the tumble. First, early April has been a seasonally weak period. Second, April was the first month in which stocks purchased right before the huge run-up began were eligible for long-term capital gains treatment. Third, sentiment was wildly bullish—itself a cautionary sign. Fourth, the stock index futures had reached the top of a four-year channel and then developed a "triple-bottom" formation which was very similar to the pattern formed after the highs of July 1983. A familiar chart pattern involved a series of ever-weaker rallies from a "triple bottom" base, and then a sharp selloff which occurred when futures traders began panic selling as soon as the triple bottom was pierced. (The comparable sell-off when 1983's triple bottom was pierced occurred before arbitrage was sufficiently widespread to have been blamed). Eventually, furious selling pushed futures prices to discounts. At this stage, arbitrageurs undoubtedly sold stocks and bought futures, thus pushing stock prices lower. But the initial sell-off was induced by technical factors—not arbitrage. The arbitrage was an *effect* of the sell-off, not its *cause*.[5] The arbitrage opportunity did not exist until after prices had already begun tumbling.

Arbitrage itself presents no great danger. But what may be dangerous is that the mysteriousness and complexity of the arbitrage seems

---

[5]Nor is this analysis all hindsight. I established a short position gradually in the few days before the market broke.

to fascinate the media and policymakers, and therefore may distract attention from what may prove to be more serious problems with stock index futures. My own view is that the stock market may well eventually crash—and that stock index futures will be blamed—*but for all the wrong reasons*.

I believe that stock index futures will not cause a crash, but might accelerate it for two reasons that are unrelated to arbitrage.

First, I frequently hear the argument that we cannot have another 1929-style crash because stock margin is 50% today versus approximately 10% in 1929. But consider that stock index margin rules allow an investor to "buy the market" for less than five percent down. Too many margin calls in the stock index futures market could engender a selling wave in futures that would spill over into stocks. One could argue that with today's dominance of the market by institutions which do not buy stocks on margin, such a concern is remote. On the other hand, if you consider the dollar value of open interest in stock index futures as a percentage of the "float" in NYSE shares, it suggests that margin calls on futures positions could prompt enough selling to push the market below the stop-loss levels set by institutions engaging in dynamic portfolio hedging, thereby triggering a cascade of additional selling.

Second, I think that the stock market could eventually be harmed by the infiltration into the stock market of what I call a "commodities mindset." As suggested in Chapter 5, futures market participants and equity market investors have different time horizons and views as to value. Moreover, I believe that commodity traders have a tendency to test how far in one direction prices can be pushed. Trend-following trading systems reinforce this tendency. This is fine as long as a bull market is in progress. But when a shift in fundamental economic forces leads to unsustainably high stock prices, the tendency to see how far prices can be pushed in the other direction could be very harmful to the stock market itself. But not to the trend-followers. A short seller makes as much when the futures drop 10 points as a long makes when the futures rise 10 points.

Non-Arbitrage Program Trades

A sudden wave of buying or selling of stocks is not necessarily arbitrage-related. Many institutional money managers use buy programs or sell programs as a means of establishing or liquidating a large portfolio as inexpensively as possible. Consider the manager of a passively-managed S&P 500 index fund who receives $50 million of new money to invest after the S&P 500 closes at 250. His goals are to closely track the index and to minimize transaction costs by buying the index as close to 250 as possible. He knows that NYSE specialists may not be able to fill all of his orders for blocks of stock at the last sale or even at the most recent offered price, so he may wind up buying the index for considerably more than 250.

His alternative is to ask one or more major brokerage firms to guarantee a fixed maximum price for the entire portfolio. Generally, a brokerage firm would be willing to earn commissions by guaranteeing a maximum average price of 1/8 to 1/4 above the last sale on each stock. The brokerage firm is willing to make such an aggressive guarantee because it is in a unique position to find the other side of block trades, judge market conditions, and to hedge itself as necessary until the portfolio can be purchased. If the market opens weaker, the brokerage firm might withhold buy orders or at least wait until its bids are hit, so that its buy program is barely noticeable. But if the market appears to be strong, the buy program might be executed just as rapidly as a cash-futures arbitrage program. This similarity in manner of execution is the main reason that some market commentators have failed to distinguish arbitrage trading from unrelated program trading.

Program trading is often the most efficient means of reaching a variety of goals, including re-allocation of assets or investment of new cash.

PRICE RELATIONSHIPS AMONG FUTURES CONTRACTS

As noted, it is difficult to engage in cash-futures arbitrage with certain contracts, especially the Value Line futures, and, to a lesser extent, the NYSE Composite futures. If such arbitrage with these contracts is minimal, what keeps their premiums or discounts from becoming excessive? More importantly, how does one profit when these prices deviate too far from fair value?

It stands to reason that, if two underlying indexes have a close correlation, the corresponding futures contracts should not move too far out of line. This is particularly true of the S&P and NYFE contracts, because the underlying indexes have a .99 correlation. Since there is both an expected price relationship between these two contracts and four years of price history which can be used to evaluate trading opportunities, arbitrageurs are willing to jump in whenever the S&P and NYFE contracts do not move in tandem.

Assume that both the S&P and NYFE contracts go to excessive premiums. Cash-futures arbitrageurs buy stocks and sell enough S&P futures to push that contract back into its fair value. The NYFE contract has experienced no cash-futures arbitrage and remains overvalued. An arbitrageur (often a different actor than a cash-futures arbitrageur) will sell NYFE contracts and buy S&P contracts in the hope of profiting from what he perceives to be a temporary aberration in the price relationship between those contracts.

In fact, there is considerable arbitrage activity between the S&P 500 futures and the NYFE futures. Traders in the NYFE trading pit have assistants who spend all day on long-distance calls to counterparts at booths near the S&P trading ring in Chicago. They indicate prices in the corresponding market by flashing hand signals to their traders, who take advantage of extremely short-term price aberrations.

For example, assume that a NYFE trader realizes that an S&P 500 futures contract is usually valued at about 1.72 times of a NYFE contract. When he sees the last sale of a NYFE contract at 100.00, and the S&P future at 172.00, he does nothing. Suppose, 15 minutes later, the NYFE contract had rallied ten ticks, or fifty basis points, to 100.50, and the S&P contract had also rallied ten ticks to 172.50. Now Chicago is priced at only 1.716 times of New York. An arbitrageur sees an abnormal spread relationship between the two prices. He need not have an opinion about the general direction of the market to attempt to profit from this abnormality. He would simply buy S&P

contracts, sell NYFE contracts, and hold them all until the price relationship returned to normal.

Suppose, in his very first arbitrage, he buys one S&P contract and sells one NYFE contract before the prices return to where they were initially. His $250 gain on his short position in New York would have been completely offset by the $250 loss on his long position in Chicago. Since the Chicago contract has a higher dollar value, it takes fewer of them to offset contracts held in New York. Most "arbs" use a seven to four ratio, or multiples thereof, when arbitraging the S&P versus the NYFE.

Had our trader calculated an even more exact arbitrage ratio and bought 17 NYFE contracts while selling only ten S&P contracts, he would have made .50 on each of 17 NYFE contract, for a gain of 8.50, or $4,250. On the ten S&P contracts, he would have lost .50 per contract, for a loss of 5.00 or $2,500. He would have generated a net profit of $1,750 upon a return to a normal spread relationship, regardless of the general market direction.

That precise ratio can be altered slightly with little risk. Suppose he had bought four S&P contracts and sold seven NYFE contracts. He would have made .50 on each of the NYFE contracts, for a gain of 3.50 or $1,750. On the four S&P contracts, he would have lost .50 per contract, for a loss of 2.00 or $1,000. This produces a net profit of $750.

A seven to four spread translates to a 1.75 arbitrage ratio. In other words, the S&P contract is given slightly more weight than is appropriate in ideal circumstances. Our example shows, however, that an arbitrage can still be profitable if the arbitrage ratio is slightly skewed toward the losing leg of the arbitrage.

Of course, one problem with arbitrage is that one can never be sure that the spread relationship will ever return to the familiar historical level, or that it will do so soon enough to produce a profit. Suppose, for whatever reason, that the S&P were gradually to drop to a level of 1.70 times a NYFE contract. On a properly constructed arbitrage, that could get costly—to the tune of about $3,250 in our example with the seven-to-four ratio. In such a situation, profit from arbitrage requires nerves of steel, financial staying power, or perhaps an understanding banker.

The best way to judge whether a change in the proportional relationship between futures contracts is justified is to examine the relationship between the underlying indexes. A move in the S&P 500 index up to 1.75 times the NYSE Composite Index fully justifies a similar percentage premium in the futures.

Even though the correlation between the two indexes is high, price disparities may last for several weeks or months. For instance, the S&P 500 index usually increases its premium over the NYSE Composite Index when oil stocks rally because of those stocks' higher weighting in the S&P 500. Therefore, one who arbitrages one stock index contract against another is playing a probability game. Based on a knowledge of the correlation between two contracts, he assesses the probability that a spread relationship will return to some norm before expiration of the contract, or within a longer time frame if positions are rolled forward. In contrast, a cash-futures arbitrageur is not playing that type of probability game. Rather, he is playing a convergence game: if his cash position eliminates "tracking error," he is certain to earn his spread at expiration.

Two types of arbitrageurs trade one futures contract against another. Those on the floor play a short-term game of the sort described above. They need only a two- or three-tick aberration to trade, making their money by taking positions when spreads reach the limits of very short-term trading bands. When such a trading band is violated, the price relationship between two contracts can vary by several hundred dollars. The short-term arbitrageurs unwind their positions as soon as a short-term trading band is exceeded by a preset amount.

The second type of arbitrageur takes over when the price relationship reaches extremes measured over several weeks or months. This type of arbitrageur is commonly called a "spread trader."

Arbitrage between the S&P 500 and the NYSE Composite has become especially popular because of the near-perfect correlation between the two indexes. In fact, "locals" on the NYFE floor have estimated that approximately 35 percent of trading activity on that floor is arbitrage against the S&P contract. Thus, short-term movements in the NYFE contract are heavily influenced by price changes in Chicago. The reverse is not necessarily true. The influence of the arbitrageurs is much more diluted in the S&P pit because of its far higher volume and because each arbitrage involves fewer S&P contracts. For this reason, one can very often observe the NYFE pit lagging price changes in Chicago by fifteen to thirty seconds or so.

Numerous arbitrages are possible between other contracts. However, the lower correlations between other indexes, and therefore the futures contracts, increase the risk to an arbitrageur of an already wide spread moving even wider and perhaps staying there until or beyond expiration. But as the easy form of arbitrage becomes a saturated game, more resources are being devoted to such arbitrages. These arbitrages are more likely to be done by institutional traders or individual speculators than by "locals" since the profit opportunities tend to arise from major aberrations in the spread rather than from minute-to-minute deviations.

Let us briefly consider some of these opportunities for intermarket spreading. One involves the relationship between the blue-chip stocks in the Major Market Index and the broad market or secondary listed stocks represented by the S&P 500 or NYSE Index. This strategy is rooted in the fact that the performance of blue-chip stocks and secondary issues diverge during different periods. Secondary issues often out-perform the more mature corporations in bull market periods. But when investors are more apprehensive, they may shy away from secondary issues. If you spot what you perceive to be an unwarranted divergence between a blue-chip index such as the MMI and a broad market index, you may wish to short the relatively overbought segment of the market and buy the relatively underbought segment.

The Value Line/S&P spread is also attractive to speculators. Moreover, some analysts look to the spread as an indicator of the market's direction. I must confess that such analysts see things I do not. Conventional wisdom is that the premium of the Value Line contract over the S&P futures increases when the trend is bullish and narrows when the market moves lower. Figure 7–3 puts the conventional wisdom to rest, at least for a while. Notice that in the Dow's great bull rampage through the 1300s and the 1400s, the S&P futures came within 500 basis points of the Value Line contract. Later in 1985, the spread fell to under 200 basis points. In the same year, that spread had been as wide as 2,000 basis points.

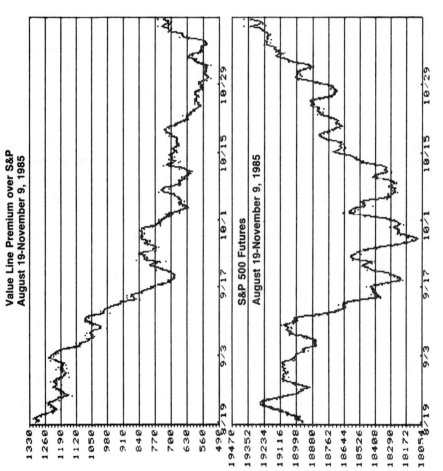

Source: Videcom Service, ADP Comtrend, Stamford, Conn.

FIGURE 7-3.

The newest example of potential profit from spreading involves spreading blue-chip/Fortune 500 stocks versus low-capitalization/growth companies through trades such as the MMI versus the NASDAQ-100 on the Chicago Board of Trade or the S&P 500 versus the SPOC-250 on the Chicago Merc. However, the viability of such spreading strategies depends upon those new contracts exhibiting more liquidity than they did at the end of 1985.

A spread such as the S&P 500 versus the S&P 100 provides another way to play the broader market against the blue chips with the protection of a reasonably high correlation between the indexes. However, one side of this spread must now be done with options since the S&P 100 futures are dormant.

Ironically, the efficiency of the markets is reduced by certain exchanges themselves, which refuse to permit arbitrageurs to post spread margins on arbitrage positions carried overnight. Spread margin requirements, common in the commodity markets, are substantially lower than normal margins because the two offsetting positions greatly reduce the risk of holding either position outright. Each exchange has the power to grant or deny spread margin treatment to the leg of an arbitrage established on its floor. For example, the NYFE allows a member to post initial spread margin of $400 per contract to maintain its leg of an arbitrage against the S&P contract, but the CME requires the full $6,000 deposit per contract to maintain the offsetting leg. One may surmise that this policy has more to do with the CME's desire to maintain market share by discouraging additional trading in the New York contract than it does with an assessment of market risk. The situation will probably not change unless the CME is threatened with an antitrust suit.

CALENDAR SPREADS

Spreading can also be done within one market rather than between markets. A spread done in the same market is known as a "calendar spread" because it consists of a long position in one month and a short position in another. Calendar spreads can yield a profit in traditional commodity contracts for a variety of reasons, including expected seasonal price variations. Calendar spreads in stock index futures are designed to profit from adjustments in the premium that reflect changes in short-term interest rates or in market sentiment. These adjustments sometimes occur unpredictably and suddenly. Waiting a week (or more) for a calendar spread to adjust to changes in short-term rates can be frustrating, and liquidity in the out months is lower, so the bid-ask spread is often two ticks instead of just one.

Yet calendar spreads are attractive for a few reasons. First, the spread involves little risk in that if the spread is not justified by current short-term interest rates, it is very likely to correct and produce a profitable trade sooner or later. In the meantime, the trade ties up very little capital because, as Table 7–1 indicates, margins for calendar spreads are very low.

TABLE 7–1. CALENDAR SPREAD MARGINS

	Initial	Maintenance
S&P 500	$400	$200
NYSE Composite	200	100
KC Value Line	400	200
Major Market Index	mark-to-market	

DOES IT EVER MAKE SENSE TO BUY OVERVALUED CONTRACTS?

Clearly, selling overpriced futures contracts and buying under-priced ones can yield profit. Are there ever times when it makes sense to buy a contract that is overpriced or to sell one that is underpriced? In other words, are contracts trading at large premiums because the smart money knows the market is going up? Do discounts foreshadow bearish trends?

It appears that a large premium does not reliably predict higher prices. Therefore, it generally would not make sense to buy an over-priced contract. Moreover, because the level of premium or discount does not appear to have any significant positive correlation to subsequent market direction, the law of probability works in favor of the speculator who takes outright long positions in undervalued contracts and outright short positions in overvalued contracts.

PREDICTIVE POWER OF PREMIUM OR DISCOUNT

One early study concluded that S&P futures correctly anticipated 14 key turning points in the stock market, but missed ten such moves. That study by a subsidiary of Donaldson, Lufkin, and Jenrette, Inc. covered the first 241 days of trading in S&P futures. It found that the forecasting reliability of S&P futures depends heavily on the period measured.

A review of major turning points and subsequent trends between 1982–1985 suggests that the prevailing sentiment, as reflected in a premium or discount, has been wrong more often than not! If that is so, a speculator who buys undervalued contracts and sells overvalued contracts will profit in two ways: (1) upon return of the contract to fair value, and (2) often upon favorable movement of the underlying index. In other words, premium or discount may be a useful tool to contrarian speculators. However, that review also illustrates the danger of relying too heavily on the premium or discount as a market timing device. It can be summarized as follows:

Period	Premium/Discount	Actual Trend
August 1982	Bearish	Bullish
October 1982	Bearish	Bullish
February 1983	Bullish	Bearish
April/May 1983	Bearish	Bullish
July 1983	Bullish	Bearish
January/February 1984	Bullish	Bearish
August 1984	Neutral/Bearish	Bullish
January 1985	Neutral	Bullish
Summer 1985	Bearish	Bearish
October/November 1985	Bearish/Neutral	Bullish

Let us take a closer look at each of these periods.

August 1982

The beginning of the bull market in August 1982 was not predicted by stock index futures. On August 16, the day before the 38 point rise in the Dow, S&P futures traded at a .39 point or .4 percent discount to that index while the NYFE futures carried a .35 point or .6 percent discount. Even after the first boom of August 17, the S&P futures still managed to close at a rather substantial .70 point discount. That day recalls one of the more interesting divergences between the S&P and the NYFE contracts because the latter managed to close the day at a .60 point premium. On day three of the great bull market, both futures contracts retreated again to close at discounts to the cash index.

On numerous occasions throughout the month of August, the S&P discount exceeded 1.00 points during a trading session and occasionally sold at a 1.50 point discount! In fact, the S&P futures traded at a discount more often than at a premium during the first two weeks of the bull market.

While the discount was a good contrarian tool, the extreme discounts were not the most useful. At point A in Figure 7–4, the discount was not quite at an extreme when the market first soared. Point B, an extreme low point for the discount, would not have been a profitable entry point without a fairly wide stop order. Point C, the market's top in August, did not feature an extreme discount or premium, and Point D, a possible buy signal for a contrarian, was not an occasion to buy in retrospect.

October 1982

. Notice in Figure 7–5 (point A) that the future's basis was extremely bearish before October's sharp run-up began. Point B shows that the market's peak for this month was achieved just as the premium exceeded

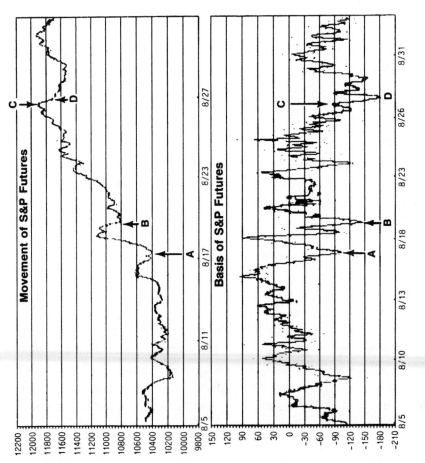

Source: Videcom Service, ADP Comtrend, Stamford, Conn.

FIGURE 7-4. AUGUST 1982

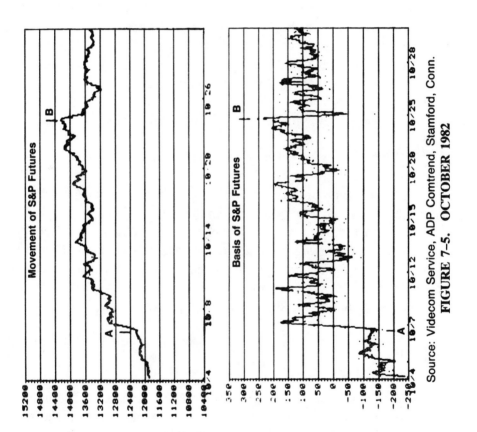

Source: Videcom Service, ADP Comtrend, Stamford, Conn.

FIGURE 7–5. OCTOBER 1982

its high point of 200 for the first time that month. The Dow tumbled 36 points shortly thereafter.

February 1983

Another good time to bet against the prevailing sentiment. A sharp selloff coincided with the highest premiums of the month. The premium suggested that most market participants did not think that January's selloff would continue. The premium was also rather high throughout January, presenting many good opportunities to get short in that month as well.

April/May 1983

An examination of the futures-cash spread throughout April 1983 shows that the futures failed to predict the magnitude of the market's steady rise in that month. In fact, S&P futures traded at a discount during much of that month with the discount again exceeding 1.00 points at times. Figure 7–6 depicts the level of the discount immediately before some of the market's major upward thrusts. It also shows the premium at peak levels as the market finally petered out in mid-May.

July 1983

High premiums again foreshadowed a sharp decline, but the premium failed to provide a precisely timed sell signal. Had you shorted the market when the premium climbed to the 220 level (Figure 7–7, point A), you might have covered that short. Moreover, point B indicates that no extremely high premium presaged the sharpest selloff, and point C illustrates the danger of a premature contrarian reaction to a sharp drop in premium. Presumably, most traders would have avoided that mistake since the premium of 60 at point C was nowhere near the bearish levels accompanying earlier turnarounds.

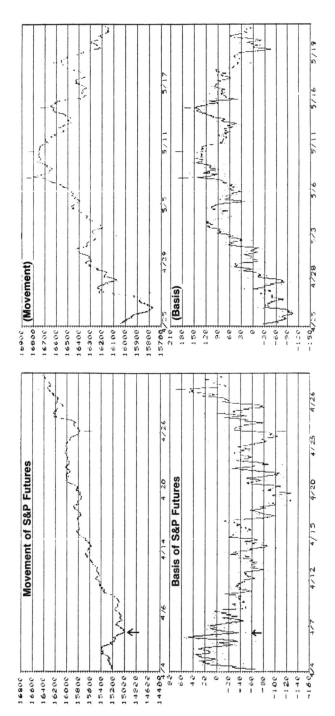

Source: Videcom Service, ADP Comtrend, Stamford, Conn.

FIGURE 7–6. APRIL/MAY 1983

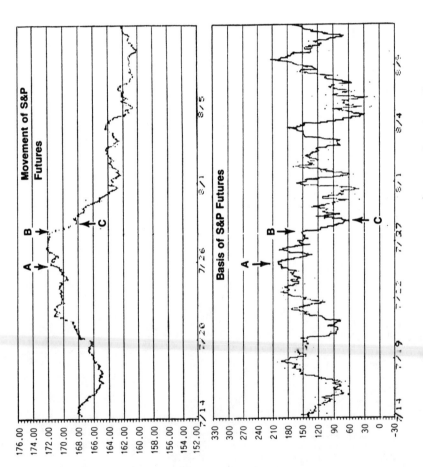

Source: Videocom Service, ADP Comtrend, Stamford, Conn.

FIGURE 7-7. JULY 1983

January/February 1984

Premiums were fairly high through January's slow decline from first-week heights. As Figure 7-8 illustrates, the premium was at its high for January (point A) right before the sharp selloff occurred. The other signals given by other premiums during that period were basically noise.

August 1984

This period suggests that premium has clear limitations as a precise market timing device. The premium was not extreme in any direction in the period before the market caught fire. The S&P staged a 20 point rally in just a week and a half in late July and early August 1984 (Figure 7-9, point A). As discussed in Chapter 6, the key to this rally was the triple bottom point tested on July 25 and the ensuing Dow breakout above 1140. However, once again, premium was useful during this rally in that its steady decline reflected the majority view that the rally could not last.

Throughout the rally, even during several Dow advances exceeding 30 points in a day, the premium of S&P futures to the S&P 500 Index stayed within a range of 0 to 120 cents. Not until the morning of August 6 did the premium move to a range of 120 to 240 as the Dow climbed another 20 points in the opening hour. The highest premium of the rally (Point B) presaged its end as the Dow closed lower that day and then consolidated for awhile.

January 1985

The premiums in December had been quite bullish. While premiums remained bullish, the year opened with three down days. Then, as the premium dropped 1.50 points, the market began a month-long rally. The premium indicated only that sentiment became increasingly skeptical of the rally's staying power as it continued. The premium

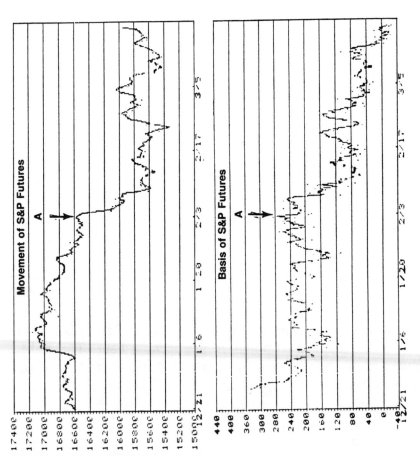

Source: Videcom Service, ADP Comtrend, Stamford, Conn.

FIGURE 7-8. JANUARY/FEBRUARY 1984

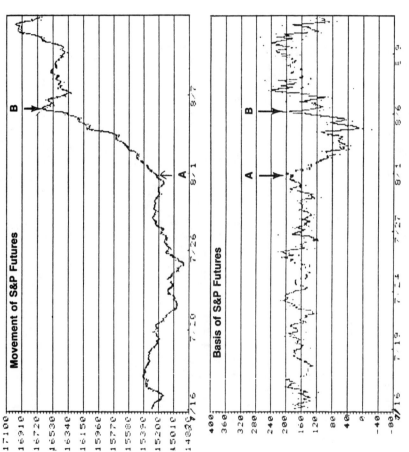

Source: Videcom Service, ADP Comtrend, Stamford, Conn.
FIGURE 7-9. AUGUST 1984

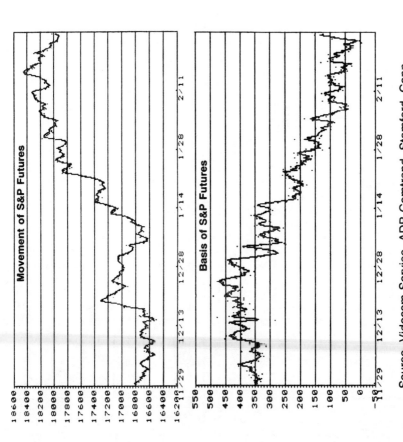

Source Videcom Service, ADP Comtrend, Stamford, Conn.

FIGURE 7-10. JANUARY 1985.
(DECLINING PREMIUMS SUGGEST FUTURES PLAYERS WERE
SKEPTICAL OF RALLY—ANOTHER GOOD BET AGAINST THE CROWD)

provided absolutely no euphoric peak to serve as a sell signal at the rally's end.

Summer 1985

As Figure 7-11 shows, the peak in the premiums came shortly after the market began to retreat from its all-time highs in mid-July. The double top in the premium still enabled one to get short near the 197 level, though that short might have been covered in the one last run-up.

The premium levels gave no abundantly clear signal of the precipitous 22 point drop in the Dow on August 6, 1985. The premiums had come down markedly from their levels of two weeks earlier, but neither the Chicago nor the New York futures traded at a discount. They moved in a narrow and fairly neutral range right before the sharp drop.

In September 1985, however, the discounts were indeed prescient—and they provided plenty of warning time. As Figure 7-12 shows, the September S&P futures traded at a discount before 2:00 p.m. on September 9 (point A); the market's break began shortly before 2:00 p.m. on the following day (point B). Moreover, the September futures traded at a discount all day for several days during the previous week and never traded at a substantial premium during that time. The vertical line in Figure 7-12 shows that the discount indeed provided sufficient time to get short. In fact, the premium went negative for the last time before the big selloff began. It ended with the S&P futures about nine points lower. A contrarian could have gotten his fingers burned this time.

October/November 1985

Just a month later, the market began to recover. Stock index futures managed to remain at a discount for most of the Dow's successful assault on the 1400 level in late October and early November 1985 (see Figure 7-13). In fact, substantial premiums began to appear

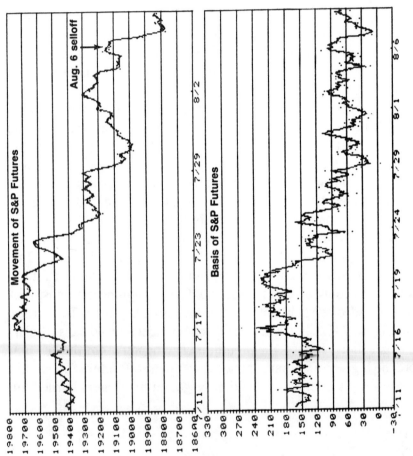

Source: Videcom Service, ADP Comtrend, Stamford, Conn.

FIGURE 7-11. SUMMER 1985

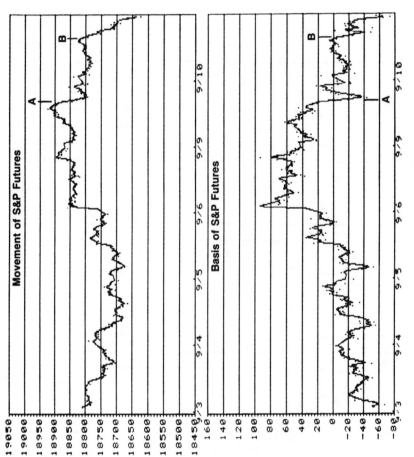

Source: Videcom Service, ADP Comtrend, Stamford, Conn.

FIGURE 7-12. SEPTEMBER 1985

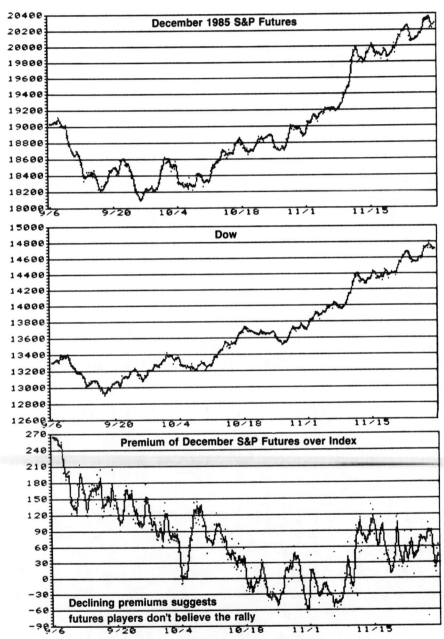

Source: Videcom Service, ADP Comtrend, Stamford, Conn.
FIGURE 7-13. SEPTEMBER/OCTOBER 1985

only in mid-November when the Dow reached 1440 and the S&P futures broke through the 200 barrier. In the week that the S&P futures flirted with and broke above 200, the premium fluctuated wildly between zero and 120. On the first three occasions that the futures traded up to 200 during that time, the premium fell quickly.

Figure 7-14 shows the premium as the Dow assaulted and blew away the 1500 barrier. On all three charges to 1500, the S&P premium remained in a rather neutral 60–120 range, but as soon as the Dow began a retreat from 1515 back toward the 1500 magic number, fear quickly overcame greed and turned the premium into a discount. That discount created another terrific contrarian play as the Dow resumed its bullish ways.

WHICH PREMIUM MAKES THE BEST INDICATOR?

The prior discussion explored only the spread between futures and cash for the S&P contract. Does any other contract's spread more reliably forecast market trends, by being either consistently right or consistently wrong? Apparently not. Here are some initial results of a study.

In May 1985, when the Dow first penetrated 1300, the different futures markets disagreed more than usual about whether the uptrend could continue.

Ranked in order of most bearish to most bullish, the premiums on May 31 were as follows:

Contract	Theoretical Premium	Actual Premium	Bullish/Bearish Factor*
June S&P	43	8	.19
June NYFE	23	22	.96
June MMI	60	75	1.25
June Value Line	66	157	2.37

*Calculated as actual premium/theoretical premium. A figure of 1.00 would indicate neutral sentiment. A negative result would occur any time the actual premium is negative.

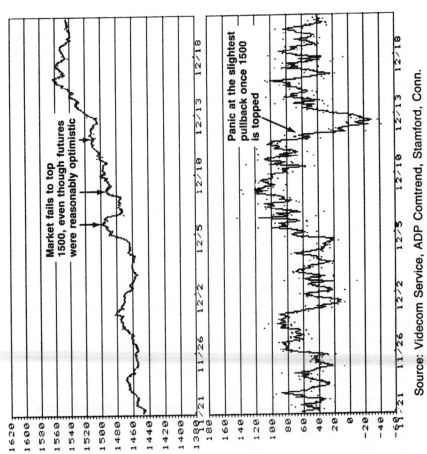

Source: Videcom Service, ADP Comtrend, Stamford, Conn.

FIGURE 7-14.   NOVEMBER/DECEMBER 1985

For the subsequent hour of trading, Value Line provided the best forecast due to an opening surge attributable to a point-and-a-half rally in the bond market. But for the day overall, the S&P and NYFE premiums were the most accurate gauges as the Dow finished four points lower and the broad market was flat. By the end of the week, the Value Line was again the most prescient as the Dow briefly touched 1330, before declining to 1290 in the ensuing two weeks.

The close on December 5, 1985 provided another interesting divergence in sentiment among the contracts. On that day, the Dow rose 16 points and briefly pierced 1500 before falling back in the final hour to close at 1483. Could the 200 point rally continue, or was this 181-million share day the final blow-off? Here is what the premiums said:

Contract	Expected Premium	Actual Premium	Bullish/Bearish Factor*
December MMI	78	10	.13
December S&P	55*	47	.85
December Value Line	47	47	1.00
December NYFE	31	38	1.23

*The expected premium on the S&P contract exceeded that of the Value Line contract because at that point in time, the dividend yield to December expiration was higher on the Value Line Index than on the S&P 500 Index, even though the S&P 500 has a higher annualized dividend yield.

The MMI was right in the short term as the market opened several points lower the next morning, but it closed only slightly lower on the day so the S&P premium measured results a day away most closely. The NYFE contract won the week-away prize as the Dow was already at 1511.

The procedure was repeated after the close on another momentous Friday the thirteenth, December 13, 1985, when the major stock index futures contracts roared to the top of their long-term trading channels. Could the market break out? Here is what the March 1986 contract premiums said:

Contract	Expected Premium	Actual Premium	Bullish/Bearish Factor
March MMI	242	273	1.13
March S&P	163	346	2.12
March Value Line	203	461	2.27
March NYFE	96	232	2.41

The first hour of trading on the following Monday, December 16, was simply choppy, but the NYFE contract was the clear winner after a day, one in which the Dow soared another 17 points to a new record of 1553. After a week, the Dow was still at 1543. Ironically, the Major Market and the S&P were the only futures to close higher on December 20 than they had on December 12, and they had been the least bullish premiums.

PREMIUMS AND INTRADAY TRADING

I do not make day-trading decisions based upon the level of a premium. That is due in large measure to the fact that premiums are rarely at an extreme, and I do not find them helpful otherwise. My best advice for day-traders is not to trade against a premium or discount in an effort to call intraday market turns. However, you might watch the premium level in order to develop a sense of when cash-futures arbitrage programs are likely to hit the floor.

TRACKING THE PREMIUMS

Premium analysis can be a valuable tool for the small investor looking to catch five or ten good moves in stock index futures in a year. It is easy to tabulate each day's closing premium by subtracting the closing index price from the futures settlement prices as they appear on the financial page of a major newspaper. To get intraday highs, you cannot simply subtract the high on the index from the high on the futures, because the two highs probably did not occur simultaneously.

That will, however, give you an approximation. A good broker should be able to supply you with more precise information.

CONCLUSIONS ABOUT PREMIUMS

I use the premium only in formulating a long-term position trading strategy rather than as a day-trading tool. For position trading, I consider premium or discount a useful barometer primarily in two circumstances.

First, when premium or discount is at an extreme over a period of 20 to 60 days, it often (but not always) gives a good contrarian signal. But the sizable arbitrage programs related to the level of the premium or discount, which became influential in 1985, can temporarily push the stock market in the direction "predicted" by that premium or discount. As cash-futures arbitrage becomes more prevalent, an element of self-fulfillment is present in a discount or a large premium. Arbitrage is likely to sustain a movement for a bit longer, but will often provide a final burst of activity.

This suggests biding one's time before buying into a sharp downtrend when futures are still trading at a discount and similarly, waiting for the arbitrageurs to finish before getting short in a rally accompanied by excessive premiums. Premium is just another indicator. Although it may assume greater importance when at an extreme, a speculator should never make it the sole basis for a trading decision.

Second, a discount or very low premium during a rally is often a signal that the rally is not over. Perhaps it is a sign that a "wall of worry" may still be climbed.

CHAPTER 8

Hedging

The principal reason for CFTC approval of any new futures contract is to facilitate the legitimate hedging needs of commercial users of the commodity underlying the futures contract. From an investor's standpoint, the purpose of hedging in financial markets is generally to "lock-in" a price, profit, or rate of interest. Generally speaking, hedging either offsets an existing position in the underlying cash market or temporarily substitutes for a position one expects to take at a later time in the underlying market. The cash market underlying any stock index futures contract consists of the component stocks of the particular stock index.

The basic categorization of hedging transactions distinguishes between a long hedge and a short hedge. A long hedge protects the hedger against the adverse economic impact of a rise in prices. Conversely, a short hedge protects the hedger from the adverse impact of a decline in prices.

We have the familiar example of the wheat farmer who knows he needs a 15 percent profit on his crop for his business to remain viable. Because he incurred certain costs at the time he planted the crop, he wants a guarantee of a certain profit level. He can procure this guarantee through a short hedge by selling the wheat he has just planted and promising to deliver it several months down the road at harvest time or sometime thereafter. By selling a contract for future delivery of wheat, he has locked in a satisfactory price for his crop.

The worst he can do if the price of wheat rises is to incur a loss on his short position in the futures market. But when he closes out his futures position with an offsetting purchase in the futures market at delivery time, he can then go sell his actual grain to a distributor for a higher price than he had anticipated at planting time. Thus, the loss on the futures transaction is really an insurance cost of sorts. The loss in the futures market will be offset by the gain on the sale of the wheat crop itself, and the farmer will be left with the profit margin he had envisioned at planting time. The farmer does this because he is willing to incur an insurance cost in order to guard against the bad year when the price of wheat drops between planting time and harvest time, leaving him with a cash shortfall that might affect his ability to make his mortgage payments or pay for equipment procurement or other expenses.

Why Hedging Can Be Valuable

One major motivation for hedging in the stock market is not so different. In plenty of investment decisions, the investor wishes to limit the downside risk in a portfolio. For instance, so-called "market timers" have continually moved money between stocks and the money market in an effort to miss short-term down cycles in stocks and to catch short-term uptrends. Such market timers may use stock index futures as an efficient means for temporarily switching out of the stock market.

In contrast, other money managers engage in dynamic portfolio hedging on the theory that they cannot predict short-term market trends, but can protect assets by gradually reducing market exposure in a declining market. By selling futures to reduce exposure as a market declines, dynamic portfolio hedging attempts to replicate a hedge that uses put options. For a pension fund manager who must make sure that a fully funded pension plan does not incur major losses, dynamic portfolio hedging guarantees a specified minimum return. Discussion of whether dynamically-hedged portfolios outperform unhedged portfolios either absolutely or on a risk-adjusted basis has been inconclusive. Critics say that dynamic portfolio hedging amounts to "buying high, selling low" and can accelerate market declines if too many portfolio managers sell futures at the same time.

Other institutional investors are gradually learning how to use stock index futures to lock in a rate of return higher than that available in the fixed-income market. A dividend-based hedge would be extremely attractive to many corporations since they are permitted to exclude 85 percent of dividends from taxable income under section 243(a) of the Internal Revenue Code. Currently, a corporation that owns stock in another company would qualify for this dividend exclusion if it holds common stock for 46 days or preferred stock for 91 days.

Such a corporation could lock in an almost tax-free stream of dividends by constructing a portfolio which bears a reasonable resemblance to an index and offsetting that portfolio with hedged positions in stock index futures. Expert advice would be needed to assess any added risk of tracking error in a high-yield portfolio. Such a strategy can not only lock in an attractive dividend stream while minimizing market risk, but can also gain maximum flexibility in adjusting market exposure at times when that is desirable.[1] In summer 1985, approximately 40 non-utility stocks on the NYSE yielded dividends over 7 percent. Thus, a corporation in a 46 percent tax bracket holding a stock portfolio with a 7 percent yield should be indifferent between equally well hedged stock and bond positions when the bonds yield 12.1 percent, assuming credit equal risks.

Suppose an investor considers himself a stock picker rather than a judge of the direction of the market as a whole. If he selects 20 stocks that he believes will outperform the market, a short position in stock index futures might be an appropriate hedge. Our investor might be uncertain or even pessimistic about prospects for the market as a whole, but anxious to invest in some promising companies. For the sake of simple round numbers, let us hypothesize an investor who is optimistic about the prospects for 20 growth stocks priced at $50 each. On January 2, he buys 100 shares of each stock, committing $100,000

[1]If market risk is virtually eliminated, the 46-day holding period may be suspended pursuant to Section 246(c)(4) of the Internal Revenue Code. Thus, many dividend capture investors prefer to hedge with options.

of capital. The investor, confident that the 20 stocks will outperform the market, wishes to be protected against the risk of a market decline while he owns the stocks. He chooses to hedge with Value Line futures because five of the stocks are on the NYSE, and fifteen trade over-the-counter. Moreover, he determines that his portfolio has about the same historical volatility as the Value Line Index, so that a dollar-for-dollar hedge is proper. Let us assume that on January 2, the September Value Line contract was trading conveniently at 200. By selling one contract (worth $100,000), our investor would have fully hedged the portfolio against a market decline.

Now let us assume that on July 2, each stock had dropped to $45, reducing the value of the portfolio to $90,000, but the Value Line contract also dropped during that time to 165 (worth $82,500). So our investor who sold a futures contract for $100,000 can now buy it back for $82,500, earning a $17,500 profit. This more than offsets the $10,000 loss on the stocks. He profits because even though his stocks declined, they outperformed the market. The stocks dropped 10 percent while the market, as measured by the Value Line contract, dropped 17.5 percent. Since the stocks outperformed the market by 7.5 percent, our investor earns 7.5 percent (or 15 percent annualized) on $100,000—i.e., the $7,500 difference between his $17,500 profit on the futures contract and his $10,000 loss on the stocks.

This strategy would have been equally effective in a rising market where a loss incurred on the futures transaction is more than offset by the gain on the stock.

A final type of hedge is called an "anticipatory hedge." Such a hedge temporarily substitutes futures for a transaction to be made in the cash market at a later date. An anticipatory hedge is distinguished from an actual hedge, which offsets an existing position. Why would an investor want to hedge a position that does not exist?

Suppose you know that you are due to receive a gift of $100,000 in three months and that you intend to spend the money to buy stocks. If you anticipate a substantial market rally in those intervening three months, it will cost you only $6,000 of margin deposit (for one S&P contract at 200) to participate in the market during those months. You get in before the purchasing power of your $100,000 is reduced. This is an example of an "anticipatory hedge". The rally in October–December 1985 exemplifies the value of such a hedge.

Before the advent of stock index futures, opportunities for hedging a stock position were limited. Beginning in 1973, certain opportunities for hedging arose with the introduction of exchange-traded stock options. Those options tend to cover only the most widely traded stocks, however, and do not serve as a viable mechanism for the hundreds of other equity shares one might want to hedge. The advent of stock index futures has broadened hedging opportunities enormously.

As the hypothetical Value Line hedge indicated, the mechanics of hedging stocks are essentially, but not exactly, the same as hedging wheat. In that real-market example, the investor bought stocks and sold futures in the belief that the stocks would outperform the market. In that example, things worked out as planned. Even though the stocks went down, they outperformed the market. By shorting stock index futures, the investor's fundamental research and expertise were rewarded with an annualized return far in excess of both the overall return in the stock market and the risk-free rate of interest. But hedging with stock index futures is not always quite so simple.

Pure Hedging and Cross Hedging

The real world has some twists that are not always fully developed in hypothetical examples. Our example did not account for different tax treatment of stocks and futures contracts, although taxes are not relevant to many institutional hedgers. Nor did it contemplate that a futures contract does not always have the same dollar value as the portfolio to be hedged. Nor did it consider that the portfolio might have been more or less volatile than the Value Line stocks as a whole. These problems are not at all insurmountable, but they do require a more in-depth understanding of the process of hedging, so read on.

Although hedging wheat and hedging stocks are mechanically similar, there is one significant practical difference between them. The wheat example demonstrates a *pure* hedge (assuming that the wheat sold in the spot or cash market is the same type of wheat hedged in the futures market).

The stock example involves a *cross* hedge because the asset traded in the cash market (i.e., a portfolio of stocks) is not the same as that traded in the futures market. A small portfolio of stocks is not equivalent to the large, albeit theoretical, portfolio of stocks underlying the futures contract. The aggregate price of that portfolio is not likely to experience the same percentage change as the Value Line Index or the S&P 500 Index, either on a daily basis or over a longer period of time. The same is true for any single stock. As we shall see, *stock index futures should rarely, if ever, be used to hedge a position in a single stock.*

Hedging with stock index futures is generally most feasible when one is hedging a well-diversified portfolio. The more diversified a portfolio becomes, the more closely its price movement is likely to track the movement of the market as a whole. Eventually, a portfolio can become sufficiently diverse as to closely approximate the movement of a market index. In fact, if one were to own the equivalent number of shares of all 20 MMI stocks, the portfolio would track the Major Market Index exactly. Here, we would have a pure hedge. If, however, the portfolio were to consist of just 19 of the 20 MMI stocks, we would be back to cross-hedging.

Basis Risk

Even a so-called pure hedge is not risk-free. In our MMI example, a risk remains that the MMI futures may not perfectly track changes in the Major Market Index itself. This risk is termed "basis risk." "Basis" is another word for the difference between the stock index itself and the price of the futures contract it underlies at any point in time. When the futures price exceeds the index price, the basis is generally called a "premium" or "contango." When the futures price is less than the index price, the basis is generally called a "discount." Since movements in the futures price will not necessarily reflect movements in the index itself, a hedger will assume basis risk.

Failure to understand basis risk can be costly. For example, consider a $1 million portfolio that consists of equal numbers of shares of each stock in the Major Market Index. On August 7, 1985, our portfolio manager turns bearish and decides to protect his portfolio at the close by selling approximately $1 million worth of MMI futures[2], or 38 September MMI contracts, at the closing price of 261 3/8. At the time, the September futures carried a premium of only .29 of a point over the Major Market Index, which closed at 261.09. The bearish sentiment expressed by the narrow premium was justified, because a week later on August 15 the index closed at 256.70. This represents a drop of approximately $16,814 in the original $1 million worth of the MMI portfolio. Our portfolio manager had offset this loss with a profit on the short sale of MMI futures, which he can buy back at 258. This yields a profit of $2,337.50 per contract, or $12,825 on 38 contracts, but this is not enough to offset the $16,814 loss on the portfolio.

Why did the portfolio manager still incur a net loss of $3,989? Notice that when he covered his short position, the premium on the September futures over the Major Market Index itself had expanded to 1.30 points. In other words, the futures did not drop as much as the index itself. The basis of the futures over cash changed. This is the primary reason that our portfolio manager was unable to offset his entire loss, even with a dollar-for-dollar hedge.

Clearly, basis risk can be substantial. In fact, the futures contract on the Value Line Index has fluctuated from a basis (or premium) of 10.00 points to 4.00 points in just one month. This translates to a potential maximum loss for a hedger of $3,000 per contract. Viewed another way, one who is hedging a $1 million portfolio with ten Value Line contracts worth $100,000 each would have been exposed to a basis risk of up to $30,000, or 3 percent of the value of the portfolio.

A hedger should be aware of the "theoretical" basis at any point in time. In other words, by knowing the intrinsic value of the futures contract, one can establish what the basis or premium should be, as discussed in Chapter 7. Then, a hedger who knows the likely duration of his hedge can also establish what the basis should be when the hedge is due to be terminated. Thus, a hedger can correct for the difference

---

[2]Example uses "old" MMI futures with the $100 multiplier, which were the active MMI contract at that time.

between the theoretical basis and the actual basis by calculating the expected profit or loss, assuming that the future will be at or near its intrinsic value when the hedged position is unwound. Needless to say, the only time at which theoretical basis is guaranteed to equal the actual basis is at expiration of the futures contract. An attempt to correct for basis risk is itself a somewhat risky endeavor for hedges that will not remain in place until expiration of the futures.

Cross Hedging

Unfortunately, basis risk is not the only risk that a hedger must understand. Remember that once a portfolio differs from the relevant index, we are back to cross-hedging. A pure hedge no longer exists because the individual stocks composing a portfolio do not generally move up and down together.

To illustrate the risk of cross-hedging, let us modify the example used in discussing basis risk. We will assume a constant premium of 29 cents so that basis risk is not an issue. But now let us assume that our $1 million portfolio consists of 1,650 shares each of only ten of the 20 MMI stocks. On August 7, we once again sell 38 MMI September futures at 261 3/8. By August 15, the index has dropped by 4.39 points, so we will assume that the futures dropped that much as well. Our results are shown on the following page.

Even when hedged, we still incurred a net loss of $10,600, 1.1 percent of our portfolio. *The example illustrates the difficulty of hedging individual stocks or an insufficiently diversified portfolio with stock index futures.* To dramatize the point, I picked the ten worst-performing MMI stocks of that week. Even so, the hedging did protect us from over 60 percent of our portfolio losses.

Systematic and Unsystematic Risk

In order to create an optimal hedge, we need to explore the factors that cause the price movement of a stock to deviate from the movement

Stock	Opening Price	Opening Value	Closing Price	Closing Value
American Express	43 7/8	$ 72,394	42 7/8	$ 70,744
AT&T	21 1/4	35,062	20 5/8	34,031
Du Pont	60	99,000	57 1/4	94,462
Kodak	45	74,250	44 1/8	72,806
GE	62 1/8	102,506	60 3/8	99,619
IBM	127 3/8	210,169	126 3/8	208,519
International Paper	49 3/4	82,088	48 5/8	80,231
3M	79 7/8	131,794	77 3/8	127,669
Philip Morris	85 1/4	140,662	81 1/8	133,856
U.S. Steel	30 1/4	49,912	29 1/2	48,675
Total		$997,837		$970,612

Net loss on stocks: $27,225
MMI Index August 7: 261.09
MMI Index August 15: 256.70

Sale of 38 September MMI futures: 261 3/8
Cover short on 38 September MMI futures: 257
  (assumed price)

Net profit on futures: $16,625

of the market as a whole. All price movement of a stock (or portfolio) can be attributed to two basic elements, systematic and unsystematic risk. Systematic, or market, risk results from economic, sociological, and political factors that affect all stocks. Such factors may range from sudden unexpected events (e.g., a presidential heart attack or an oil supply crisis) to influences that might be felt over a longer period of time (e.g., changes in the capital-gains tax rate, in the level of interest rates generally, or in margin requirements). On the other hand, unsystematic risk refers to factors unique to a particular company that affect only its stock. Such factors might include a poor earnings report, labor difficulties, or supply problems.

In a well-diversified portfolio, unsystematic influences on the price of one stock tend to be neutralized by offsetting influences on the prices of other stocks. For instance, a decline in oil prices tends to boost airline shares, but generally weakens the shares of oil companies. As a result, the portfolio as a whole will exhibit less price variation than the individual stocks that make up that portfolio. While diversification can eventually eliminate unsystematic risk, it cannot eliminate the systematic risk which exists due to factors which affect the market as a whole.

Systematic risk can be quantified statistically. The systematic risk of a particular stock (or portfolio) is measured by what is known as "beta." Beta is the amount by which the price of a particular stock changes for a given change in the stock market as a whole over a particular period of time. More precisely, beta is the ratio of the variability of the total return of a given stock over a particular period to the variability of the total return of the stock market as a whole (as measured by a particular index) over that same period.

Use of Beta and Correlation in Cross Hedging

Even though beta is not easy to measure, it cannot simply be ignored because it is the most suitable measure for determination of the "hedge ratio" to be used in establishing a particular hedged position. A hedge ratio indicates the appropriate dollar value of a futures position needed to fully hedge a stock portfolio of a stated amount. If a portfolio is expected to change in value by two percent for every one percent change in a particular index, a dollar-for-dollar hedge would not protect the portfolio fully.

Beta of a portfolio to be hedged is calculated by first figuring the beta of each constituent stock and then finding the appropriate weighted average of those betas. Thus, though it is generally not wise to hedge individual stocks with stock index futures, it is useful to have some familiarity with the rudiments of beta calculation for individual stocks. Since estimates of beta are provided by many full-service brokers and certain investor services, the reader need not absorb any math that gets too heavy.

Conceptually speaking, a stock has a beta of 1.00 when it moves the same percentage and in the same direction as the index being used to represent the market. For example, if the NYSE Composite Index climbed from 100 to 110 during the month of February, a $10 stock with a beta of 1.00 would rise to $11 during the same time period. If the stock rose only to $10.50, it would have a beta of .50 for that time period. If the stock jumped to $12, it would have a beta of 2.00. If it tumbled to $9, its beta would be negative.[3]

For a hypothetical situation, suppose that you wish to hedge 500 shares of IBM purchased for $100 per share. Your portfolio is worth $50,000. Assuming that NYSE futures are priced at 100.00, you could short one futures contract worth $50,000 and be hedged against systematic risk. But not fully hedged if IBM has a beta greater than one. Suppose that, on average, when the NYSE Composite Index moves five points, IBM moves seven points in the same direction. Your results from a dollar-for-dollar hedge when the NYSE Composite Index drops 5 percent would, on average, be as follows:

Long 500 IBM at		$ 100
Opening value ($100)	=	$50,000
Closing value ($93)	=	$46,500
Loss on stock	=	($ 3,500)
Short one NYSE Future at		$100
Opening value (100)	=	$50,000
Closing value (95)	=	$47,500
Gain on futures	=	$ 2,500
Overall loss	=	($ 1,000)

In this case, a hedge ratio equal to the beta of 1.4 would have left you fully hedged. Understand that "fully hedged" just means that *on average* you'll come out even. Practically speaking, such a hedge will usually generate either a small profit or leave you with a small loss, but can occasionally produce a larger net loss or profit. In any circumstance, deriving beta is critical to being fully hedged, because an improper hedge ratio increases the possibility of unacceptably large losses (or windfall profits). Hedging is not as simple as selling $50,000 worth of futures for every $50,000 in a portfolio.

[3]For simplicity, these examples ignore the dividend component of total return.

Suppose you wish to hedge a $1 million portfolio consisting solely
of equal amounts of A Corporation and B Corporation, which have
betas of 1.0 and 2.0, respectively. Your portfolio would have a beta
of 1.5. You would use a hedge ratio of 1.5 to be fully protected against
a market downturn. You would have to sell $1.5 million worth of stock
index futures contracts to protect against the probability that your stocks
would decline by 50 percent more than the market as a whole. If the
portfolio were to consist of $800,000 of A Corporation (1.0 beta) and
$200,000 of B Corporation (2.0 beta), the portfolio's weighted beta
would equal 1.2, since the beta of a portfolio is a weighted average
based upon the market value of the component stocks. In this case,
you would sell $1.2 million worth of stock index futures to be fully
protected against a market downturn.

Beta is generally measured with reference to historical data. To complicate things, the measurement of historical beta can vary significantly
depending upon several variables.

The first variable is the particular stock index used as a proxy for
the market as a whole, against which price movements of a particular
stocks are compared. A stock can have one beta when measured against
the S&P 500 Index and a different one when measured against the Value
Line Index.

The second variable is time. Beta can be measured over different
time periods, commonly over a year to five years. A few institutions
have developed sophisticated computer models in an effort to find the
optimal time period for measuring beta. A measurement involving much
less than six months of weekly calculations may not yield a reliable
statistical sample. On the other hand, a beta coefficient reflecting more
than five years of data may overemphasize influences on a stock's
volatility that no longer exist or are dormant. Certain institutions derive
a weighted beta for an individual stock by assigning more importance
to more recent data within the optimal time period selected. A prudent
hedger will recognize all the risks associated with measuring beta when
formulating a hedge ratio.

Regression analysis may indicate that a stock's beta has changed
over time, perhaps dramatically. For example, the beta of Homestake

Mining versus the NYSE Composite Index was calculated as .41 from January 1973 to December 1977, and as 1.81 from January 1978 to December 1982. The increased volatility of the stock reflected volatile gold prices rather than a sudden increase in Homestake's sensitivity to the price movement of other NYSE stocks. In fact, its price bore almost no correlation to movements of the NYSE Composite Index during 1978–1982. This increase in beta is one type of statistical quirk that a hedger should recognize. This element of unsystematic risk provides a good example of why it is dangerous to hedge a single stock with stock index futures.

Other apparent changes in beta over different time periods can be attributed to sampling error. Any calculation of beta provides only an estimate of a stock's "true" beta. In a portfolio of stocks, sampling errors tend to cancel each other out so that the estimated beta for a large portfolio is more likely to reflect that portfolio's true beta.

Once an appropriate index and time frame are selected, the calculation of beta is accomplished by solving a linear regression equation. The formula is:

$$Y = A + BM + E$$

where

Y   stands for the total return on a security; price change plus dividends,
A   stands for alpha, the portion of total return attributable to non-systematic risk,
B   represents the beta coefficient (i.e., the portion of total return attributable to systematic risk),
M   represents the total return to a particular market index, and
E   (epsilon) represents the error inherent in any estimation.

In English, you have:

Security Return = Alpha + (Beta × Market Return) + Error

Several brokerage houses, and investor services such as Value Line, run beta regressions and provide betas for most common stocks.

It is wise to have some knowledge of the methodology of a particular service. At a minimum, you should know the index used in the calculations. For instance, betas provided by the Value Line Investment Survey are calculated with reference to the NYSE Composite Index rather than the Value Line Average. Since betas can change, it is prudent to ensure that those provided by a service are current. IBM's beta with respect to the NYSE Composite Index was .76 between January 1978 and December 1982 and .99 between January 1973 and December 1977.

Various academics and market participants have attempted to improve the measurement of beta through various adjustments. However, one paper concluded that adjusting betas with the best techniques provides statistically insignificant gain and that a bad technique can cause a significant loss.[4]

In sum, no assured means will establish whether a particular beta will be reliable in the future. First, of several methods of measuring the beta of a particular stock or portfolio, none has been proven clearly superior. Second, even when a single method of measurement is consistently applied, betas frequently change over time. Such changes can be quite sudden and of large magnitude.

Beta suffers an additional shortcoming that, although it implies a linear relationship between the price of a stock and the movement of the market as a whole, it gives no indication as to whether the stock prices are really on that line or widely dispersed around both sides of it. In other words, beta tells you where a stock is likely to wind up given a certain change in the overall market, but it doesn't tell you whether the stock will get there by tracking the market closely or by zigging and zagging all over the place in the interim. A hedger would clearly benefit from more information as to how much of the stock's movement is explained by systematic influences, or, in other words, how closely its movements correspond to (or are "explained by") those of the market as a whole. Statisticians use a correlation technique to judge the efficacy of a beta-based hedging strategy.

[4]Hawawihi and Vora, "Is Adjusting Beta Estimates an Illusion?" *The Journal of Portfolio Management* (Fall 1983), p.23.

This assessment of reliability is derived from regression analysis, which produces a *coefficient of determination* and a *correlation*, the square root of that coefficient. The coefficient of determination (or R^2) is a statistical measure of the strength of a relationship between a stock and the overall market. It measures how much of the movement in a particular stock is explained by the movement in the index. Similarly, the correlation coefficient measures the degree of linear association between a stock and an index, 1.00 indicating a perfect correlation.

To a statistician, "explained" does not mean that one price movement is necessarily caused by the other. Rather, statistician can only gauge the association between two price movements. The investor must draw his own inferences about causation from that degree of association.

The greatest possible value of R^2 is 1.00. If IBM has an R^2 of .378 as measured against the NYSE Composite Index, as it did over the period January 1978 to December 1982, then IBM's price movement can be said to have been associated with the movement of the NYSE Composite Index with 37.8 percent reliability over that period of time. A statistician would say that 37.8 percent of IBM's movement is associated with the movement of the NYSE Composite Index. No opinion is expressed as to whether that association is causal or merely coincidental.

A simple illustration follows of the difference between beta and R^2: Assume that, during the month of February, the Dow Jones Industrial Average climbs from 1000 to 1100 by rising five points on each of 20 trading days in that month. Meanwhile, IBM begins the month at 100 and languishes between 98 and 102 for 19 trading days, then on February 28, it soars to 110 on reports of sharply higher earnings. For the month, it might appear to have a beta of 1.00 as measured against the Dow, but the coefficient of determination would be very low because IBM moved quite independently of the daily movement in the Dow. (The difference between beta and R^2 is depicted graphically in Figure 8–1.)

One should not blithely assume that one can skip over correlation and come out ahead on average by selecting a proper hedge ratio. Perhaps the following example will clarify this point. Consider

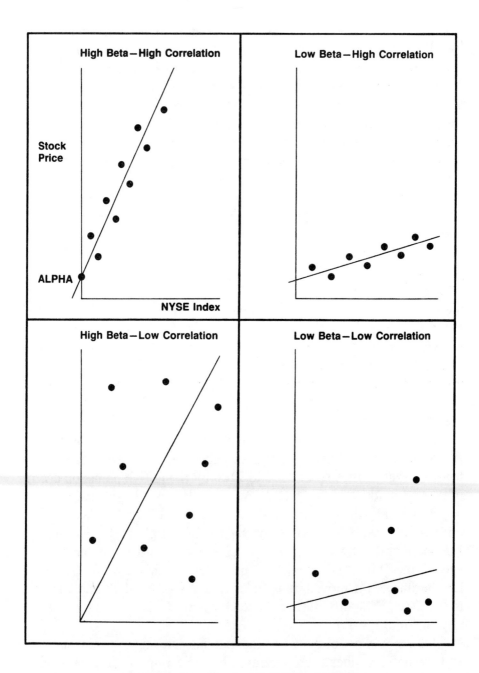

FIGURE 8-1. BETA AND CORRELATION

a stock that you think will outperform the market in the near future and that has historically been quite volatile. So you take a position and decide to hedge that position in case of a downturn in the overall market. Here are five weeks of price information:

Week	Widget International	NYSE Composite
1	50	100
2	53	101
3	55	102
4	54	103
5	52	104

Under a simplistic calculation, we would find a beta of .97. This can be determined on an HP-12c or other business calculator by entering both series of numbers into the statistics register. The calculator can determine the change in the Y variable (Widget International) for a given change in the X variable (the NYSE Composite Index). The slope of the beta line is found by dividing the percentage change in Widget by the percentage change in the index.

Now we'll assume that you correctly calculated this estimated beta of .97 for the period. To hedge a $50,000 stock position, you sell one NYSE Composite future (at the initial price of 100 shown above). After five weeks, you broke even because the stock did not outperform the market. But certainly no harm was done, so who needs to bother with correlation?

Well, the stock did not move entirely in tandem with the market, even though both were in uptrends. If we examine the results of the hedge from week to week, we can see that our "hedge" would have been quite costly in weeks 4 and 5, and would have provided windfall gains in weeks 2 and 3. Had we established the position in week 3, and unwound it in week 5, we would have lost $4,000. The weekly results are as follows:

Week	Net on Stock	Net on Futures	Total
1			
2	+3,000	−500	+2,500
3	+2,000	−500	+1,500
4	−1,000	−500	−1,500
5	−2,000	−500	−2,500
Totals	+2,000	−2,000	0

The importance of correlation is that it indicates how smooth your week-to-week results are likely to be. In this example, our correlation coefficient is .41. A low correlation increases the likelihood of uneven results from week to week.

A sense of what correlation and the coefficient of determination mean—and what they do not mean—may be best illustrated with a graph. The plot of actual changes in IBM for a given change in the NYSE Composite Index in the late summer of 1984 is shown in Figure 8-2.

A regression line does not necessarily touch any of the points. It is plotted to minimize the squares of the total vertical distances between the regression line and each point. More precisely, the regression line is a least squares line that minimizes the distance between each point and itself. Not surprisingly, the slope of the regression line is IBM's beta.

Now look at the point in the upper right corner of the graph. That point is some distance above the regression line, i.e., higher than its expected level when a correlation is perfect. Statisticians say that this distance is "unexplained" by the regression and thus a "residual" variation. On the other hand, the distance between the regression line and the mean price of IBM is explained by the regression line and is termed explained variation. The entire distance between the mean and the point in question is called total variation. The coefficient of determination is the ratio of the sum of the explained variations to the total variations.

Look at it intuitively. Consider first the intersection of the mean price line (A) and the regression line (B). That intersection says that

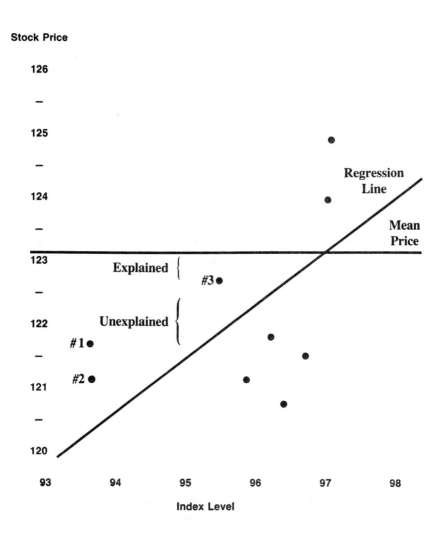

**FIGURE 8–2. IBM WEEKLY CLOSE PLOTTED
AGAINST NYSE COMPOSIT INDEX**

when the NYSE Composite Index is at 96, we would expect IBM to be at 123 1/4. As the market rises, we would expect the price of IBM to increase at the rate of change (i.e., the beta) depicted by the regression line. Similarly, if the market declines, IBM would be expected to fall, on average, by the amount depicted by the regression line. For example, if the NYSE Index were to go to 93.50, the regression line indicates that we could expect IBM to trade for about 120 1/2.

Now look at the two points furthest to the left. Our expectations were almost exactly right. Dot 1 shows IBM at 121.75 when the index is at 93.45. Dot 2 shows IBM at 121.125 when the index is at 93.58. Neither dot is exactly on the regression line, but as the market declined, IBM dropped pretty close to its expected value along the regression line. If IBM were to fall exactly to the regression line, we might infer that it did so because that's the percentage by which it typically has dropped during market declines of the same magnitude. So we say that a drop to the regression line is "explained" by the stock's beta, but we can't prove a causal connection between the market's drop and IBM's drop. Maybe IBM dropped because the Japanese cut computer prices. All we can do is make inferences using the information we have.

IBM did not land exactly where we predicted at dot 1. How do we explain the distance from the point to the line? We can't, because the point does not coincide exactly with our expectation. The distance between the point and the regression line represents unexplained variation.

On the other hand, the stock fell from its mean price to almost exactly where we expected it would fall. In this case, the distance from the mean to the point itself is termed "explained variation."

Dot #3 is also between the mean and the regression line. Here, the coefficient of determination "explains" more of a movement away from the mean than actually occurred—it "explained" too much in this case. The "unexplained" distance is still the distance between the regression line and the point itself.

If that is too much analysis, remember this much: If the price of the stock or portfolio you are hedging has bounced far and wide around the regression line, chances are you will not be a happy hedger. In other words, if the price is widely scattered during an overall trend in the market, a perfect offset is less likely in a hedging transaction.

Several studies have concluded that the correlation between the movement of any broad stock index with virtually any individual stock is so small as to make it quite risky to hedge a single stock with futures.[5] Some institutional investors are comfortable hedging a portfolio of approximately twenty stocks with S&P futures. Others prefer to begin with a portfolio of at least 100 stocks. Clearly, the efficacy of a hedge using stock index futures increases with the diversification of a portfolio.

A good financial calculator will calculate correlations for you with relatively little pain. For a large data series, a computer will be even less painful. Investment advisory services or brokerage firms that provide beta figures will also generally supply correlation data.

To summarize our discussion of basis risk and systematic risk, a hedge using stock index futures would be free of risk only in the unlikely event that it satisfied two conditions: (1) the price movement of a portfolio matched perfectly that of a particular stock market index and (2) the price movement of that index matched perfectly that of the corresponding futures contract. The risk that condition (1) will not be fully satisfied is termed "systematic risk" or "beta risk." The risk that condition (2) will not be fully satisfied is called "basis risk."

The risks associated with cross-hedging using stock index futures can be best appreciated by separating systematic risk and basis risk. Some investors short-cut this process simply by calculating the beta against the futures contract itself. The process is no different than anything we have already done. Our time series would substitute futures prices for index prices and, the regression analysis would then use futures prices and stock prices.

Variation Margin

One remaining problem can make hedging difficult in the stock index arena. This is variation (or maintenance) margin, which must be posted when the futures leg of the hedge loses a predetermined

---

[5]See Stephen Figlewski, "Hedging with Stock Index Futures: Theory and Application in a New Market," New York University, June 1983.

amount of money, regardless of corresponding profits on the stock or portfolio being hedged. For example, consider an investor who thinks that the market is due for a correction after a six-month bull market of unprecedented proportion, but who also wishes to invest in a hot new company called Digital Switch. On February 1, 1983, the investor buys 10,000 shares of Digital Switch for $50 per share, committing $500,000 of capital. Assume a beta of 1.5 for the stock. Leaving aside for the moment the substantial risk of hedging a single stock with futures, the investor could have hedged by establishing a short position in $750,000 of Value Line futures. Value Line June futures settled at 166.60 that day, so the investor could have shorted nine contracts worth $749,700. This hedge would have yielded excellent results after three months. The following results are based on closing prices on Monday, May 2:

Bought 10,000 shares Digital at 50	$ 500,000
Sold 10,000 shares Digital at 110	1,100,000
	$ 600,000
Sold nine KVH at 166.60	749,700
Bought nine KVH at 189.40	852,300
	$ (102,600)

   Net Gain: $497,400

Before rushing headlong into hedges of this sort, it is necessary to fully appreciate the flow of funds that would have resulted from the Digital Switch example. Monday, April 4, half-way through the period of the hedge, Digital Switch was at 89 1/2, producing a gain of $395,000. The Value Line futures were at 179.35, however, producing a loss of $6,375 per contract or $57,375 total. Under the margin rules of the Kansas City Board of Trade, we would have posted margin of only $2,500 per contract, the initial margin requirement for hedgers.

Notwithstanding the fact that our profits on Digital Switch more than offset the losses on the futures leg of the hedge, we would still have had to meet several calls for maintenance margin on the futures position. Our profits on the stock could not have satisfied the margin call, since they were only paper profits as opposed to realized profits, except in the unlikely event that our clearing firm had been willing to accept our appreciated stock as collateral and to post its own cash with the clearinghouse.

Many hedgers try to minimize the cash-flow burden associated with maintenance margin calls by underhedging. In other words, they use the hedge ratio to determine the total capital at risk in a given situation, then they hedge only a pre-set portion of it.

WHO DOES HEDGE?

So much for the theory of hedging. A real question remains as to whether there is much practical demand for such hedging, since it is at least arguable that people buy stock with money reserved for speculation. No doubt, it is true that few individuals use stock index futures as a hedging device.

However, the stock market is now dominated by institutions such as pension funds, mutual funds, insurance companies, and trust accounts. Institutional use of stock index futures varies considerably by size and type of institution. For instance, one report revealed that nearly one-half of the pension funds with assets exceeding $1 billion hedge with stock index futures.[6] In early 1985, only about ten percent of all pension funds used stock index futures. Users reported that these futures primarily serve to adjust equity exposure in the expectation of big market moves and to increase returns through arbitrage or other incremental income strategies. By mid-1986, approximately $40 billion[7] was protected under portfolio insurance programs, which are generally implemented through a short hedge using stock-index futures.

Much demand arises from the anticipatory hedging activities of passively managed index funds. Passive managers may use futures to

[6]"Who's Using Stock-Index Futures?" *Institutional Investor* (April 1985), p. 105.

[7]"Intermarket's 1986 Portfolio Insurance Directory," *Intermarket* (September 1986), p. 26.

get into the market quickly or to get in inexpensively at times when the futures are undervalued. In 1985, funds tied to an equity index increased approximately 70 percent to over $85 billion from about $50 billion at the end of 1984. Indexed money was less than $10 billion as recently as 1980.[8]

Additionally, specialists, market-makers, underwriters, and other market participants with a short-term time horizon often have reason to hedge a position. CFTC statistics show that commercial users account for an appreciable portion of the open interest in stock index futures. However, commercial users are not necessarily bona-fide hedgers. It is difficult to ascertain what percentage of open interest in stock index futures consists of positions of bona-fide hedgers. For example, the CME does not tabulate such data for S&P futures. However, the CME reports the following breakdown of volume in S&P futures: locals (floor members), 50 percent; give-up business (one member for another), 10 percent; clearing member proprietary trading, 7 percent; and public customers, 32 percent. Although the public customer category is not broken down into retail and institutional trades, it is believed that most customer trades are for institutional investors.

WHO CAN HEDGE?

Broker-dealers are essentially free to use stock index futures as they see fit. However, some institutional investors are constrained by a variety of legal impediments to investment in stock index futures, even for hedging their portfolios.

One general caveat is in order. The laws and rules applicable to the use of stock index futures by most institutions are still only gradually evolving. The brief discussion that follows is meant only as an overview or checklist of issues and should not be considered as a substitute for legal advice or a written legal opinion as to whether stock index futures would be a legal or prudent investment for any particular type of institution.

[8]Pension & Investment Age, December 23, 1985

Depending upon the type of institution involved, barriers might arise under federal securities laws, federal commodities law, tax law, a variety of prudent-man standards, regulations of banking authorities, state statutes such as blue-sky laws, or laws governing particular entities such as insurance companies or state-chartered banks. Sometimes these legal barriers prohibit the use of stock index futures outright, and sometimes they establish conditions that must be satisfied when investing in stock index futures.

Most of these laws and regulations apply to investment in futures contracts generally and were in force before stock index futures were introduced. The interpretation of various laws and regulations as applied to stock index futures is gradually evolving toward a liberalized view which would facilitate the use of stock index futures by institutional investors.

The evolution of CFTC regulations is an example of an increasingly favorable regulatory climate with respect to the institutional use of stock index futures, at least to hedge a portfolio. Until recently, many institutions were discouraged from using stock index futures because in so doing, an institution would have been classified by the CFTC as a commodity pool operator (CPO) and thereby subjected to a morass of regulation.

This stance led many institutions to seek "no-action" letters from the CFTC, in which the CFTC gave its assurance that a particular institution would not be deemed a commodity pool. To the extent that such "no-action" letters provide more leeway than subsequently adopted regulations, addressees of such "no-action" letters may continue to rely on them. Other institutions decided that in view of the expense and inconvenience of obtaining such letters from the CFTC, use of stock index futures was not worthwhile.

In 1985, the CFTC adopted a more realistic outlook, deciding that it was unnecessary to subject institutional investors to duplicative (and sometimes inconsistent or conflicting) regulations governing their use of stock index futures. Thus, the CFTC removed an area of great uncertainty for institutional investors by decreeing that "certain otherwise regulated" institutions would be excluded from the definition of a CPO. This freed them from the burdensome registration, reporting, record-keeping, disclosure, and operational requirements with which a CPO must comply. CFTC Regulation 4.5 specifies "otherwise regulated institutions" as registered investment companies; insurance companies; most pension plans; and banks, trust companies, and other financial depository institutions subject to state or federal regulation. The otherwise-regulated institution generally must still file a notice with the CFTC stating that it is excluded from the definition of a CPO under Section 4.5. That notice becomes effective upon filing.

But Section 4.5 does not provide carte blanche for the use of stock index futures. In additional to certain other conditions, an institution wishing to avoid CPO status must not commit more than 5 percent of its total assets as initial margin for trading stock index futures and must trade solely for bona fide hedging purposes.

Satisfaction of the bona fide hedging condition for purposes of either Reg. 4.5 or other regulatory concerns is not always as straightforward as it might appear. Different regulators may have slightly different standards for judging particular transactions. Generally speaking, a bona fide hedge boils down to three basic elements: (i) a purpose to offset price risk incidental to cash market operations, (ii) a temporary offset of (or substitute for) cash market positions, and (iii) a futures position which is substantially related to the cash market position. Let us discuss each element in turn.

Purpose. At the time the hedge is established, the hedger's purpose must be a present intent to offset price risks incidental to his stock portfolio.

Temporary Offset. A hedge is not a permanent substitute for a spot market position. Nevertheless, there are no set parameters on the maximum duration of a hedge. Generally, it is permissible to roll over a futures contract to a more distant month. Several rollovers on the same hedge would generally be viewed as legitimate.

Substantially Related. The CFTC has not formally interpreted the phrase "substantially related to the fluctuations in value of the actual or anticipated cash position." However, the phrase "substantially related" means reasonably expected to reduce risk. There is no requirement that a futures market position must virtually eliminate or even minimize market risk in order to be a bona fide hedge. Neither the

CFTC nor any exchange has set any minimum acceptable correlation for gauging whether a futures position is "substantially related" to a spot position and thus a bona fide hedge. Regulators prefer a flexible approach which encompasses use of futures that do not have an optional correlation with the cash position, but which may be more advantageous to a hedger in terms of liquidity, basis risk, or otherwise. Thus, a qualitative standard of a "reasonable correlation" is generally accepted. This correlation should be measured over a sufficient period of time in order to avoid questions about the validity of that measure.

Some institutions like to engage in what is known as "anticipatory hedging." For instance, a university may receive a pledge of $1,000,000 to be received on the last day of the year. If the university's portfolio manager has already selected the stocks to be bought with the proceeds and wants to lock in present prices before an anticipated "traditional year-end rally," he could buy stock index futures and later roll that money into the individual stocks. Or, if the manager had the $1,000,000 in hand but was still deciding which stocks to buy, a temporary purchase of the futures could still be an anticipatory hedge.

To qualify as an anticipatory hedge, a transaction must satisfy CFTC and exchange standards. In an anticipatory hedge, the hedger must intend to eventually replace the futures market position with a corresponding position in the stock market. However, regulators wish to accommodate hedgers who alter their strategies in light of changed circumstances in the market or in internal cash flow and therefore do not insist that the cash market position always be assumed.

The CFTC's most detailed consideration of the requirements for an anticipatory hedge was in the context of exclusion of certain hedgers from the definition of a commodity pool operator pursuant to Regulation 4.5 (rather than in the context of speculative position limits or hedge margin treatment). The CFTC concluded that for a transaction to be a bona fide anticipatory hedge for purposes of Regulation 4.5, the party must: (i) intend to complete all of its anticipatory hedges by actually buying the spot market position and (ii) must in fact buy the spot market position 75 percent of the time. However, the CFTC is unlikely to be unduly rigid in enforcing the so-called "75 percent test" where good faith seems apparent. Moreover, a staff member characterized the 75 percent test as an arbitrary number which may be more conservative than the standard that the CFTC would use in a context other than with respect to Regulation 4.5. A somewhat lower completion ratio would generally be acceptable given circumstances such as regular involvement in the stock market, unexpected developments in the stock market after the anticipatory hedge was established, or unexpected decreases in internal cash flow.

Substantial legal effort has been expended on subtleties of what is a hedge and what is not. Generally speaking, the CFTC will not question a position where a stock portfolio is offset. But an institution hedging stock options with futures or employing other elaborate strategies could be on thinner ice. Similarly, institutions engaging in over-hedging, i.e., hedging more than 100 percent of their assets, could conceivably have trouble showing that their hedging is bona fide. Since, however, stock hedge ratios are not necessarily one-to-one, as is the case with traditional commodities, it is likely that the CFTC would condone what might appear to be overhedging. For instance, hedging a $1 million portfolio that has a beta of 1.5 with $1.5 million worth of stock index futures should be acceptable.

As noted, commodity laws are only one hurdle to the institutional use of stock index futures. Moreover, the hurdles can be much higher for an institution that wants to speculate in stock index futures. Since legal restrictions vary depending upon the type of institution, it is most sensible to discuss each type of institution separately.

ERISA PENSION FUNDS

ERISA Pension Funds make up the largest class of institutional participants in the stock index futures market. Almost all private sector pension plans are regulated by the Employee Retirement Income Security Act of 1974, as amended (ERISA). ERISA governs investment decisions and other fiduciary conduct of plans established by private sector employers, whether the employer or an outside professional manager invests fund assets. Despite these explicit rules of fiduciary responsibility, ERISA pension funds enjoy more latitude than some other institutional investors.

There have been four major issues to be considered with respect to an ERISA pension plan's use of stock index futures. They are (1) whether the use of stock index futures conforms to the ERISA prudent man rule, (2) whether futures trading would have any undesirable tax consequences, (3) whether margin deposits are "plan assets" that must be held by a trustee, and (4) who may make trading decisions on behalf of a pension plan.

Prudence

The most critical concern for a discretionary manager of an ERISA pension fund is satisfaction of the prudence standard set forth in section 404(a) (1) (b) of ERISA. That prudent man standard mandates that the plan manager use the

> care, skill, prudence, and diligence under the circumstances then prevailing that a prudent person acting in a like capacity and familiar with such matters would use in the conduct of an enterprise of like character and with like aims.

Department of Labor (DOL) regulations elaborate on this prudence standard. Those regulations that the ERISA requirement is satisfied if the fiduciary

> (i) Has given appropriate consideration to those facts and circumstances that, given the scope of such fiduciary's investment duties, the fiduciary knows or should know are relevant to the particular investment or investment course of action involved, including the role the investment or investment course of action plays in that portion of the plan's investment portfolio with respect to which the fiduciary has investment duties; and
> (ii) Has acted accordingly.

On the basis of the literal wording of the statue, this standard is sometimes referred to as the "prudent expert rule." It supersedes the common law prudent man rule that governs other fiduciaries, although it is derived from that rule. Under the traditional prudent man rule, a fiduciary may be held personally liable for any single investment that, viewed in isolation, is imprudent. Under the ERISA prudence rule, as interpreted by the Department of Labor, no investment is viewed in isolation. Rather, the approach is to focus on the appropriateness of the decision in the context of the overall investment strategy and investment conduct of a plan's fiduciaries. For example, if the risk-reward ratio on a particular investment is reasonable in relation to the overall risk-reward for the portfolio, and assuming all other factors are neutral, the individual investment can be prudent although it might be considered risky if viewed independently. Hence, a plan manager should consider the role of a particular investment in the context of the overall investment strategy and composition of the plan portfolio and should document such consideration. In so doing, a pension fund manager is protected from claims of beneficiaries based upon adverse results from a particular investment (such as a stock index futures contract) if the investment was part of an overall strategy that was thoughtfully considered and deemed appropriate, even if the investment proves unsuccessful.

Given that this level of comfort is attainable, plan managers have been willing to hedge with stock index futures and, to a lesser extent, to speculate on them. The ERISA prudence rule is generally considered to allow sufficient latitude for fund managers, despite the absence of a specific statement, to define investments in futures contracts as prudent. ERISA and its interpretive authority contain no legal list of permissible or impermissible investments and the regulations neither expressly approve nor prohibit the use of stock index futures.

Of course, the trading of stock index futures may be considered imprudent for certain plans. Legal advice is recommended for any pension plan manager who wishes to initiate trading in stock index futures both because existing imprecise guidelines mean that prudence depends on numerous subtle factors and because the possibility remains that new guidelines can be issued or precedents set at any time. A threshold prudence consideration is that a strategy involving stock index futures should not be implemented without express authority in a pension plan document or trust instrument.

Tax

The major tax consideration is the theoretical possibility that income a pension plan derives from stock index futures could be deemed unrelated business taxable income (UBTI) if that activity were extremely substantial or the investment speculative. It is also theoretically possible that substantial speculation could be deemed inconsistent with the tax-exempt purpose of the plan. However, the IRS has determined in specific cases in a series of private-letter rulings that gains from trading futures should be excluded from UBTI.

Commodity Pool

As noted earlier, fiduciaries of pension plans are eligible for exclusion from the definition of a commodity pool operator (CPO). Moreover, the CFTC recognizes that a noncontributory ERISA plan (i.e., one in which all contributions are made by the employer) should not be considered a commodity pool because no funds are solicited from employees. So-called "defined-benefit ERISA plans" are not considered commodity pools, even if employee contributions are permitted, providing that no employee funds are used to trade futures. This is because such plans generally require the employers to cover investment losses, either directly or indirectly.

Custody

It is now relatively clear that ERISA and DOL regulations allow depositing margin for futures positions directly with a FCM. Until recently, it was unclear whether margin funds constituted plan assets, which, at a minimum, had to be held by a trustee in escrow for an FCM, rather than by the FCM itself. However, amounts in excess of required margin should not be simply left on deposit with a FCM. The float on excess margin ought to directly or indirectly benefit the plan and a plan fiduciary should leave such margin on deposit with a FCM only in such amounts as are negotiated and as might be reasonably necessary to meet near-term calls for variation margin.

Investment Authority

ERISA expressly requires that only certain persons exercise managerial discretion over the disposition of a pension plan's assets. Such fiduciaries include a named fiduciary of a plan, such as an employer's in-house investment management committee or an individual serving as the plan's trustee, or an outside investment manager who is registered with the SEC as an investment advisor and has acknowledged in writing that he is a fiduciary with respect to the plan.

A plan sponsor may well decide that it does not have the in-house expertise to trade in stock index futures. The plan trustee may either lack such expertise or be unwilling to make trading decisions with respect to commodity futures. In these cases, a plan will have to obtain the expert advice of a futures commission merchant (FCM) or a commodity trading adviser (CTA) in order to participate in the futures markets. If the FCM or CTA exercises discretion over the management or disposition of the plan's assets, as a CTA usually does, the plan should consider registering the adviser with the SEC as an investment adviser, naming that person as a fiduciary in the plan instrument or, if legally possible, appointing him or her as a trustee. Acting in a discretionary capacity without registering or taking one of these other steps exposes the plan sponsor and/or appointing fiduciary to risk that they have appointed an improper, *de facto* fiduciary. At a minimum, the plan sponsor and/or appointing fiduciary would realize with some discomfort that appointment of a *de facto* fiduciary left the sponsor jointly and severally liable for every investment decision the appointee made.

ERISA strictly prohibits transactions that may involve self-dealing or conflicts between the interests of the plan beneficiaries and those of anyone who is a fiduciary of that plan or who provides services to it. A thorough familiarity with the prohibited-transactions provisions of ERISA (Sections 406, 407, 408, and 502) is recommended to anyone involved with the management of plan assets. For example, the DOL apparently believes that performance or incentive fees may violate the prohibited-transactions rules, even if the SEC might approve such fees. The DOL's position is not based on an explicit statutory ban on such fees, but on an inference drawn from Section 406(b) (1).

Separate Accounts

Pension money is frequently commingled for investment purposes with the assets of other fiduciary accounts. The fiduciary requirements of ERISA apply to pension monies commingled in a trust fund maintained by a bank or in an insurance company pooled separate account. However, if such assets are invested in shares of a mutual fund, the mutual fund would not be subject to the fiduciary requirements of ERISA.

The Department of Labor has not yet promulgated final regulations regarding the applicability of ERISA to other types of pooled investment vehicles such as limited partnerships. Any collective investment vehicle that trades futures must be closely analyzed to determine whether the assets of a plan that invests in such a vehicle consist solely of the security representing an interest in the vehicle, or whether the plan's assets will be deemed to include any of the assets owned by the vehicle. In the latter case, the sponsor and manager may be *de facto* fiduciaries. That may mean that they have irreconcilable conflicts of interest.

MUTUAL FUNDS

Senior Security

Until recent clarification of the Investment Company Act of 1940 (1940 Act), which governs mutual funds, it was unclear whether those funds could invest in stock index futures. The uncertainty arose because some lawyers thought that the obligation to pay variation margin on the futures contract might constitute the issuance of a senior security in violation of Section 18(f) of the 1940 Act. In recent no-action letters, however, the SEC has made it clear that a mutual fund may hedge with stock index futures.

A mutual fund which is hedging an existing portfolio may sell stock index futures having a dollar value equal to the value of its stock portfolio. Furthermore, the SEC staff has indicated that it would be appropriate to use a hedge ratio in excess of 1 to hedge a high-beta portfolio. Thus, mutual funds enjoy the ability to fully hedge themselves using stock index futures as long as appropriate disclosure is made to holders of the mutual fund shares.

The SEC has also condoned anticipatory hedges and even speculative purchases of stock index futures by mutual funds, as long as certain conditions are met regarding segregation of funds equal to the value of futures positions less margin posted.

Due Authorization

Unlike a pension fund, where the key issue is prudence, a mutual fund can engage in high-risk plays as long as the manager makes full disclosure of such tactics. A fund would make such disclosure by filing with the SEC and distributing to shareholders an amendment to its registration statement describing its strategies and objectives in using stock index futures. Thereafter, a majority of shareholders of the fund would ordinarily have to approve the new investment policy, pursuant to Section 13 of the 1940 Act.

Commodity Pool

A related question is when might a mutual fund engaging in extensive hedging in stock index futures become a commodity pool? As noted earlier, the CFTC has the power to revoke an exclusion of a mutual fund manager from the definition of a commodity pool operator.

Custody

Section 17(f) of the 1940 Act requires that fund assets be placed and maintained in the custody of a bank, a member of a national securities exchange, or the investment company itself. This requirement presented an apparent conflict with the segregation requirements of CFTC Regulation 1.20, which requires that the futures commission merchants have possession of margin deposits. The solution developed by the SEC and CFTC staffs has been to permit an account maintained with an acceptable custodian to be specially arranged so that the FCM can directly deposit customer monies into the commodity account if the account should become undermargined and the customer has not made the margin payment. See CFTC Financial Segregation Interpretation No. 10, 1 Comm. Fut. L. Rep. (CCH) ¶ 7120.

Tax

To qualify as a regulated investment company (RIC) under Subchapter M of the Internal Revenue Code, a mutual fund must, among other things, satisfy the following tests:[8]

1. The 90-percent test: At least 90 percent of its gross income must be derived from dividends, interest, payments from securities loans, and gains from the sale or other disposition of stock or securities;
2. The 50-percent test: At the close of each quarter of the taxable year, at least 50 percent of the mutual fund's assets must be in cash, government securities and other securities;
3. The 5-percent test: At the close of each quarter of the taxable year, not more than 5 percent of the total assets of the mutual fund can be invested in the securities of any one issuer; and
4. The 30-percent test: Less than 30 percent of the fund's gross income in a taxable year must be derived from the sale or disposition of stock or securities held for less than three months.

The issue arising under the 90-percent test is whether a futures contract on a stock index would qualify as a security. Although

[8]In addition to those discussed here, an RIC must pass certain tests that do not pertain directly to tax matters relating to stock index futures.

"security" is not defined within subchapter M, the subchapter refers to the definition contained in the 1940 Act. There, a security is defined in relevant part as:

> Any note, stock, . . . evidence of indebtedness, . . . any put, call, straddle, option, or privilege on any security . . . or on any group or index of securities (including any interest therein or based on the value thereof), . . . or in general, any interest or instrument commonly known as a "security."

In a private-letter ruling[9] (which may not be cited as precedent), the Internal Revenue Service concluded that the

> broad, general language of the above-quoted definition of a security would seem to imply that a futures contract on a stock index would qualify as a security . . . Further, an option on a stock index futures contract would also constitute a security since the statute explicitly provides that any option on a security is itself a security.

Therefore, gains from stock index futures or stock index option contracts can be counted toward gross income to meet the 90-percent test. Under the same rationale, investments in stock index futures and option contracts can be counted toward satisfaction of the 50-percent test.

The 5-percent test raises a different question: who is the issuer of a stock index futures contract? The IRS has concluded that generally the entities whose stocks are listed in the index should *not* be treated as the issuers of the index instrument of purposes of the 5-percent test. Rather, stock index instruments are deemed to be self-issued securities. Futures and options contracts derived from each stock index are considered to be separate securities but are aggregated in the same manner as stock and stock options on the same company. For example, to meet the 5-percent requirement, a $100 million mutual fund could own no more than 55 S&P 500 contracts valued at $90,000 (180.00) each. The fund would not be permitted to own another $100,000 worth of S&P futures contracts expiring in another month or option contracts on the S&P 500 Index. However, the fund would be permitted to own another $5 million worth of NYSE composite futures and/or options.

[9]Index No. 0851.00-00 (September 27, 1984).

The only question that is at all troublesome arises with the 30 percent test. The question is whether a constructive gain realized as a result of year-end marking-to-market of futures contract under Section 1256(a) of the Code will be considered gain realized from securities held less than 3 months. The same private letter ruling referred to above concluded that the holding period is not terminated when gain results from a constructive sale of futures or option contracts pursuant to the mark-to-market rule of Section 1256. Thus, only an actual sale or disposition will terminate the holding period of a regulated futures contract or a nonequity option.

While normally the 30 percent limitation should not interfere with legitimate hedging activities, during periods of significant market volatility it is possible that an RIC could derive substantial short-term income from futures positions (even though they were offset by securities positions that generated related losses).

With respect to the following institutions, we must draw a distinction between proprietary investing of their own money versus investing the money of others (e.g., pension fund money or individual trust accounts) in their capacity as fiduciary. Let us first consider proprietary hedge trades.

Nationally Chartered Banks

Since nationally-chartered banks may not, as a general rule, purchase or sell corporate stock for their own accounts, they may not engage in proprietary trading in stock index futures or stock index options. However, several bank holding companies have won Federal Reserve Board approval to trade stock index futures for customers through their respective wholly-owned futures subsidiaries. The Fed determined that the execution and clearing of futures contracts and options is closely related to banking and that such activities would be unlikely to have such adverse effects as undue concentration of resources, conflicts of interest, and unsound banking practices.

Insurance Companies

Insurance companies are regulated under state laws which are usually quite restrictive with respect to investment of general account assets (i.e., money from premiums as distinguished from money managed under contract) in the futures markets generally. An example of a liberal provision is found in Illinois, which permits insurance companies to invest in "financial-futures contracts," which are defined to include stock index futures. Any such investment must be part of either an actual or anticipatory hedge.

Although New York law is regarded as fairly liberal with respect to insurance company investments, stock index futures are excluded from the provisions which allow life insurance companies to hedge with other financial futures. Thus, although New York permits life (but not property/casualty) insurers to hedge portfolios with bond futures, they may not hedge stock portfolios with stock index futures. Further, New York law applies to any insurer doing business in New York and thus may bar numerous major insurance companies from investing general account assets in stock index futures.

Certain states have a "legal list" of specifically enumerated permissible investments, which may permit investment in stock index futures.

Use of stock index futures could be permitted in states which have "catch-all" provisions that allow a small percentage of an insurance company's admitted assets to be invested in "additional investments." Such provisions may still restrict transactions to bona fide hedges or set forth other restrictions.

Thrift Institutions

Since nationally chartered thrift institutions may not purchase or sell corporate stock for proprietary investment, they may not engage in proprietary trading in stock index futures or options.

Bank Trust Departments

Bank trust departments act in several fiduciary capacities, such as trustee, executor or managing agent, for various types of accounts, such as employee benefit trust accounts and personal trust accounts. The legal restrictions facing bank trust departments when investing the assets of their fiduciary accounts vary depending on the terms of the trust instruments as well as the applicable state or federal law.

Although most states employ the rule of prudence, several states use "legal lists" of permissible investments for trusts. Only a few states have a legal list which includes stock index futures. These legal lists apply to personal trust accounts and to public sector pension trusts.

Even where the applicable law expressly permits the investment of trust monies in stock index futures, the governing instruments (i.e., trust agreements) must permit stock index futures. This often necessitates an amendment of that document to specifically permit the use of stock index futures.

For pooled investment accounts, the investment must be legally permissible for *all* participating accounts, and the plan of the investment fund must state that the fund may engage in stock index futures transactions. Moreover, it is a prudent practice to obtain an opinion of counsel that the governing instrument permits their use.

The Comptroller of the Currency issued Trust Banking Circular No. 14 on October 16, 1981, which sets forth minimum guidelines that must be followed by a trust department of a national bank. It would apparently permit stock index futures on essentially the following terms:

1. The trust department should obtain an opinion of counsel concerning legality of any investment in stock index futures.
2. The board of directors of the bank should adopt specific written policies and procedures on the permissible scope of the use of these contracts.
3. Record keeping systems must be sufficiently detailed to determine whether trades were authorized and appropriate to the needs of the trust account.
4. Limitations (e.g., dollar limits, position limits, and escrow receipt limits) should be set for each trust account.

5. All open contracts and underlying cash positions should be marked to the market at the same time for valuation.
6. To prevent unauthorized trading, bank trust departments should establish appropriate internal controls, including periodic reports, segregation of duties and an internal audit program.

The Federal Reserve has also issued guidelines regarding the prudent use of financial futures for trust and other fiduciary accounts. The guidelines apply to fiduciary accounts of state member bank trust departments and trust companies and also to the fiduciary activities of non-member trust company subsidiaries of bank holding companies.

The FRB staff stated that such contracts, when permitted, should represent additional tools for reducing overall portfolio risk or for increasing portfolio yield without subjecting account assets to unwarranted risk; futures should never be used solely to generate trading profits on the basis of anticipated market movements.

The FRB staff has indicated that hedging should be undertaken only when the futures contract bears a high correlation to the underlying security (i.e., the portfolio of stocks) and the hedge should be as close to a dollar-for-dollar hedge as is practicable. Although stock index futures may be sold to hedge the systematic risk in a customer's portfolio, the FRB staff stated that, except in special circumstances, it would be difficult to envision a prudent strategy involving a long position in stock index futures.

In a later memorandum, however, the FRB staff stated that its pronouncements were intended as guidelines and examples and not as formal or inflexible rules.

Insurance Company Separate Accounts

Insurance companies are the other major type of institution to act in a fiduciary capacity for trust monies. These monies are held in so-called "separate accounts," which are not subject to the rules governing the investment of the assets of the insurance companies themselves. Other than the terms of the individual investment contract and a general requirement of good faith and prudence, insurers in most states may invest separate account assets subject only to the same general restrictions as any other fiduciaries or trustees.

MONITORING A HEDGING PROGRAM

An improperly supervised trading program raises a wholly separate risk of hedging—that of human error or even dishonesty. For example, one insurance firm lost approximately $100 million in the bond market when senior company officials were unaware of the size of bond positions established by trading personnel. Prudence dictates a system of well-defined guidelines, internal and outside audits, and renewal of market positions by senior management. Other practical advice includes:

— Each individual trader must have position limits with each brokerage house. This should be a part of his written trading authorization.

— Numbered order tickets and transaction slips should be used. This makes it hard for a trader to hide a bad trade.

— A serious "red flag" is the typed confirmation. This is very suspicious and should be immediately looked into by management.

— The financial institution's personnel should be prohibited from taking a position in the futures instruments that will be traded by the institution as part of its hedging program. This is because there is a possibility of a trader trading for his own account at an FCM used by the entity.

— Trading errors, fails and what are known in the futures industry as "D-Ked Trades" are a "red flag" if they are more than an occasional event with a specific trader. Trends and patterns should be quickly investigated, particularly if they repeatedly involve a trader and a particular brokerage house.

— Last but not least, it must be clearly understood by all personnel in the hedging program that there is no such thing as an "automatic pilot" hedge. Each position requires constant attention.[10]

---

[10]John S. Stoppelman, "Hedging in Financial Futures—Prevention of a Blow Out," *Commodities Law Letter* (Vol. V, No. 8) October 1985.

NEW HEDGING TOOLS

New hedging tools are being developed for investors who are not permitted to use stock index futures or options or who want to lock in protection or upside participation for a longer term than is available with exchange-traded futures and options. For instance, an investor can now purchase a note with a below-market coupon that has a redemption price that increases in proportion to decreases in a stock index. The hedger owns an instrument that is legally a security rather than a commodity which, when dissected, is essentially a low-coupon note coupled with either an index put option or futures contract.

Firms such as Shearson will sell to an investor a note that has a redemption price that increases in proportion to decreases in the value of a particular portfolio. Such an instrument might be an especially useful hedging device for an investor whose portfolio does not have a high correlation to any stock index on which futures are traded.

CHAPTER 9

Stock Index Pools

For one who has neither the time nor the inclination to actively manage his own money, investment in a commodity pool that speculates in stock index futures may serve as a viable alternative means of participating in that market. A stock index pool is the commodity world's answer to a mutual fund. Legally, a stock index pool is typically organized as a limited partnership, while a mutual fund is organized as an investment company. Moreover, the leverage, and thus the risk and reward, are greater in a stock index pool. Perhaps for these reasons, over $1 billion was invested in public commodity pools by late 1985. A stock index pool is organized and administered by a commodity pool operator (CPO), who is usually the general partner of the limited partnership. The CPO normally contracts with one or more commodity trading advisors (CTA) to be the trading manager(s) and make the trading decisions for the pool.

ADVANTAGES OF A POOL

Investing in stock index futures through a pool has certain advantages. First, as a limited partner, your liability will be limited to the amount of your initial investment. This gives you the same basic protection you would have in buying options with all of the advantages of the greater fluctuations of futures price movements. Some commodity pools achieve annual appreciation that substantially exceeds that offered by stocks, mutual funds, or bonds.

For a second advantage, your money will be managed by professionals who have, presumably, studied the market for some time and who may have more of a trading edge than you could provide. Another advantage of a pool is that you need not be distracted from your own job responsibilities as someone is watching the market for you.

RISKS OF A POOL

Although commodity pools provide certain advantages for the stock index futures investor, one must weigh those advantages against certain risks before investing. The following discussion mentions certain factors that should be considered. It is not intended to be an all-encompassing list.

Illiquidity

No secondary market allows the sale of your interest in a commodity pool. Instead, you simply cash out at the net asset value per unit of the fund at the time you redeem your interest. You may be unable to redeem your interest during some minimum holding period established by the partnership agreement.

Possible Large Trading Losses

Past performance does not guarantee equally good future performance. As the saying goes, even the professionals sometimes read their charts upside down. Profits and losses of some commodity pools tend to fluctuate dramatically.

Additionally, some proprietary traders anticipate the buying and selling patterns of trading managers and attempt to profit by trading against them. Any resulting profits need not result from some dark conspiracy among traders to "gun for stop orders." Rather, floor traders simply develop a sense of what market levels are likely to trigger a fund's buy or sell mechanism. For example, a trading manager may program a computer to sell anytime the futures contract pierces a twenty-day moving average line. If such a decline is accompanied by heavy volume or other indications that the selloff is real, pit traders may not trade against apparent selling by fund trading managers. If, however, the market just drifts through a twenty-day moving average line on minimal volume, some pit traders are likely to wait for computer-generated selling to slow and then go long.

The danger with some commodity pool trading systems is that no human emotion is permitted to interfere with the system. But human discretion in the market is hardly infallible, either. Take your pick.

High Administrative Costs

The administrative costs of a commodity pool usually exceed charges of a mutual fund. These costs can appreciably affect the bottom-line performance of your pool.

Three major categories of charges are generally assessed against members of a commodity pool: (1) management fees, (2) incentive fees, and (3) brokerage commissions. The trading manager will generally receive a management fee regardless of whether the pool realizes any profits. This fee will typically range from four to six percent annually of the amount of funds under management in a publicly-offered pool.

The trading manager also usually receives incentive fees based upon the appreciation, if any, in the net asset value of a unit at the end of each accounting period. Such incentive fees typically range from 10 to 15 percent of new appreciation in the value of the fund. Incentive fees may be based in part upon unrealized appreciation in open positions and those fees will generally be retained even if the pool experiences losses before that appreciation is realized and distributed. However, a trading manager will not be entitled to additional incentive fees unless and until those losses are recouped and additional profits are generated.

Brokerage commissions can amount to a substantial charge against the assets of a commodity pool due both to commission rates and to the frequency of trading. Although commissions are generally set at a slight discount from the rates published by full service brokers, commission rates paid by the pool may be substantially higher than the rates actually paid by most public customers.

Commission charges can be especially high when the pool's trading manager has a very short-term orientation. Conceivably, this kind of short-term orientation may be encouraged when the general partner is a corporate affiliate of the broker receiving the commission. Even though an affiliated general partner benefits from commission income from frequent trading, commodity laws permit such affiliations.

No Guaranteed Distribution of Gains

Many commodity pool partnership agreements put the general partner under no obligation to distribute realized net profits from a successful quarter or year. Nevertheless, a limited partner will have tax liability for all gains of the partnership, whether or not they are realized. It could be inconvenient, to say the least, to have a tax liability without the cash flow that generates it from which to make the payment.

Further, there is no guarantee that the income upon which you are taxed is fully recoverable, even by redeeming some or all of your shares. Some funds permit redemption only once a month. By the time your redemption is actually in the works, these trading profits could conceivably have disappeared.

Other Conflicts of Interest

No law requires a trading manager to devote all of his attention to a particular pool. Often, a trading manager manages other funds, and the risk always remains that he will be devoting primary attention to that other money during the fifteen minutes when stock index futures move dramatically.

Double Taxation

An opinion of counsel in the pool's prospectus should state that the pool is a validly constituted limited partnership and will be taxed as such. Without such an opinion, the risk increases that your investment will be subject to double taxation. First, the pool's profits could be taxed at the corporate tax rate, and then your distributions could be taxed as dividends.

Fraud

Losses caused by unlucky or downright poor trading may be unavoidable. But losses due to fraudulent misrepresentations should be avoidable if you have the diligence to take some basic precautionary steps. The most basic step is to read the prospectus describing the stock index commodity pool. Anyone who offers an interest in a public commodity pool is required by law to provide you with a prospectus. If you are tempted to invest in a commodity pool without even seeing a prospectus, you might as well mail your $5,000 to me and forget about it. Your net loss is likely to be the same and your money will go to a worthier cause. If it serves no other function, a prospectus at least permits you to determine whether the broker and the trading advisor are all properly registered under the Commodity Exchange Act.

JUDGING PERFORMANCE

Statute requires that the trading advisors who make trading decisions for commodity pools disclose their prior trading records. Before investing, examine the past track record of the advisor(s) who will be in charge of day-to-day trading of the commodity pool's assets. Look for the bottom-line dollar figure. If you are handed a chart showing that the market guru divined every market bottom, make sure you get a copy of the guru's profit-and-loss statements as well. The track record is required to show actual dollars made and lost in response to trading signals generated, rather than depicting the performance of a hypothetical portfolio.

It is worth inquiring whether performance data has been adjusted to reflect various fees and commission costs. Also, check to see whether the trading manager includes interest earned on T-bills in calculating overall return.

In short, be careful of trading advisors whose strongest skills are in marketing rather than in trading.

Check other points before you sign on with a particular trading advisor. Make sure that you get a sense of how well the advisor does in declining markets. An advisor who is a habitual bull might do just fine — but only as long as a bull market lasts.

Also, make sure you know whether performance figures are time-weighted or dollar-weighted. Some managers present dollar-weighted performance figures, in which the figures are weighted by the amount of money invested at the time.

A favorite lament of trading advisors is that their trend-following system was unable to generate a profit because the market was "trendless" and stayed in a narrow trading range. You might ask if the advisor's trading system can anticipate periods in which the market is likely to be trendless. With options on stock index futures, a trading manager should be able to profit from a trendless market by writing straddles in that options market.

An investor may wish to inquire whether an advisor's trading signals are based upon data from the stock market or from the stock index futures contracts directly. My own prejudice is that certain statistics relating to the stock market itself are outmoded for two reasons. First, some of these figures are distorted by the influence of stock index futures. For example, the ratio of specialist shorts to public shorts is probably distorted by index-related arbitrage so that a high proportion of today's public shorts are really just hedged positions (e.g., short stocks with long futures).

Second, many stock index futures traders confine their technical analysis to analysis of the futures prices. If you subscribe to the notion that technical analysis works to the extent that prophecy is self-fulfilling, stock market data is less likely to influence large numbers of futures traders.

Before investing, get a good sense of the performance of commodity pools in general. Performance has varied widely, both in terms of average results for all pools from year-to-year and among pools in any given year. Funds posted an average gain of only 1.8 percent in 1982 and dropped in value by an average of 14.2 percent in 1983. But in 1984, pools gained an average of 12 percent and rose an estimated 14 percent in 1985. Among pools in 1985, the two top pools registered gains of 89 percent and 56 percent, while the two worst performing pools showed losses of 24 percent and 37 percent.[1] Of the 72 pools tracked by Norwood Securities, 53 posted gains in 1985. An officer of the CTA with the year's best performance stated: "This year we were just lucky there were trending markets. When there aren't any, you're happy just to break even."[2]

Commodity funds could easily turn in performances in upcoming years which match those of the halcyon days of 1978 through 1982. Particularly in light of the stock market's recent tendency to move over 100 points on the Dow rather quickly and to trend in the same direction for a long period of time, it is very possible that the performance of stock index funds will be superior to the performance of commodity funds generally.

Finally, check into whether any administrative, civil, or criminal actions have been brought against any promoters of a fund in which you are considering an investment.

As indicated, most commodity pools are organized as limited partnerships. As a limited partner, you will not have an active role in managing the investment. An active role could lead to forfeit of your limited liability. If you want an active management role, a limited partnership is not for you.

INVESTMENT OPPORTUNITIES

There are two ways of investing in a stock index pool. One is through private channels. Suppose you and your three golfing partners

[1]Norwood Securities, Chicago, Il.
[2]"Commodity Funds Post Respectable Gains", The Wall Street Journal, January 2, 1986.

decide to get together and form your own exclusive limited partnership to invest in stock index futures. Can you just go ahead, or must you comply with any statutory or regulatory requirements? No registration with the CFTC is required if the endeavor involves no more than $200,000 and no more than fifteen participants. Even without registration with the CFTC, the operator of the private pool must still provide monthly financial reports to the other participants.

The other means of investing in a stock index pool is through a publicly offered fund. Several commodity pools trade stock index futures as part of a diversified array of commodity interests. I am aware of only three publicly available pools that trade stock index futures exclusively. Table 9–1 gives basic information about them.

Although some set no amount for a minimum investment by individuals, many pools require a minimum participation of not less than $5,000 plus a percentage sales charge, often as high as an additional 8 percent. Due to tax laws governing Individual Retirement Accounts, the minimum participation for IRAs is $2,000 plus applicable sales charges.

TABLE 9–1. PUBLICLY-OFFERED STOCK INDEX POOLS

Name	Underwriter(s)	Trading Advisor(s)	Starting Date	Initial NAV	1/31/86* NAV
Stock Index Futures	Paine Webber	James Orcutt	5/84	$936	$749
Market Directions	Gruntal & Co.	California Index Associates	3/85	954	979
Dominion Stock Index Fund	Bateman Eichler; J.C. Bradford	Kohl Lane Seibens	9/85	902	872

*Source: Managed Account Reports, 5513 Twin Knolls Road, Suite 213, Columbia, MD., as reprinted in *Futures* Magazine, March, 1986 (vol. 15, no. 3).

CHAPTER 10

Impact of Commodity Laws and Industry Norms

Now we have a basic understanding of what stock index futures are and how they trade. We must remember, however, that they are regulated by the Commodity Futures Trading Commission (CFTC) and by commodity laws, and they are traded according to commodity practices and customs. The more familiar securities laws and practices do not apply.

The Commodity Futures Trading Commission is still regarded by many as a fledgling agency. It has neither the budget nor the staff of its sister agency, the Securities and Exchange Commission. Moreover, it is regarded as having adopted a more laissez-faire attitude toward the industry. Some have argued that futures trading abuses have not been rectified as quickly as they might have been.

CFTC JURISDICTION

Why are stock index futures considered to be commodities in the first place? The answer has more to do with bureaucratic politics and political compromise than anything.

The world regulated by the Commodity Exchange Authority, the CFTC's predecessor agency, had little in common with the world regulated by the SEC. However, since the CFTC was created in 1974, the commodities markets and the securities markets have become

275

increasingly interrelated and the distinctions between the instruments traded in those markets have sometimes blurred. As a result, the SEC and the CFTC have engaged in a bureaucratic turf battle involving their respective jurisdictions over stock index futures and options as well as certain other instruments having attributes of both securities and commodities, such as futures on foreign currencies, Treasury bonds, and GNMA's.[1]

The tensions heightened when commodities exchanges proposed to trade futures contracts on stock indexes. In fact, stock index futures did not gain approval until nearly 4 1/2 years after the initial formal application was filed with the CFTC. Finally, the chairmen of the two agencies announced a truce, dubbed the "SEC-CFTC Jurisdictional Accord," on December 7, 1981. Pursuant to this accord, which was codified at 7 U.S.C. Section 2 by the enactment of the Futures Trading Act of 1982, the agencies agreed that (1) the CFTC would have *no* jurisdiction over options on any security, and (2) the CFTC would have *exclusive* jurisdiction over all futures contracts (including futures on exempt securities) and over all options on such futures contracts, and (3) the CFTC could approve futures trading on stock indexes or sub-indexes, provided that certain requisites, including input from the SEC, were satisfied.

The SEC and CFTC resolved their jurisdictional dispute on a product-by-product basis, rather than on a functional basis. As a result, functionally similar instruments that serve similar economic purposes may be subject to markedly different regulations. For example, the SEC now has jurisdiction over options on a stock index while options on a stock index future are the province of the CFTC. The absurdity of this arrangement is highlighted by the fact that both option products, which are functionally similar investment vehicles, are traded in adjoining trading rings on the floor of the New York Futures Exchange. Moreover, since one option is a "security" and the other a "commodity," they may be taxed at different rates and ineligible for cross-margining treatment.

[1] See Russo, Thomas A., *Regulation of the Commodities Futures and Options Markets*, Vol.1 (New York: Shepard's/McGraw-Hill, 1983) Sections 10.22–10.24.

One's natural enthusiasm for the potential benefits of trading stock index futures must be tempered by an appreciation of certain risks, both market-related and legal, inherent in commodity trading.

SUITABILITY

Until recently, there has been no counterpart in the commodities world to what securities regulators call the "Suitability Rule." The National Association of Securities Dealers (NASD) and different securities exchanges have promulgated rules prohibiting member firms from recommending any securities transaction to a customer unless the member has reasonable grounds to believe that the recommended transaction is not unsuitable for the customer. The member's belief that a transaction is not unsuitable must be based upon information furnished by the customer concerning the customer's investment objectives, financial situation, and needs. The NASD rule requires "reasonable inquiry" concerning those matters.

The NASD's counterpart in the commodities world, the National Futures Association (NFA), has recently promulgated a narrower suitability standard for its members. In essence, the NFA's Compliance Rule 2-30 requires each NFA member to ascertain a customer's age, estimated annual income, net worth and such customer's previous investment and futures trading experience. But the rule does not require an NFA member to consider the suitability of particular futures transactions. Presumably, this is because any investment in a commodity futures contract is on the high-risk end of the risk-reward spectrum, so that it is difficult to call a transaction involving one commodity less suitable than a similar transaction in another commodity. Since, however, securities can lie virtually anywhere on the risk-reward spectrum, the notion of suitability can be applied more feasibly to securities. In the commodities game, you pay your money and take your chances.

A number of plaintiffs have alleged violation of some duty of adherence to a suitability standard, but only recently have such claims met with any success. There is no express right under the Commodity

Exchange Act to sue a broker because he let you invest in stock index futures on a day when you were feeling particularly risk-averse.

However, an administrative law judge has recently ruled that a suitability standard is implied in Section 4b of the Commodity Exchange Act. It is not yet clear whether this ruling foreshadows a trend. Under current law, one would expect it to be quite difficult for a customer to prevail in a suitability-based legal action involving commodities.

LIQUIDATION

A commodity customer agreement typically gives a broker the right to liquidate a position at any time in his sole discretion if he believes that you cannot or will not pay initial margin or maintenance margin immediately when it is due. Conceivably, though it is exceedingly rare in practice, your broker could close out your position despite your expressed intention to provide sufficient funds to maintain the position. If the contract begins to move back in your favor shortly after you have been liquidated, you can do little except to re-establish the position. Commodity brokers may be more concerned than stockbrokers about timely receipt of margin payments because of the enormous leverage and volatility in commodities.

UNAUTHORIZED TRADING

Aside from trades involving liquidation, numerous court cases allege unauthorized trading.[2] Unauthorized trading claims may arise from simple price errors (e.g., a stop order entered at 233.50 rather than 234.50), or a broker who unilaterally assumes discretionary authority or continues to exercise such authority after it has been revoked. Unauthorized trading may be a breach of fiduciary duty or a violation of the anti-fraud provisions of the Commodity Exchange Act. Since commodities orders are typically given by telephone and

[2]For citations, see, 1 Comm. Fut. L. Rep. (CCH) ¶ 12,685.54.

orally reported back with written confirmation of the execution mailed, disputes arise over whether a telephone call was ever made or what was said on a particular conversation.[3]

Determination of an unauthorized trade will generally depend either on the credibility of the witnesses or, in cases where a broker tapes telephone conservations, on those recordings. A customer must make a timely objection to an allegedly unauthorized trade, or the trade may be deemed ratified.[4]

DISCRETIONARY TRADING ACCOUNTS

In discretionary trading accounts, trading decisions are made by the broker rather than by the customer. On occasion, a large loss in a discretionary account has produced litigation in which the customer alleges churning or unauthorized trading (e.g., trading beyond agreed upon limits or after an alleged revocation of discretionary authority). Such a customer will often allege several violations of anti-fraud provisions of securities laws as well, on the theory that a discretionary account is an ''investment contract'' and thus a security as defined in the securities laws.

Pursuant to the landmark case of *SEC* v. *W.J. Howey & Co.*, 328 U.S. 293, 298 (1946), an ''investment contract'' is deemed to exist if the following three elements are found:

1. An investment of money
2. In a common enterprise and
3. With profits to come solely (or primarily) from the efforts of others.

[3]But failure to provide oral confirmation is not necessarily a breach of fiduciary duty, at least under the rule in *De Cruz v. Shearson Hayden Stone, Inc.* [1977–1980] Comm. Fut. L. Rep. (CCH) Section 20,522 (CFTC, 1979).

[4]*Schang v. London Futures, Ltd.* [1977–1980] Comm. Fut. L. Rep. (CCH) Section 20, 613 (CFTC, 1978).

However, a majority of courts have decided that a discretionary account does not satisfy the "common enterprise" element of the *Howey* test, because there is neither horizontal commonality (involving pooling of customer accounts) nor sufficient vertical commonality (under which the broker shares in the profits of the enterprise and thus benefits in some manner other than merely commissions paid). Moreover, case law has recognized that an account in which commodities are traded is also a "commodity" under the exclusive jurisdiction of the CFTC, as provided in the Commodity Exchange Act.

CHURNING

A futures commission merchant (FCM) can breach fiduciary duty to a customer by executing trades in an account controlled by the FCM with volume or frequency that is excessive in light of the customer's objectives, for the purpose of generating commissions. Churning is difficult to prove in a commodity futures account, though. First, the broker must control the account. A signed discretionary account form, which is required when an FCM or person associated with an FCM is given discretion, would show control. A broker may exercise control over an account even without a written discretionary account agreement, but a customer who is intelligent, educated, and sophisticated in general business affairs may have difficulty showing that a broker exerted this kind of *de facto* control. Finally, even if such control is shown, a broker could claim the defense of ratification by the customer.

Second, a suit must demonstrate that a broker's predominant purpose was to generate commissions rather than to make profits for the customer. This is generally done by showing a turnover rate and/or the commissions as a percent of average equity balance in the account. However, no litmus test will determine what constitutes unacceptably high ratios under either of those standards. The objective of the account is germane in determining what ratios would be excessive. If you mark "speculation" as your objective on new account papers, it would be difficult to prove that your objective was preservation of capital or conservative investment.

There is little authority on which to draw for benchmarks concerning these ratios because so many disputes are settled by unwritten decisions of arbitrators. However, churning based on excessive commissions in relation to the size of the account has been found in the following cases: *Miller* v. *Kinch*[5], in which commissions of $7,762 were generated on $12,500 of equity in less than one month; *Aronson* v. *Cayman Associates Ltd.*[6] where commissions of $3,415 were generated in two weeks on equity of $3,500; and *In re. Cayman Associates Ltd.*[7] where commissions ranging from $745 on a $1,500 account to $11,440 on a $20,000 account were generated in a period of 20 to 30 business days. Clearly, most successful churning cases demonstrate quite outrageous commission ratios — anywhere from 39 percent to over 2000 percent annualized, of equity in the account.

The turnover ratio is a more difficult test to apply to commodity case because of the extreme leverage in futures trading.[8] Cases dealing with stocks and options, rather than futures, have held that turnover rates of 1.87 (for a covered writing account) and 1.85 (for a trading account) were not excessive. A turnover rate of approximately six is generally regarded as excessive in a securities law context, but court decisions "vary widely"[9] on this point.

Finally, it should be noted that even with a successful churning claim, damages may be limited to recovery of commissions, and would not necessarily include recovery of trading losses. A separate showing that trading losses were proximately caused by the churning is generally required.

[5][1980–982] Transfer Binder] Comm. Fut. L. Rep. (CCH) Section 21,488 (Sept. 24, 1982).

[6][1980–1982 Transfer Binder] Comm. Fut. L. Rep. (CCH) Section 21, 268 (Oct. 5, 1981).

[7][1980–1982 Transfer Binder] Comm. Fut. L. Rep. (CCH) Section 21, 277 (Oct. 23, 1981).

[8]*Dwyer v. Murlas Brothers*, [1977–1980 Transfer Binder] Comm. Fut. L. Rep. (CCH) Section 20, 520 (Nov. 21, 1977).

[9]Note, Churning by Securities Dealers, 80 Harv. L. Rev. 869, 876 (1967).

REMEDIES AGAINST A BROKER

The Commodity Exchange Act provides an express private right of action. Three private remedies are available when you incur a loss that is fraudulently caused by a broker or other registrant under the Act. These remedies are arbitration, reparation, or a civil suit in court. Let us briefly review the advantages and disadvantages of each alternative.

Arbitration

Many regard arbitration as the simplest, quickest, and least expensive form of dispute resolution. Arbitration is particularly useful for small disputes. An arbitration involving a small dollar amount may cost as little as $50 if you represent yourself. Each of the commodity exchanges on which stock index futures are traded, the NFA and the American Arbitration Association (AAA) all sponsor arbitration forums. Formal rules of evidence do not apply to arbitrations in order to keep the proceeding informal and comprehensible to non-lawyers. However, each party is entitled to be represented by counsel and also to examine other parties, witnesses and all relevant documents. The hearing is conducted according to rules of the sponsoring exchange in a manner consistent with CFTC Regulation 180.3.

Public customers generally must have some degree of choice in the selection of the arbitrator or panel of arbitrators. The customer must consent to arbitration in a separately signed document rather than in the customer agreements. Signing an arbitration agreement is not properly a condition for opening an account, but it does constitute a waiver of your right to litigate (but not of your right to a CFTC reparations proceeding).

Perhaps the major problem with arbitration is the feeling among some experts that results are too unpredictable and occasionally even arbitrary or capricious. Moreover, written decisions from arbitrators are rare. It is virtually impossible to appeal the decision of arbitrators to a court of law without a clear demonstration of bias or conflict of interest. However, my own prejudice as a sometime arbitrator is that an arbitrator is more likely than a judge to be well-versed in the nuances of stock index futures and options and may thus grasp complicated facts of a dispute more fully.

An aggrieved individual can handle a simple arbitration without the assistance of counsel. Decisions in an arbitration can turn on considerations of fundamental fairness, even if procedural technicalities might produce a different result in a court of law. Only pecuniary damages, interest, and filing fees will be awarded in an arbitration. Punitive damages and attorney fees will not be awarded.

Reparations

A reparations hearing is a sort of mini trial before an administrative law judge employed by the CFTC. Once you've endured a rather backed-up calendar, a reparations trial takes approximately one-fifth the time and costs approximately one-tenth as much as a normal civil trial. In many cases, the parties never even appear before the judge, but rather submit all their claims in writing.

A customer can file a reparations claim only to remedy a violation of the Commodity Exchange Act or a CFTC regulation or order. Violation of an exchange rule or some other claim cannot form the basis of a reparations proceeding. But section 4b of the Act does contain a fairly broad anti-fraud provision. As with arbitration, only pecuniary damages, interest, and filing fees will be awarded in a successful reparations case.

Only firms registered with the CFTC may be sued in a reparations proceeding. If you give your money to some fly-by-night confidence man to buy stock index futures, a reparations proceeding will do you no good when the market heads north and the con-man heads south. It is irrelevant that the self-proclaimed broker should have been registered with the CFTC if he is not in fact registered.

A ruling by an administrative law judge is reviewable by the CFTC. The ruling of the commission is subject to review by a federal circuit court, which will generally uphold any findings from the reparations proceeding as long as such findings are supported by the weight of the evidence. A federal court will not undertake a *de novo* review of the facts.

Civil Suit

The most expensive and cumbersome private remedy, a civil suit, can drag on for years. It may be difficult to find a lawyer specializing in commodities who is willing to file a civil suit for a commodity fraud claim on a contingency basis. However, some lawyers with general litigation experience might take a case on such a basis.

SAFETY OF CUSTOMER MONEY

The safety of your money deposited to meet margin requirements depends upon the integrity of the clearinghouse and also upon the solvency of your brokerage firm.

Integrity of the Clearinghouse

Suppose your (or your broker's) counterpart on a particular trade is someone who experiences one forced liquidation too many. On certain foreign commodity exchanges, that would be a legitimate fear. For example, traders on the London Metals Exchange (LME) are presently responsible directly to each other for making good on trades. Traders on that exchange concern themselves with the financial stability of their counterpart in each trade, as evidenced by the losses incurred during the LME's tin crisis of late 1985 and early 1986.

The clearing system in effect on domestic commodity exchanges minimizes the need for such concern. Once a clearinghouse compares a trade and accepts it a valid, no privity of contract remains between the opposites in any particular stock index futures trade. Rather, each party has a contract with the clearing corporation for the exchange.

Once trades are reconciled, the clearinghouse substitutes itself as the buyer to every seller and as the seller to every buyer. In turn, clearing members are liable to the clearinghouse for full performance on all contracts they submit for clearance. The clearinghouse, rather than any individual or institutional trading counterpart, is obligated to pay your broker sums due you.

The clearinghouse does not pay you directly. The clearinghouse makes no guaranty directly to a defaulting firm's customers; rather, that guaranty runs to the members of the clearinghouse. Therefore, two questions regarding the integrity of the clearing system arise: (1) what happens if the clearinghouse becomes insolvent? and (2) what happens if your individual broker (or his clearing broker) becomes insolvent before you get your money out?

A series of fail-safe devices insures the solvency of each exchange clearinghouse. Solvency is predicated upon each clearing member depositing margin money with the clearinghouse to guarantee its ability to perform all outstanding contracts it holds for its own account or for the accounts of its various clients, once those trades are reconciled.

Exchange clearinghouse rules differ with respect to the amount of margin money that each clearing member must post to cover the open positions carried on its books. The Chicago Mercantile Exchange has adopted the most conservative system, known as a gross margin system. A clearing member must forward margin money to the clearinghouse to cover all of its positions that remain open at the end of each trading day. If the aggregate futures positions of all customers of ABC Clearing Corp. on the CME amount to 1,000 long positions and 500 short positions, ABC Clearing would forward $9 million to the clearinghouse at the close of the business day (i.e., $6,000 margin per contract times 1,500 contracts).

The other exchanges (NYFE, KCBT, CBOT) use a net margin system, under which ABC Clearing Corp. could calculate that with 1,000 long positions and 500 short positions, its customers hold a net long position of 500 contracts. In this case, ABC Clearing Corp. would forward to the clearinghouse margin money representing its net long position of 500 contracts.

While a net margin system ties up less money (allowing the clearing members to earn more interest on customer money), it has been criticized for not providing sufficient security when a clearing member's long and short positions become either perfectly balanced (so that no funds are forwarded to the clearinghouse) or severely imbalanced due to a few large customers on the same side of the market.

It would not be surprising to see other exchanges adopt a gross margin system or a modified net margin system, under which a clearing member would have to deposit margin money for the full amount of the larger position. In other words, in our example, ABC Clearing Corp. would post margin money for the 1,000 contract long position for a total of $6 million.

The clearinghouse is further insulated in the event that a clearing member fails to meet a margin call from the clearinghouse. Clearing members must be well capitalized and they are usually some of the largest trading or brokerage firms on a particular exchange. They would normally have sufficient reserves to call upon when a customer fails to meet a margin call. Moreover, the clearinghouse generally assesses each clearing member to establish a reserve fund to cover any obligations of a defaulting clearing member to the clearinghouse. Should that fund prove insufficient to cover a shortfall, clearing members will ordinarily be assessed additional (though not necessarily unlimited) sums to make up the difference. To date, the existing system has been satisfactory insofar as no clearinghouse has ever collapsed.

Integrity of Each Clearing Member

Nevertheless, on some occasions clearing members have collapsed. While such an event would not normally cause losses to other clearing members or their customers, the collapse of a clearing member can cause losses to its own innocent customers. The CFTC has tried to prevent such problems by requiring a mechanism to keep such funds from being misappropriated.

Under CFTC Regulation 1.20, a commodity broker is required to segregate and separately account for each customer's funds, i.e., money, securities, and property received to margin or secure trades, and all money accruing to customers as a result of profitable trades. In contrast to the securities world, brokers are also prohibited from using or permitting the use of the property of one customer to margin or settle the trades of any person other than that customer.

This segregation requirement would seem to protect an innocent customer, even in the event of the bankruptcy of his clearing firm. However, innocent customers of Volume Investors, including investors who had no open positions but who merely had cash or collateral on deposit, were faced with a drawn-out legal imbroglio to recover their assets in the wake of that firm's failure. How could this happen? Your funds could be jeopardized under three scenarios:

1.   You have open positions; your margin is forwarded to the clearinghouse. Suppose you are long one S & P future and you deposit $6,000 with your broker. Your broker forwards that money to the clearinghouse. The clearinghouse is entitled to keep that $6,000 if the debts of your clearing member to the clearinghouse are unsatisfied. If another customer of your clearing broker incurs huge losses, and neither that customer nor the clearing member comes up with margin to pay the clearinghouse, the clearinghouse may use any money already received from the defaulting clearing member (including your $6,000) to pay amounts due other clearing members.

2.   You have no open positions, but have a $5,000 credit balance; your $5,000 is improperly forwarded to the clearinghouse. Even if your money is improperly forwarded to the clearinghouse, the clearinghouse is still entitled to use it to pay amounts due other clearing members. True enough, your funds should never be forwarded to the clearinghouse under such circumstances because the CFTC requires that your assets be segregated. But as Russo warned, the CFTC's

underlying assumption, that the debtor commodity broker's books and records will be reasonably accurate, is not necessarily correct. Notwithstanding various CFTC regulations which require documentation that ideally permits specific identification of open commodity contracts and customer property, a debtor commodity broker quite probably will have kept inadequate records or even have destroyed records which would have documented identification of customer property.[10]

The 1985 bankruptcy of Volume Investors Corp. underscored the significance of Russo's observation. Volume Investors did in fact use money of other customers to meet margin calls issued by the exchange clearinghouse to cover the losses of three gold options traders.

3.   You have open positions; your money is kept by your clearing member, who has a balanced account and thus owes nothing to the clearinghouse under a net margin system. You are short one S&P future while another customer of your clearing broker is long 5,000 S&P contracts and still other customers are short a total of 4,999 S&P contracts. The market plunges 10 percent in one day, moving the S&P from 200 to 180 and leaving the guy long 5,000 lots with a loss of $50 million—some $20 million more than his initial margin. Down goes the clearing broker. If the same record keeping problem described in scenario 2 surfaces, you could again have difficulty getting your money back.

Protection Afforded under Bankruptcy Laws

Suppose your commodity brokerage firm does go bankrupt. How can you protect yourself? Much of the answer lies in taking protective measures before the fact, by dealing with a well-capitalized firm. In the securities world, after-the-fact measures are not too late because the Securities Investor Protection Corporation (SIPC) presently insures the claims of an individual securities investor up to $500,000, including up to $100,000 for claims for cash (as distinct from securities).

Commodity laws afford no such protection. In fact, several years ago Congress considered establishing an entity akin to SIPC, but declined to do so. At that time, several legislators noted that the amount of losses incurred by commodity customers has been very small relative

[10]Russo, *Regulation of the Commodities Futures and Options Markets*, Vol. 1, p. 18.50.

to the losses of securities customers.[11] Even if your bankrupt broker is also registered as a securities broker-dealer and is a member of SIPC, you still will not be reimbursed by SIPC for any loss of funds in your commodity account. Instead, your rights are governed by a new and essentially untested section of the Bankruptcy Code that specifically governs the bankruptcy of futures commission merchants.

The basic goal of this new bankruptcy law is to give nondefaulting customers a priority claim to their own segregated and specifically identifiable property on deposit with the FCM and to virtually all remaining assets of the bankrupt FCM.[12] This statutory priority places the claims of public customers ahead of those of officers or principals of the bankrupt firm who might have kept their own commodity trading accounts at the firm. Claims of public customers would not conflict with claims of bank creditors, the taxman, and the like, at least in theory.

The intent of the new bankruptcy law is to facilitate the recovery of property of innocent customers as well as the transfer of open positions to a different commodity broker.

If all customer property can be accounted for, each customer's account will be made whole. In the event of a shortfall, each customer will receive his pro rata share of all customer property on deposit with the bankrupt broker, whether or not that property is specifically identifiable to particular customers.

These new commodity broker bankruptcy provisions should expedite the proper handling of specifically identifiable property deposited by individual customers. Normal bankruptcy proceedings can last for years and can essentially freeze assets during that time. Such a freeze of assets could have harsh consequences when rapidly fluctuating commodities or options approaching expiration are involved.

[11]For example, between 1938 and 1981, a total of some $7.7 million in regulated commodity customer funds were lost. This sum is less than the amount paid out by SIPC annually and far less than the $109 million SIPC paid out between 1971 and 1986.

[12]Customer claims have second priority behind the payment of legal and administrative costs associated with the administration and distribution of customer property.

The new law gives the trustee in bankruptcy extensive power either to carry out customer instructions for the desired disposition of outstanding contracts or to exercise discretion in the best interests of a customer. For instance, a trustee would insure that one leg of a hedged position is not unexpectedly liquidated in the confusion of a bankruptcy proceeding. Also, a trustee would minimize the danger of options being frozen as their value wastes away. Often, the trustee will simply transfer such assets to another commodity brokerage firm.

Any customer may notify his broker that he wishes to have his account either transferred or liquidated in the event of the broker's bankruptcy. In the event of a shortfall that requires a pro rata distribution of assets to customers, the trustee will request each customer to pay in his share of the shortfall before transferring that account to another FCM. A customer is well-advised to notify the trustee promptly to maximize the chances for satisfactory handling of his specifically identifiable property.

It is important to know what constitutes specifically identifiable property should you want assets transferred to another brokerage firm. All open commodity contracts themselves are specifically identifiable property. But what about the margin you put up for those contracts? Regulations promulgated by the CFTC (17 CFR 190.01(kk)) define the term narrowly for purposes of classifying collateral used for margin. Specifically, the CFTC excludes cash, cash equivalents, T-bills maturing within 180 days and certain other assets from the definition of specifically identifiable property. Nonexempt, fully paid securities identified on the books and records of the debtor as held for or on behalf of the commodity account of a particular customer would be considered as specifically identifiable property. The rules get worse from there.

If your FCM goes bankrupt, you must fill out a claim form to recover your assets. Remember that your most recent account statement will probably reflect your account balance at some point before the bankruptcy. If you have had a net gain since that statement date, remember to claim that amount as well, since at least some chance remains that the gain will also be recoverable.

Of course, one should try to avoid bankruptcy as a major risk. Sounds easy, but in their hurry not to miss the market, some people get careless. Just so you know what can go wrong, I have reprinted part of a 1984 letter to the Action column of the *Seattle Post-Intelligencer*:

> ...our Smyth-Wheatley salesman assured us as late as Feb. 17 that the company was in a solid position and had met all requirements of the U.S. Commodities & Futures Trading Exchange [sic] based in Los Angeles. But on Feb. 21 when I called our salesman, there was no answer. To this date, we have had no remuneration of any amount on our investment. We'd appreciate any information you have on the status of this company. H.S., Northwest Seattle

> Dear H.S.
>
>   * * *
>
> Arther Salzberg, regional counsel for the CFTC, says that in spite of what the salesman told you, Smyth-Wheatley was never registered with either the CFTC or any other federal or state agency.

What preventive steps should you take to protect your assets? First, as the column implies, a clerk in the registration office of the National Futures Association will tell you whether the person or firm contacting you is registered with the CFTC as an FCM or introducing broker. The telephone number is 312-781-1410.

Second, do not leave too much excess cash, collateral or accrued profits on open positions on deposit in a commodity futures trading account. Limit funds on deposit to an amount that will cover anticipated margin requirements and no more.

Third, check the financial statements of the commodity brokerage firm. Try to find out whether it has any customers who could jeopardize the firm's position almost overnight, as happened in the 1980 Hunt silver debacle and in the Volume Investors situation in 1985.

Fourth, private insurance of a commodity account is available, though rarely used. Fifth, at least one outfit (The Vanco Group, Elk Grove Village, Illinois) will provide you with an assessment of the financial condition of major commodity brokers. Sixth, if the protections afforded by the bankruptcy laws applicable to commodity brokers leave you worried, stick to trading stock index options. As discussed in Appendix A, those options are traded in regular securities broker-age accounts covered by SIPC.

Some final caveats regarding the application of bankruptcy law to commodities firms. First, this area of bankruptcy law is still in a state of flux. Changes may be made in the statute or in its interpreta-tion in the near future. Second, the law as it stands is infinitely more complex than this summary would suggest. It would be prudent to seek the advice of counsel if you believe that you may have substantial assets in jeopardy.

MINIMAL CUSTOMER PRIORITY

Trading practices in commodity futures contracts, including stock index futures, vary from trading in stocks in subtle but significant fashion. In the commodities world, no particular individual is under any obligation to buy from you even if you instruct your broker to sell at the market. Although as a practical matter, someone will bid for your contract, no law or exchange rule obligates anyone to do so. Traders in a commodity ring are obliged only to trade in an open and competitive manner. Although legal interpretation of the open and com-petitive requirement is minimal, it means only that a bid or offer must match or improve the current bid or offer and be made known to all traders in the ring.

By contrast, someone on a stock exchange trading floor is indeed obligated to bid when you instruct your broker to sell at the market. That someone is the specialist in the particular stock, who has the demanding obligation to insure that trading in the market is "fair and orderly" rather than just "open and competitive". Part of that man-date involves the obligation to make a two-sided market, i.e., to be willing to bid and offer at all times. This insures that there will be a buyer at a reasonable price when you want to sell and vice versa. As a practical matter, a willing buyer or seller can be found virtually always in a commodity ring, but the comfort of a guarantee is absent.

Separately, a customer has no assurance that his limit order will be filled, even if the futures contract trades at the price the limit order specifies. In the securities world, a customer's limit order entered on a specialist's book receives priority in that floor traders may not jump ahead of it. However, in the commodities world, no specialist book or any other device assures that your order receives priority. Getting execution of a limit order depends even more on the skill of your broker than would be the case on a securities exchange. Certainly, it is in the interest of every exchange member to try to facilitate a limit order held by a broker, but no guarantee assures that each such order will be executed if the market moves quickly away from the limit price.

Commodity law embraces a system under which, unlike on a securities exchange, any exchange member may trade for his own account and perform brokerage functions for customers almost simultaneously in the same product. A CFTC Advisory Committee concluded in 1975 that dual trading was beneficial in that it promoted both market liquidity and expertise among floor brokers. Such dual-trading has led to certain abuses, such as "trading ahead of a customer" in commodity trading pits. Such trading has been difficult to monitor because most exchanges have had no procedure for accurately recording trades made by exchange members at the time of execution. This has made it difficult for market surveillance personnel to reconstruct accurately any exact trading sequence. Potential for and allegations of trading ahead of customers have been a source of many complaints about the commodities industry.

Let us take a moment to see how such an abuse might occur. Consider the time and sales sequence shown in Figure 10-1. Between 9:30 and 9:44 on that day, the S&P futures traded in a 50 basis point range. Now look at the copy of a trading card, which each trader or broker uses in the trading ring. Up top, where it says "member," I have entered "BTB," the letters on my trading badge. I have also marked an X in the box with the letter "C," indicating that all trades shown on the card occurred in the 9:30 to 10:00 time bracket.

Suppose that on December 23, 1985, you sat in front of a computer screen at 9:30 feeling basically bullish. You see the first trade flash on the screen at 213.50. You sit tight for five minutes until the futures settle into an even cheaper range of 213.15 to 213.25. You call your broker with instructions to buy five contracts at the market.

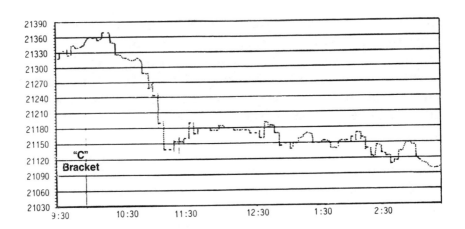

CME S&P 500 Stock Index Futures, March 1986

9:30	213.50	213.55	213.50	213.45	213.50	213.55	213.50	213.45	213.40
9:31	213.45	213.50	213.55	213.60	213.55	213.50	213.45	213.50	
9:32	213.45	213.50	213.45	213.40	213.35	213.30	213.25	213.30	
9:33	213.25	213.20	213.15	213.20	213.25	213.20	213.15	213.10	
9:34	213.10	213.15	213.20	213.25	213.30	213.25	213.20		
9:35	213.15	213.20	213.25	213.20	213.15				
9:36	213.20	213.25	213.20	213.15	213.20	213.25	213.20		
9:37	213.15	213.10	213.15	213.20	213.25	213.20	213.25		
9:38	213.30	213.35							
9:39	213.30	213.35	213.40	213.35	213.40	213.35	213.30	213.35	
9:40	213.35	213.40	213.30	213.35	213.30	213.35	213.30	213.25	213.30
9:41	213.35	213.40	213.35	213.30	213.35				
9:42	213.40	213.35	213.30	213.25	213.30	213.35	213.30		
9:43	213.35	213.30	213.35	213.40	213.35	213.30			
9:44	213.35	213.30	213.35	213.30	213.25				

Source: Videcom Service, ADP Comtrend, Stamford, Conn.

FIGURE 10–1.

ABC FUTURES

BTB
MEMBER

12/23/85
DATE

A [B] ⊠ [D] [E] [F] [G] [H]
[I] [J] [K] [L] [M] [N] [O] [P]

GIVE UP	BOT.	✓	SOLD	SYMBOL	PRICE	CONTRA
ME	5			SPH	213 15	JOE
YOU	5			H	213 20	DAN

FIGURE 10–1 (concluded).

A clerk at your brokerage firm fills out an order ticket, time stamps it to show that the order was received at 9:36, and hands the order slip to me in the trading ring. It instructs me to buy five at the market.

Meanwhile, I've decided that I like the market also and I am trying to buy five contracts for my own account. I'm obligated to execute your order first. But I am permitted to execute trades for myself as long as I execute your trade first. The trade at 213.10 at 9:37 strikes me as a fluke, so I bid 213.15 for ten contracts. A trader whose badge says "JOE" yells "sold five." I write down the trade on the trading card reproduced in Figure 10-1. That trade can also be seen on the computer printout in Figure 10-1, marked with an A.

Since I still want to buy five contracts for my own account, I continue bidding 213.15 for five contracts. But the whole pit seems to be bidding 213.15, so I raise my bid to 213.20. One trade has already been executed at 213.20 as a result of an offer being lifted, but I am the first person in the ring actually to bid that price. A trader with badge "DAN" sells me five contracts at 213.20 (trade *B* in Figure 10-1).

These two trades occurred less than a minute apart. Meanwhile, I've handed your order ticket back to a clerk who time stamps it at 9:37, showing the time at which execution of your trade was reported.

Now comes the clincher. I figure that had your order not been in my way, I'd have been able to buy Joe's contracts for my own account at 213.15. I fudge my entries just a little bit in the column on the trading card marked "Give Up." (I had managed to leave that column blank when I bought the first five at 213.15.) The trade term "give up" refers to a number assigned to identify a particular buyer or seller to facilitate automated clearing of trades. To simplify the examples, I have entered "ME" and "YOU" instead of numbers. I show that I bought contracts at 213.15, apparently only seconds before receiving your order. Also, note that even though your trade gets recorded at 213.20, I still managed to execute your order "at the market".

In fact, I might suggest, you should be happy because other customers who entered market orders to buy at the same time wound up paying 213.25 for their contracts. You are appropriately grateful for my skill in execution, which "saved" you $125 ($25 per contract times five contracts). But I was a little too skillful in that I managed to reverse the proper sequence of two trades that occurred in the same minute, pocketing $125 that was rightfully yours. Due to the frenzy of the trading pit, it is almost impossible to reconstruct that trading sequence. Moreover, my proprietary trades have never had to get time-stamped.

That is not the only way in which abuses can occur. Consider the following. Now it is 9:38. You are a bullish floor broker and would like to buy some contracts for your own account at your side of the market, which is now 213.30 bid, offered at 213.35. A customer wishing to take profits phones your clerk with an order to sell ten contracts at the market. You can't sell them to yourself, so you do the next best thing. Without making any effort to sell them at 213.35, you turn to your best buddy in the trading ring, who is also bidding 213.30 for ten contracts, and say, "I sold you ten." He knows you did him a favor because a lot of people would have liked to buy ten contracts at 213.30. Thirty seconds pass and you look at him and say, "thirty bid for five." If he's a friend, particularly a smart friend who knows you have a lot of customers who buy or sell at the market, he might well accommodate you and sell back five lots at 213.30. The net result is that both pit traders got five lots on their side of the market. In so doing, they indirectly took advantage of a customer order.

My trading card provides no way of knowing that I've bought back five contracts only thirty seconds later. As long as 213.30 traded again sometime during that half hour time bracket (which it did), a market surveillance person would have no way of proving that the latter was not my trade. An audit trail is very difficult to reconstruct since an auditor's only tools are customer ticket order, broker trading cards with the half-hour bracket indicators, and price-change registers. These tools are sometimes sufficient, particularly in markets where price changes are frequent. But if the same price recurs a number of times within a half-hour bracket, it is very difficult to know when within that time a floor trader made particular trades.

However, even if a surveillance person can show that the trade occurred thirty seconds later, it does not necessarily follow that the transaction was not an arms-length trade. So even time stamping would not completely resolve all issues relating to untoward trading against customer orders.

It is hardly inconceivable that there will be times when your market order is filled a tick or more away from where you thought it should be. Usually this will be the result of a rapidly fluctuating market and nothing more. But it will be nearly impossible to differentiate those trades from the rare occasion where some abuse has taken place.[13]

In response to this problem, the CFTC planned to require that all trades be time-stamped to the nearest minute, even if no customer order is involved. Floor traders have maintained that such a time-stamping rule would disrupt trading, reduce liquidity, increase the frequency of so-called "out-trades," and produce reams of inconsistent trading data, particularly with respect to "fast markets." A compromise between the CFTC and the exchanges should produce a more thorough audit trail beginning in late 1986. The goal is to be able to reconstruct virtually all trades, probably by making traders record a specific time rather than just a time bracket for each trade. These trading cards would be matched with an exchange time and sales run to create complete trading sequence record. Nevertheless, as noted, certain of the above-described abuses could probably occur even in the space of one minute.

If you remain wary of trading abuses, one way to protect yourself is to give your orders to a firm that does not allow its brokers to trade for their own accounts. Certain brokerage firms have adopted such a policy.

Despite the drawbacks of the present commodity trading system, it does offer certain advantages. In a trading ring with 150 or 200 traders present at any given time, it is quite likely that any number of people will be bidding or offering simultaneously. This assures that prices are as competitive as possible in a free market. In fact, the bid-ask spread in a stock index futures trading ring is almost always the minimum possible spread. In other words, the difference between bids and

---

[13]Another analysis suggests that abuses may be somewhat more frequent than I have been able to observe in New York. "Traders . . . readily admit that 'fiddles' occur." "America's Futures: Out of the Pits?" *The Economist*, January 10, 1986, pp. 61–63. For a cogent discussion of futures trading practices, see "Chicago Versus The World", *Institutional Investor*, August 1986, pp. 235–241.

offers is generally one tick, that is, the minimum allowable price fluctuation. By contrast, the bid-ask spread in a securities market is often
wider than the minimum tick.

LIMIT MOVES

Daily price limits on certain commodity futures contracts were
imposed in an effort to prevent unwarranted price movements caused
by panic or rampant speculation. Once a limit price is reached, trading
will slow or virtually cease, making it very difficult to liquidate a position. A small investor can lose a small fortune when several consecutive limit moves make closing out a position impossible. When silver
prices crashed in the Hunt debacle of 1980, small investors with long
positions in silver couldn't sell during a series of downward limit moves.

This risk no longer exists with stock index futures because they
are bound by no limit moves. The CME and KCBT rescinded their
limit-move rules in 1983. Presumably, they recognized the fact that
daily limits might impose artificial price constraints in the marketplace.
Such artificial futures prices would have the ironic impact of discouraging hedging transactions under just the volatile conditions in which
hedges are thought by many to be particularly useful. The NYFE and
the CBT never imposed price limits on their stock index contracts.
Although the limit-move risk has been eliminated from the stock index
futures market, the corresponding risk of higher potential losses in a
single day cannot be overlooked. Again, I stress the importance of stop-
loss orders!

TAX CONSEQUENCES

Presently, the tax treatment of stock index futures differs from
that of other capital assets. Like most exchange-traded derivative
products, stock index futures are subject to the mark-to market regi-
men of section 1256 of the Internal Revenue Code, enacted initially
as part of the Economic Recovery Tax Act of 1981 (ERTA).

This distinct treatment results from corrective action taken in response to certain abuses that were associated with commodity futures trading before the introduction of stock index futures contracts. The 1981 legislation was intended to prevent commodity traders from engaging in what are known as "tax straddles." A tax straddle was a transaction in which a person would establish a straddle position (e.g., a calendar spread or a butterfly spread) in futures contracts and close out the losing leg of the position prior to year-end. In the case of a calendar spread, the "closing-out" procedure involved establishing a new position in a more distant month in order to minimize the risk of losing the unrealized profit on the open position from the original spread. Such a transaction enabled the taxpayer to roll forward his capital gains while recognizing sizable paper short-term capital losses in a current year, which were used to offset unrelated income. The unrealized gain would become realized when the taxpayer closed out the position bearing the gain the subsequent year. The goal was to defer the gain, yielding time-value benefits, and to convert it into long-term capital gain.

A typical tax-motivated transaction in stock index futures, if it were possible today, might have been a simple spread trade. Assume that in November you established an initial position as follows:

Buy ten March futures at 200.
Sell ten June futures at 202.

There is at least some nominal risk that the spread relationship between the two months will change. A month later, with the market up five percent, your P & L would have been approximately:

Ten March futures at 210:   +$50,000.
Ten June futures at 212.10:   ($50,500).

So you would have sold the June position and realized a $50,500 loss. Meanwhile, the goal was to keep the profitable March position intact but unrealized until the following year. Since you would not have wanted your unrealized gain of $50,000 to evaporate due to adverse market conditions, you would have offset your long March futures position by selling 10 September futures. The transaction involves a minimal market risk, particularly in relation to the tax benefits that could be derived, because you are dealing in contracts which are sub-stantially identical and which tend to move almost dollar-for-dollar.

The ERTA reforms replaced traditional capital-gains treatment of commodity futures contracts with two principal features. First, tax liability now includes both realized and unrealized net gain or loss from all futures contracts at year-end. In other words, a futures position remaining open at the end of a taxable year is treated as if it were sold at its year-end settlement price (and then re-established at that same price on the first day of the following year). The deemed sale is referred to as a "mark to market."

Second, with respect to contracts held as capital assets, the hold-ing period of the contracts is irrelevant. All gain or loss on such a regulated futures contract, regardless of whether the position was held for a minute or a year, is treated as 60 percent long-term capital gain or loss and 40 percent short-term capital gain or loss. For the individual in a 50 percent tax bracket, the marginal rate of tax on gains from futures contracts is 32 percent, figured as follows:

$$(.60 \times \text{Long-term capital gains rate of } .20)$$
$$+ (.40 \times \text{short-term capital gains rate of } .50)$$
$$= (.12) + (.20)$$
$$= .32$$

The tax benefit attributable to any losses generated is similarly limited to 32 percent. It appears that any new tax bill would eliminate the dis-tinct treatment accorded futures contracts. Thus, both realized and unrealized gains would be taxed in the same bracket as other earned and unearned income.

If a taxpayer continues to hold the contract from one taxable year to the next, any gain or loss subsequently calculated on such a con-tract would be adjusted to reflect gain or loss reported in a prior year under the mark-to-market rules.

In addition to requiring the mark-to-market approach of Section 1256, index futures contracts that are part of straddles are subject to additional special tax accounting rules under Section 1092 and Sec-tion 263(g). As of 1984, stocks were included as a type of property subject to these straddle rules.

Mixed Straddles

Congress had anticipated that clever speculators would quickly learn to evade the tax-straddle rules by taking positions that didn't look like tax straddles upon a cursory examination, but were in fact essentially risk-free. For instance, one might buy $100,000 worth of stock in all twenty companies comprising the Major Market Index and simultaneously sell short $100,000 worth of Major Market Index futures. Clever, but not clever enough. The tax law was amended to apply specifically to stocks that form part of a straddle.

Such a position is now considered a mixed straddle for tax purposes. It is a *straddle* "if there is a substantial diminution of the taxpayer's risk of loss" on any position as a result of one or more other positions. The straddle is *mixed* if one of the positions is a Section 1256 contract and the other position or positions are "actively traded personal property" (i.e., basically any non-Section 1256 capital asset, meaning equities or non-dealer equity options for our purposes). While the rules governing mixed straddles get complicated, the bottom line is that such positions cannot be used to dodge taxes.

The rules pertaining to mixed straddles are more complex than those that govern straddles made up solely of Section 1256 contracts. With a mixed straddle, the IRS lets you elect how you want to treat the gains and losses from such positions. The major significance of an election is deciding whether you prefer to have the net gain or loss from the straddle taxed at rates applicable to commodities. Since it appears that the 1986 tax reform bill will eliminate the difference in these rates, this election may be obviated after 1986. But under current law, the taxpayer may elect as follows:

(1) Elect Out of Mark-to-Market 60/40 Treatment. This election subjects the mixed straddle to regular capital gains treatment (rather than 60/40 treatment) and to the loss-deferral rule (along with certain wash-sale and short-sale rules applicable to straddles). Under the loss-deferral rule, the investor may recognize losses at year-end only to the extent that they exceed unrecognized gains on open offsetting positions.
(2) Straddle-by-Straddle Identification Election. The taxpayer may identify each position as a separate straddle, then calculate net gain or loss

attributable to the offsetting positions. The net gain or loss is treated as 60/40 gain or loss if attributable to the section 1256 position, or as a short-term gain or loss, if attributable to the non-Section 1256 position. (3) Mixed Straddle Account Election. The taxpayer may place the positions in a special mixed straddle account that is marked to the market daily. This is often the most convenient administrative approach for an investor who regularly trades stocks against futures positions. Under a special account cap, gains can be no more than 50 percent long-term capital gain and losses can be no more than 40 percent short-term capital loss. If the election of the special mixed straddle account is made, it cannot be rescinded without the approval of the Commissioner of the IRS. (4) Make no election. In this case, the net loss on either position is treated 60/40 while a net gain is treated as short-term capital gain. This is called the killer rule.

The application of the mixed straddle rules might become clearer with a few examples. But before you struggle through them, let me warn you that the straddle game is no longer played for tax reasons. If you are engaging in mixed straddles, you should be playing an arbitrage game. If you care to go on, consider the following:

Example (1). On April 1, 1986, A enters into a non-Section 1256 position (e.g., buys all twenty MMI stocks) and an offsetting Section 1256 contract (i.e., sells an equivalent amount of MMI futures). A then makes a valid election to treat the straddle as a Section 1092(b)(2) identified mixed straddle. On April 10, 1986, A disposes of the non-Section 1256 position at a $1,100 loss and the Section 1256 contracts at a $1,000 gain. Under these circumstances, the $1,100 loss on the non-Section 1256 position will be offset against the $1,000 gain on the Section 1256 contract and the net loss from the straddle will be $100. Since the $100 loss is attributable to the non-Section 1256 property, it is treated as a short-term capital loss.

Had our taxpayer elected to treat his Section 1256 position as a non section 1256 position as in alternative (1) above, the same netting out process would take place. Here again, a short-term capital loss of $100 would result.

The election to treat Section 1256 property as non-Section 1256 property is not always so advantageous. Had the non-Section 1256 property (i.e., the MMI stocks) generated a $1,000 loss and the Section 1256 property (i.e., the MMI futures) generated a $1,100 gain, the net gain of $100 would be taxed at 50 rather than 32 percent.

In the original example, the ''killer rule'' yields the worst-case result in that a $100 gain would be taxed at 50 percent while a $100 loss would provide a deduction at only the 32 percent rate. Thus, it is wise to make an election.

The above example illustrates the working of the mixed-straddle rules when both legs are closed out in the same year. Let us consider what happens when the positions are closed out in different years.

> Example (2).   On November 1, 1986, *A* enters into a non section 1256 position (e.g., buys all 20 MMI stocks) and an offsetting Section 1256 contract (e.g., sells an equivalent amount of MMI futures). On December 1, 1986, with an unrealized gain of $1,000 on the long position of MMI stocks, *A* disposes of the futures (i.e., the Section 1256 position) at a $1,100 loss. *A* then immediately locks in his unrealized $1,000 profit by selling ''synthetic'' positions using options in all 20 stocks. On January 2, 1987, *A* disposes of the non-Section 1256 contracts and unwinds the synthetic position at a $1,000 gain.

First of all, *A* would be bound to treat this straddle in the same manner as prior mixed straddles, but let us assume that this transaction was *A*'s first mixed straddle. Under alternative (1) above, due to the loss deferral rule, *A* would not be able to deduct the $1,100 loss in 1986. The loss on the Section 1256 property up to the amount of unrealized offsetting gains would be deferred until realization of those gains in the non-Section 1256 property. Thus, only the $100 in excess of unrealized gains would be deductible in 1986. Since the $100 portion was attributable to Section 1256 property, it would receive 60/40 treatment.

When an election is made, it applies to all subsequent straddle transactions. In other words, the IRS does not permit a retrospective heads-I-win,-tails-you-lose game on a case-by-case basis. The easy advice is to avoid the killer rule. Selection of the identified straddle rule, while it may yield the best tax result, is often cumbersome and costly to implement for taxpayers engaging in numerous mixed-straddle transactions. Such a taxpayer will accept the less favorable tax treatment of the mixed-straddle account for its relative ease of implementation. Many investors will find it worthwhile to engage tax counsel to analyze the alternative elections.

To further complicate matters, it is not entirely clear exactly what is a mixed straddle and what is not. Suppose, for example, that an erstwhile investor who has shorted $10,000 worth of Major Market Index futures buys $10,000 worth of stock, but in only 15 of the 20 MMI stocks. The question is whether the non futures position is "substantially identical stock" within the meaning of Section 1092(d)(3)(B). Additionally, one must determine whether holding the stocks (or the future) substantially diminishes the risk of holding the futures position (or the stock) within the meaning of Section 1092(c)(2)(a). An investor holding a stock portfolio that correlates substantially with the movement of a stock index futures position held in a separate account may be subject to the straddle rules. To date, the Treasury has not promulgated comprehensive regulations governing these issues.

Other tax straddle issues arise because various stock index options (or options on individual stocks) could fully or partially offset a futures position. In this case, the issue is whether those options constitute "substantially similar or related property (other than stock)." That phrase gives the IRS more latitude than "substantially identical." The risk issue arising under Section 1092(c)(2)(a) also applies in this context. For the masochists among you, the options rules get even more complicated.

Until the passage of the Tax Reform Act of 1984, equity options were not subject to the tax-straddle rules. Congress sought to eradicate tax abuses involving mixed straddles using equity options without unduly burdening traders who use options in a variety of legitimate strategies not motivated by tax considerations. Thus, at the risk of some simplification, the net effect of the 1984 law was to subject deep-in-the-money stock options to the mixed-straddle rules while leaving out-of-the-money options exempt from those rules. The apparent rationale was that, since the price movement relationship of out-of-the-money options with the underlying index changes constantly, such options are not feasible for use in tax-oriented straddles anyway. In contrast, deep-in-the-money options tend to move almost point-for-point with the underlying index, and can be used to construct almost risk-free straddles.

Those are the basics of the mixed straddle rules as applied to options. Not surprisingly, Congress has more precisely delineated which options are exempt from the mixed-straddle rules. To be exempt, an option must be a "qualified covered call option." Generally speaking, that means that the option must not expire within thirty days and must have a strike price not substantially below the level of the index at the time the position is established. Certain options with strike prices that are slightly in the money are exempt from the mixed-straddle rules. Section 1092(c)(4) of the Internal Revenue Code contains a variety of formulae for determining which strike prices are covered by the straddle rules.

It is worth noting that since no put option positions are exempt under Section 1092, no tax straddles can be constructed using "synthetic" futures.

Remember that a spread position consisting of two futures contracts that are not necessarily substantially identical does not get you out from under the tax-straddle rules of Section 1256. Both positions are marked to market at year-end, regardless of whether they are closely correlated. So don't let the "substantially identical" technicalities involved with mixed straddles lull you into thinking that you can pull off a straddle with an inter-market spread in stock index futures. You can't, because both sides of the position would be Section 1256 property.

Institutions which use stock index futures to hedge their portfolios generally do not need to worry about the mixed straddle rules. Many of those institutions are tax-exempt anyway. But for tax-paying institutional investors, a question arises whether their hedges are subject to the mixed-straddle rules or whether they receive separate and distinct tax treatment. Section 1256 contracts held in hedging transactions are not subject to the mark-to-market rules. However, the IRS and a portfolio manager may have different notions about what constitutes a hedge. For tax purposes, hedging does not necessarily include offsetting the risk of holding a stock or a portfolio of stocks or indeed, of holding capital assets generally. A hedging transaction may be limited to a transaction which is entered into the normal course of a taxpayer's trade or business to protect gain which would be ordinary income or loss. Thus, the stock index future might constitute a hedge only if the institution were considered a dealer in the underlying securities. In that case, the institution's gains and losses from such transactions would be ordinary. See Section 1256(f) for further detailed requirements.

In concluding this tax section, it should be noted that the issues discussed have not been addressed in sufficient detail. Anyone engaging in straddle transactions should seek advice of tax counsel to determine how the law pertains to his circumstances.

When the mark-to-market rule was adopted, many in the commodities industry complained that it would arbitrarily force traders to take short-term capital gains even though they might not have intended to do so. The 60/40 treatment was adopted in response to that concern. Current tax reform proposals would eliminate this special treatment for futures contracts. But if a new tax law were to eliminate the distinction between long-term and short-term capital gains, the rationale for this special treatment would no longer exist. Thus, reformers have proposed eliminating any special rate for futures contracts.

POSITION LIMITS

Pursuant to Section 4a of the Commodity Exchange Act, each exchange has imposed speculative position limits on stock index futures contracts. These limits seek to discourage instability in the markets caused by reckless speculation. Nevertheless, a speculator could have held over $500 million worth of S&P futures at the end of 1985 without running afoul of the speculative position limit rules. Moreover, an institution may apply for an exemption from position limit rules in order to engage in hedging or spreading transactions. Such an exemption can even be granted to allow anticipatory hedging. The speculative position limits on the actively traded stock index futures contracts at the end of 1985 were as follows:

S&P 500 (CME)	5,000
NYSE Composite (NYFE)	5,000
Value Line (KCBT)	5,000
Major Market Maxi (CBT)	8,000

The applicable position limit rules include an aggregation requirement, under which all positions and accounts directly or indirectly controlled by a particular person or entity are deemed part of the same position. Aggregation issues often arise with respect to multiple customer trading programs or commodity pools offered by a single FCM or pool operator. To determine whether aggregation would be required, the CFTC staff has suggested basing aggregation determinations on owner ship, control, and trading agreements pertaining to accounts in question.

APPENDIX A

Stock Index Options*

Stock index futures are not the only tool available to hedgers and speculators in the stock index arena. Indeed, stock index futures may not always be the most appropriate instrument for a particular investor. Stock index options can provide an investor with limited risk and maximum flexibility in pursuing investment goals.

An option can relate to virtually any type of property. Options are sold on gold, and on parcels of real estate. Stock options are perhaps the most familiar sorts of options. So why not an option on a portfolio of stocks? That is essentially what a stock index option is. The primary difference between a stock option and a stock index option is the nature of the underlying asset—a single stock on one hand and an index of stocks on the others.

As with a stock index future, a stock index option is a leveraged, derivative trading vehicle that allows an investor to realize cash profits

*This appendix is intended primarily to draw the reader's attention to characteristics of stock index options which differentiate them from stock options. It is not intended to serve as an introduction to options in general or as a comprehensive guide to all options strategies. These topics are covered in a number of worthwhile books, including Donald T. Mesler's *Stock Index Options* (Chicago: Probus, 1985), which focuses exclusively on the basics of stock index options. See also McMillan, *Options as a Strategic Investment* (New York: Institute of Finance, 1980) Gastineau, *The Stock Options Manual* (New York: McGraw-Hill, 1979), and Cox and Rubinstein, *Options Markets* (Englewood Cliffs, NJ: Prentice-Hall, 1985).

from favorable price movements of a specified portfolio or index of securities. However, two critical factors distinguish an option from a futures contract. First, any loss incurred by an option purchaser is limited to the amount of his initial premium payment, and profits can accrue to the purchaser only in the event that the value of the underlying property increases by an amount sufficient to cover the premium payment. Second, an option gives its holder the *right* to take (or make, in the case of a put) delivery of the underlying property, but does not entail the *obligation* to do so.

While a long or a short position in a futures contract entail essentially equal (and potentially unlimited) risk, long and short options positions involve radically different risks. One who has a long position in any stock index option cannot lose more than what he initially paid in premium because, even if the underlying index moves drastically against him, the option price can only go to zero.

On the other hand, one with a short position in an index option faces the risk of virtually unlimited losses if the underlying index moves drastically against him. As compensation for the enormous risk, a short position in an option carries a much higher probability of producing a profit, since options are wasting assets whose value will decrease over time if the price of the underlying index does not change. Most options are worth less at expiration than at the time purchased. The possibility of three-fold or ten-fold gains on some occasions makes owning a wasting asset worthwhile.

Stock index options also offer enormous flexibility in that they permit an investor to implement a wide variety of investment strategies. For instance, with option strategies, an investor can profit from a trendless or unchanged market. Since stock index options allow one to select instruments with price swings ranging from under five to over 95 percent of the movement of futures contracts on the same index, options provide the opportunity to fine-tune one's risk-reward preference. Prices of widely traded stock index options which are at-the-money tend to have price swings of approximately 50 percent of the movement of the corresponding index.

With fair warning as to the limited scope of this appendix, let us quickly review some basic principles of options generally, and then deal with some of the unique characteristics of stock index options.

BASIC TERMINOLOGY AND CHARACTERISTICS

There are two types of options—calls and puts. A call option on a stock index gives the buyer (or holder) the right, for a limited time, to receive cash in an amount equal to $100 times the amount by which the closing level of the index on the exercise date exceeds the exercise price (or strike price) of the option. The cash is transferred from someone, (called "grantor,") who has sold ("written") a call option on that index having the same strike price and expiration date. The buyer of a call option expects the price of the index to rise. He can realize a profit if, at any time during the life of the option, the price of the index rises enough to offset the decay in the premium of the option or if, upon exercise or expiration, the cash he is entitled to receive exceeds the premium he paid for the option.

A put option gives the buyer the right, for a limited time, to receive cash equal to $100 times the amount by which the exercise price of the option exceeds the closing level of the index on the exercise date. The buyer of a put option expects the price of the index to decline. He can realize a profit if, at any time during the life of the option, the index declines by an amount sufficient to offset the decay in the premium he paid for the option or if, upon exercise or expiration, the cash he would receive exceeds the premium he paid.

Stock options and stock index options are very similar. Let us review their similarities and differences.

Underlying Asset

Practically speaking, any option confers a form of participation in the price movement of whatever asset or property underlies the option. The value of the option changes as changes occur in the value of the underlying asset or property. As noted, the fundamental difference between traditional stock options and stock index options relates to the nature of the underlying asset. The property that underlies a stock option is a right pertaining to shares of one particular stock. The asset underlying a stock index option is a right pertaining to an indirect interest in the shares of all the stocks comprising that index. In a sense, a stock index option is an option on a particular portfolio of stocks rather than on one specific stock.[1]

Source of Value

What value can these options really have if the underlying asset is intangible and not even represented by a piece of paper? The tangibility

---

[1] There is an entirely separate animal called an option on a stock index futures contract. Few people need to understand how these stock index futures options differ from regular stock index options because trading volume in the futures options is not substantial and is conducted primarily among professional traders. Unlike stock index options, these futures options are listed on commodity exchanges, regulated under the auspices of the CFTC and entail the right to buy (or sell in the case of a put) a stock index futures contract at a specified price for a limited period of time. Moreover, although futures options are valued in essentially the same manner as stock index options, the trading mechanisms associated with futures options may seem complicated to someone who is not well-versed in commodity trading. For instance, minimum ticks in futures options are in increments of .05 ($25) rather than the familiar eighths or sixteenths that are standard for stock options or stock index options. Additionally, the unfamiliar $500 multiple applies to futures options rather than the standard $100 multiple used with options.

Exercise of a futures option works differently. When you exercise a call before expiration, you will actually own a futures contract. This adds an element of risk that many options players prefer to avoid. For example, assume that one would purchase an S&P 500 195 call for 2.00 when the underlying S&P futures contract is at 195. Suppose the futures contract goes to 197 the next day. Instead of just selling your option, you choose to exercise, thinking that you have locked in a $1,000 profit (197 − 195 = 2.00 × $500). But it is possible that before you get around to selling, the market could reverse and drop to 192. All of a sudden you have lost $500 more than the premium you originally paid.

Ironically, many experts thought that futures options would be more successful than regular stock index options because exercise of the former gives you something that seems more tangible. But investors seem happy with cold cash upon exercise without the worries of disposing of an underlying futures contract.

of the underlying asset is something of a red herring. A lot of contractual rights are intangible. A Treasury bill gives you a contractual right to receive $10,000 at maturity from the government. This right has value even though you cannot touch a Treasury bill.

The value comes from your contractual right to exercise your option and the monetary benefit associated therewith. The contractual rights of a stock option and a stock index option are secured in the same manner and to the same extent by the Options Clearing Corporation (OCC). The OCC has adopted regulations designed to provide financial protection to its members and public customers under authority derived from the Securities Exchange Act of 1934. Moreover, your profits from stock options or stock index options left on deposit with your broker are protected by SIPC.

Liquidity

One critical difference between stock options and stock index options is that the latter are generally more liquid. However, the liquidity of different stock index options varies. To illustrate, consider the following bid-ask spreads that existed at the following randomly selected times:

I.–July 3, 1985 (10:40 a.m.)

Option	Series	Bid	Ask	Last	Spread as Percent of Last Sale
OEX*	July 185	2 1/8	2 3/16	2 3/16	2.9%
IBM	July 125	1 11/16	1 3/4	1 3/4	3.6
Exxon	July 50	2 3/16	2 3/8	2 1/4	8.3
American Home Products	July 60	3 1/4	3 5/8	4	9.4
Paine Webber	July 35	3/4	1	1	25

* Denotes index option

II.–January 2, 1986 (10:45 a.m.)

Option	Series	Bid	Ask	Last	Spread as Percent of Last Sale
MMI*	January 295	2 5/8	2 11/16	2 11/16	2.3%
IBM	January 160	2 5/8	2 11/16	2 11/16	2.3
OEX*	January 210	2 7/16	2 1/2	2 1/2	2.5
Value Line*	January 215	2 11/16	2 13/16	2 3/4	4.5
Exxon	January 50	4 3/4	5 1/8	5 3/8†	7.0
NDX*	January 240	3 3/8	3 5/8	3 1/2	7.1
American Home Products	January 60	3	3 3/8	3 1/2†	10.7
Paine Webber	January 35	5/8	7/8	3/4	33.3

* Denotes index option
† Last sale higher than asking price indicates no recent sale in hour during which Dow dropped ten points.

Liquidity saves you money in several ways. As these illustrations make clear, one who must pay the ask price to buy or who must sell at the bid price will incur a cost known as "slippage," which should be viewed as an indirect transaction cost. Referring back to our first illustration, suppose you buy ten OEX options and ten Exxon options in anticipation of a three o'clock rally. After an hour, the market hasn't moved at all you decide to close out both positions. You have incurred slippage of $62.50 on the OEX options and $187.50 on the Exxon options. This indicates that costs of doing business are usually much lower in the stock index options market.

Liquidity not only reflects the frequency of trading, it also measures the depth of the market. In this sense as well, stock index options are advantageous to investors who want to buy or sell a large number of options without causing an unfavorable change in the bid-ask market for those options before their order can be completed. In other words, a large order is less likely to have "market impact" in the index options market.

For another advantage of liquidity, the larger number of participants in the stock index options market reduces the chance that, under normal market conditions, an option will be substantially overpriced or underpriced. This works in favor of the nonprofessional investor who cannot afford to spend all day calculating the theoretical value of options to the nearest sixteenth.

Influence of Momentum on Premiums

This fair price premise does not necessarily hold when the futures are mispriced or fluctuating rapidly. Stock index options prices are closely tied to the prices of stock index futures contracts as well as the levels of the subject index. When futures stray significantly from their theoretical values, option prices may be skewed. Moreover, just as stock index futures prices anticipate short-term movements in the cash index, stock index option prices attempt to anticipate the direction of the futures and the index. Thus, index option prices can vary considerably depending upon whether the futures are trending higher or lower. For example, on Friday, December 13, 1985, the Dow gained 24 points to close at 1535. Compare futures prices with the prices of NDX December 245 calls (expiring in a week) at several points in time:

NDX Dec. 245 Calls

Time	Trend	SPH	YXH	Call Bid	Call Offer
3:06	Up	213.30	123.05	13/16	1
3:44	Down	213.30	123.05	3/4	15/16
4:05	Down	213.30	123.10	5/8	3/4

Accuracy of Quotes

Ironically, too much liquidity can have its disadvantages. So much action can make it difficult to get accurate quotes before you trade and equally difficult to get quick reports of execution after you trade. It is sometimes difficult to know where the "real" market is for a particular option. On that same December 13, at 3:20,[2] the specialist's quote board posted NDX December 245 calls as: 1 1/16 bid, 1 1/4 offered. I know several traders were offering those options at 1 1/8 at that time. Further, one trader offered options at 1 1/16 while that bid was posted on the board, but did not get "lifted." So much for the specialist's role in maintaining a fair and orderly market. My best advice is to find a broker you trust and give him discretion of 1/16, 1/8, or more when you place orders.

Timeliness of Execution Reports

Price might be the least of your worries if you don't know whether you're in or out of a fast-moving market because a telephone confirmation is slow. I once heard an arbitration involving a customer who waited over an hour for a report back from the CBOE floor on an OEX order. That can be harrowing. But if you leave a market order, you can fairly assume that it has been filled at some price. To protect yourself, you might leave instructions on where to liquidate your position should the market move adversely at the same time you leave your opening order. The risk of such delays is probably less serious with stock options, simply because trading in most stock options is less chaotic.

Expiration

Stock options and stock index options also differ with respect to their expiration cycles. Most stock options presently expire on a quarterly cycle while stock index options expire monthly thanks to aggressive competition among exchanges for market share. Moreover,

[2] NYSE time and sales records show the following consecutive entries:

Quote	15:18	1 1/16	1 4/16
Quote	15:22	15/16	1 1/16

much of the volume in stock index options is in the near month. This suggests that much of the activity in these options comes from speculation on short-term market movements. Because the most liquid stock index options are so close to expiration, the time premium on the most active stock index options should deteriorate at a more rapid rate than that of stock options with two or three months remaining until expiration.

Valuation

Although the valuation of any option is complex, its value will always be a function of *intrinsic* value and *time* value. Intrinsic value is simply the difference between the strike price and the current price of the underlying stock or index. The intrinsic value of an index call option equals the amount by which the price of the underlying index exceeds the exercise price. A put option's intrinsic value equals the amount by which the underlying index price is below the exercise price. An option which is "at-the-money" or "out-of-the-money" has no intrinsic value.

Time value can make options trading something of a cerebral enterprise. Time value represents the amount of premium that a buyer is willing to pay over and above intrinsic value in order to profit from any favorable price movement in the underlying index. That amount is determined by a buyer's assessment of the probability of favorable price movements of various magnitudes before the option's expiration. That probability can be assessed by two quantifiable factors: the *time remaining* until expiration of the option and the *volatility* of the underlying index.

An option is a decaying asset; i.e., its value declines as the passage of time decreases the chance of a change in the index price sufficient to be profitable for an option holder. The rate at which time premium deteriorates accelerates as an option approaches expiration.

The time value portion of option premium is largely a function of volatility, because a history of relatively substantial price moves increases both the probability of favorable price movements to a buyer and the risk of loss to the seller. An option seller seeks a higher premium as compensation for increased risk of a substantial adverse price move.

Volatility is generally expressed in percentage terms to reflect the standard deviation of the daily index closing levels over some period of time, and is generally expressed as an annualized figure. Roughly speaking, if the NYSE Composite Index has a volatility of 10 and a starting price of 100, there would be a 65 percent probability (i.e., one standard deviation) that the index would range between 90 and 110 during the year's trading.[3]

One needs a sense of the normal range of volatility in the stock index market in order to make intelligent investment decisions. In recent years, volatility has generally ranged between about 8 and 18.

The expected range of prices, given a particular volatility, can be depicted in a probability distribution graph. Most option pricing models assume a lognormal distribution of index prices, which reflects equal possibilities of the index decreasing in price by 50 percent or increasing in price by 100 percent. Most studies have concluded that a lognormal distribution reflects the actual distribution of index prices more accurately than a normal distribution, though neither mirrors prices perfectly.

The price of an at-the-money option will almost double when volatility doubles. The price of an out-of-the-money option will increase far more rapidly for the same increase in volatility because the cost of an out-of-the-money option is time premium, and volatility affects time premiums. As Table A–1 shows, volatility can exert an enormous influence on option premiums.

Suppose volatility is high, but you remain bullish and want to buy the market. Should you still buy call options? Volatility that seems high can always go higher, as evidenced by the rally in early 1986. So the purchase of call options can still be profitable. However, there are times when futures and stocks are both higher, but out-of-the-money

[3]Technically speaking, the mean of the normal distribution curve would be above 100 in this example, reflecting the expectation that the market will appreciate by a percentage greater than the risk-free rate of interest.

TABLE A-1

S + P 100 Index = 200 (January 1)

Volatility	Jan. 200	Feb. 200	March 200
6	1.75	2.50	3.25
8	2.12	3.12	4.12
10	2.56	3.75	4.87
12	3.00	4.37	5.62
14	3.43	5.06	6.37
16	3.81	5.69	7.19
18	4.25	6.31	7.94
20	4.69	7.00	8.69

call options are unchanged or even lower because traders are expecting the market to be less volatile. A high volatility period increases the possibility that you can lose money even while being correct on the direction of the market.

A high volatility period is often a good time to buy the futures rather than the options. Sometimes this strategy yields a double bonus. First, you avoid high options premiums, and second, it may be possible to buy the futures cheap just when options are particularly dear. Often enough, a rally that inflates options premiums is accompanied by discounts on the futures due to predominant investor sentiment that the rally cannot continue.

How does one know whether volatility is high or low? Of course, one solution is to use a computer, but the CBOE Time Premium Index published by *Barron's* gives a rough idea of volatility. Alternatively, one can gauge volatility by the calendar spreads between various options. Look, for example, back at Table A-1. It lists estimated prices for OEX 200 calls when that index is at 200 (under interest rate and dividend conditions prevailing in late 1985). When volatility is a low 8.00, the at-the-money premium increases $1.00 for each expiration month. When volatility reaches 16, however, the increase in at-the-money premium is approximately $1.90. You can reasonably guesstimate volatility by watching the spreads of at-the-money options, using

Table A–1 as a general reference (and adjusting for different index levels).

It is also important to be able to evaluate the worth of a particular option relative to other options on the same index. Using the preceding table for an example, if volatility is at 10, January 200 calls at 2.56 and March 200 calls at 4.87, we do not want to pay 4.00 for a February 200 call. That is throwing away $25. Yet many investors do exactly that.

The volatility of a stock index is generally lower than the average volatility of its constituent stocks. Hence, option premium levels should be lower on stock index options than on most stock options.

A good broker should be able to supply information on current volatility levels and to indicate whether a particular option is overvalued or undervalued, given the level of volatility. Many trading strategies are based on relative values of various stock index options, i.e., option prices in relation to each other. Although the price of underlying index, the strike price, time until expiration, and volatility are the key determinants of an option's value, the risk-free rate of interest and dividend rates also each have a small effect on the valuation of options.

Rapid Deterioration of Premiums

Remember that the most actively traded stock index options have a very short time remaining until expiration. Their premiums tend to deteriorate at a more rapid rate than those of stock options, which typically have longer maturities. Thus, a buyer of index options who expects a generally rising market over the course of six months or a year may wish to buy more distant call options, even though the purchase would entail payment of a higher premium. It would be frustrating to be right about the market a day or week after your option expires.

Exercise

Stock options and stock index options are both "American" options. This means they can be exercised at any time during the life of the option. (European options, such as the CBOE's recently introduced options on the S&P 500 Index, can be exercised only on their expiration day.) Upon exercise of a call option on a stock, the option holder receives shares of that stock in return for payment of the exercise price. Upon exercise of a stock index call option, the option holder receives cash based upon the value of the underlying index at the close on the day of exercise, rather than shares of any stock.

Similarly, one who exercises a put option on a stock sells that stock at the exercise price. One who exercises a put option on a stock index receives cash. Cash settlement makes the transaction less cumbersome, less expensive, and just as safe as settlement by actual delivery of stock certificates for all stocks in a particular index. Cash settlement also eliminates the risk associated with assuming direct ownership of the underlying stocks in an index, which is that the stocks might move against you between the time of exercise and the earliest opportunity to liquidate them.

Most index options are never exercised anyway. Rather, investors simply liquidate their position in a closing transaction and get cash from their broker. So why does anyone ever bother to exercise an index option? Because exercise assures that even in an illiquid market, you will always be able to sell your option at or very near its intrinsic value.

Deep-in-the-money options may become illiquid because floor traders do not like to tie up disproportionate amounts of capital in options with high premiums. To digress for a moment, assume you own a NYSE 90 call and that the index is at 100. When you are ready to take your profit, your broker will generally be able to get a bid of at least 9 7/8 for your option, because an arbitrageur is generally willing to buy at a price below intrinsic value and exercise the option on that day, making 1/8 point without tying up capital overnight. The arbitrageur can lock a profit during the trading day by hedging the position in the futures market.

Without a right of exercise at all times during the life of the option, certain options could trade at prices substantially below their intrinsic worth. That is why index options can be exercised even though it is usually simpler and more profitable just to offset your position through a normal purchase or sale.

The exercise procedure for index options is much more efficient than that for stock options. To exercise an option on IBM, you must complete a two-step process: (1) give exercise instructions to your broker, receive your shares of IBM, and pay a commission on the transaction, and (2) instruct your broker to sell the IBM shares (and incur a second commission). Stock index options streamline this process into one step. You receive a cash gain based on the last index price for the day.

Margin

Margin calculations for index options are similar, but not identical, to those for stock options. The premium must be paid in full upon the purchase of any option, on either a stock or a stock index. Differences in the margin rules arise upon the writing of an option.

Margin is always required when an index option is written because the underlying asset cannot be delivered. The margin requirement for the writer of a broad-based index option equals 100 percent of the premium plus 10 percent of the current index number times the index multiplier ($100). Thus, the writer of an OEX 200 call at $4 with the OEX at 200 could calculate margin as follows:

Index	200
10 percent	× .10
	20
Index multiplier	× $100
	$2,000
Option premium	+ 400
Required margin	$2,400

The margin required upon the sale of an out-of-the-money index option is reduced by the amount by which the option is out of the money. It cannot, however, fall below the price of the premium plus 2 percent of the current index number times the index multiplier. Margin for an in-the-money option increases by the amount by which it is in the money. The writer of an OEX 210 call at $1 with the OEX at 200 would calculate margin as follows:

Index	200
10 percent	×.10
	20
Index multiplier	× $100
	$2,000
Option premium	+ 100
	$2,100
Out-of-money amount	− ($100×10)
Required margin	$1,100

Margin calculations for naked sub-index options are the same as for stock options. The requirement is 30 percent of the index value plus or minus the amount by which the index is in or out of the money. The premium received can be applied against the margin requirement. The minimum margin is $250 per contract.

COMPARING VARIOUS INDEX OPTIONS

Now that we have a clear sense of the major differences between stock options and stock index options, let us look at the similarities and differences among the various stock index options themselves.

The most active index option, the OEX, is based on the S&P 100 index and is listed on the CBOE. At the end of 1985, there was open interest of well over 1,000,000 and average daily volume of approximately 350,000 in these contracts. During significant market moves, trading volume has surged to as high as 600,000 contracts per day.

The second most popular option is based on the Major Market Index described in Chapter 2 and trades on the Amex. These options are widely regarded as a proxy for the Dow Jones Industrial Average. At the end of 1985, open interest in the XMI options was approximately 150,000 and the average daily trading volume was in the area of 45,000 contracts per day.

Another entry in the game, the venerable but somewhat antediluvian New York Stock Exchange, lists an option directly on the NYSE Composite Index. Trading in these options had been at approximately the same level as trading in the XMI options, but began to lag the XMI options considerably in 1985. The NYSE also belatedly listed Double Index options in an effort to provide investors with options that feature greater price movements. However, another effect of this development was to diffuse trading among too many options, thus reducing liquidity in all NYSE index options. More recently, the NYSE listed options on a high beta index.

A more recent entry into the stock index options market has been the Philadelphia Stock Exchange. It lists options on the Value Line Index.

The most recently introduced options are those on over-the-counter indexes. At the end of 1985, three OTC contracts were listed.

Finally, due to temporarily distortions in supply and demand on different exchanges, one option may trade below its theoretical value while a similar option might be temporarily overpriced. Various computer models are available to help an investor spot undervalued and overvalued options. A good broker ought to be able to provide a customer with up-to-the-minute data. That sort of valuation analysis need not be the decisive factor in your selection of a particular option, but it should not be ignored.

SUB-INDEX OPTIONS

As if all this were not enough to absorb, these index options have spawned their own derivative: options on a sub-index. A sub- index measures the value of selected stocks in a particular industry group. Although these industry group options provide a potentially more accurate hedging device than indexes or options based on the market as a whole, none of the sub-index options has yet enjoyed overwhelming success. Table A–2 sets forth a complete list of all index and sub-index options with any meaningful volume.[4]

The Amex Computer Technology Index (XCI) measures changes in the aggregate market value of 30 leading U.S. computer firms. IBM alone counts for just over one-half of the value of the Index, which is market-value weighted in the same manner as the S&P 500 index. The Computer Technology Index was introduced with an initial value of 100 on July 29, 1983.

The Philadelphia Stock Exchange has entered the industry options business, with a gold/silver index. At the end of 1985, it had achieved average daily volume of approximately 500 contracts and an open interest of approximately 3,000 contracts at a time when public interest in trading gold and silver was waning. The Gold/Silver Index is a capitalization-weighted average of the prices of seven mining stocks. The largest firm, Dome Mines, accounts for approximately 22 percent of the index, which was set at 33.3 on January 1, 1979 and closed November 1985 at 84.70. Interestingly, the index has outperformed gold itself.

Parenthetically, these industry group options have given rise to renewed tension between the SEC and the CFTC due to the SEC's concern about the potential for manipulation and profiteering by insiders through industry options. The SEC worried that an insider could profit from price moves of an industry group option caused by a more drastic price move in a company's stock or option which he could not legally buy.

---

[4] Mesler's *Stock Index Options* (Probus, 1985) has an array of charts depicting the performance of various sub-indexes relative to broader indexes such as the S & P 500.

TABLE A-2

STOCK INDEX OPTIONS: WEEKLY SUMMARY
January 10, 1986

	Open	High	Low	Last	Chg.	Call Volume	Open Interest	Put Volume	Open Interest
S&P100	205.58	208.64	200.61	200.61	– 4.93	1,477,159	779,426	1,146,862	675,058
S&P500	210.65	213.80	205.96	205.96	– 4.92	76	171	35	266
S&P OTC 250	193.53	195.73	190.49	191.15	– 2.00	43	212	0	80
AMEX Major Market	293.51	297.20	286.34	286.34	– 7.45	182,796	98,144	129,569	74,457
AMEX Market Value	247.37	249.89	243.96	243.96	– 3.77	73	98	44	93
AMEX Comp. Tech.*	114.44	116.15	110.75	110.75	– 3.84	513	560	586	
AMEX Oil*	134.88	135.84	131.38	132.83	– 1.79	86	211	725	930
AMEX Airline*	103.06	105.13	102.88	103.44	– 0.81	559	1,539	229	354
NYSE Composite	121.38	123.14	118.82	118.82	– 2.68	28,057	29,545	29,138	47,813
NYSE Comp. Double	242.76	246.28	237.64	237.64	– 5.36	12,553	20,957	11.682	22,837
Phil. Gold/Silver*	81.61	89.08	81.61	89.08	+ 7.27	2,166	2,063	675	924
Phil. Value Line	215.93	218.93	210.83	210.83	– 5.42	48,720	29,054	20,944	22,920
Phil. Nat'l O-T-C	189.89	193.18	188.88	189.51	– 0.61	77	612	202	831
Pacific Tech.*	110.23	112.26	107.93	108.10	– 2.23	677	2,531	397	514
NASDAQ 100	260.71	265.58	257.60	259.13	– 1.97	2,956	1,449	2,653	1,365

Source: Barron's.
*Sub-index options.

This tension was alleviated when the two agencies agreed on certain guidelines for the listing of options on a nondiversified stock index.[5]

Although it had been widely anticipated that a fairly large number of new industry index options would result from this latest accord, the disappointing performance of sub-index options has probably changed all that.

GENERAL STRATEGIC CONSIDERATIONS

Stock index options have dramatically broadened the choice of investment strategies for investors in the equity-related markets. These strategies can involve outright positions in stock index options, as well as a wide variety of spreading and hedging strategies.

Mesler outlines strategies in great detail in his book, *Stock Index Options*. A number of other excellent books devoted exclusively to options cover the topics as well. I have limited this appendix to a few basic comments on strategy.

[5]Any industry index must be composed of domestic equity securities of at least 25 different companies. The aggregate capitalization of the securities comprising any such index must be at least $75 billion at initial approval of trading based on it. Moreover, no new trading months may be listed if the capitalization of the securities comprising the index falls below $50 billion. In a capitalization-weighted index, no single security within the index may have a capitalization exceeding 25 percent of the aggregate capitalization of all index securities. Moreover, the aggregate capitalization of the three highest-capitalization securities within the index may not exceed 45 percent of the aggregate capitalization of the index.

This accord sets separate guidelines for a noncapitalization-weighted index. Any single security in such an index that accounts for 10 percent or more of the aggregate weight of all index securities may not be part of the index if its weighted percentage exceeds three times the percentage weight of total index capitalization. Finally, the aggregate weight of the three securities having the highest percentage weight of all securities within the index may not exceed 45 percent of the aggregate weight of all securities within the index.

"Bounce"

Before selecting a particular option, decide how much "bounce" you want in an underlying index. The S&P 100 index is at a higher absolute level than the NYSE Composite index. On a day when the market goes up, the S&P index is likely to increase by a greater absolute amount (but not necessarily a greater percentage) than the NYSE Composite index. The S&P 100 option prices are likely to move more for that reason alone. While a greater amount of bounce has its greater potential rewards, remember the commensurate increase in risk.

Delta

Bounce in the underlying index will affect the absolute amount by which an option price changes. But a sophisticated options trader is more concerned with relative changes in the value of an option for a given change in the value of the underlying index. The percentage change in the value of an option for a given percentage change in the underlying index is known as the 'delta' of the option. Neutral hedge ratio is a synonym for delta. Although option prices are ultimately determined by supply and demand in the marketplace rather than by mathematical formulas, delta has been a highly reliable measure of likely movements in index option prices. Nonetheless, delta is only a guideline; other factors influence changes in premium.

The delta of an option which is at-the-money will be approximately .50. That is to say, the value of an at-the-money call option can be expected to increase by approximately one-half point for every one point increase in the underlying index.[6]

---

[6]This figure will vary with certain changes in interest rates, dividend flows, volatility, and life of the option.

Conversely, the value of an at-the-money put option can be expected to decline by one-half point for every one point increase in the underlying index.

The underlying logic of delta is best seen in an example of an out-of-the-money call option. For simplicity's sake, assume that the S&P 100 (OEX) Index is at exactly 180. You are watching 200 calls due to expire in three months that are trading at 1 3/8. An advance in the index to 182 might not budge the option price at all, for much the same reason that bettors wouldn't get too excited if a horse moved from 20 lengths back to 18 lengths back. This does not mean that the delta is zero, but is means that it is negligible, perhaps .02 or .03.

But delta won't remain negligible for long if the index keeps advancing toward the 200 strike price. Suppose the index advances again, this time from 182 to 184. Now you're starting to see just a bit more probability that the index might indeed reach the 200 strike price within the three months before expiration. You're willing to pay a bit more for that option now, perhaps 1 7/16. The option has increased in value by 1/16 or 3 percent of the amount of the change in the underlying index. It has a delta of .03. Remember that the concept of delta has nothing to do with the price of the option relative to its former price. Indeed, by jumping from 1 3/8 to 1 7/16, the option increases in value by nearly 5 percent, but the delta remains at .03.

Now suppose that the underlying index moves from 184 to 186. Your likelihood of profit is getting ever greater. Maybe now you're willing to pay 1 9/16 for the 100 call option. This time it increased in value by 1/8, or 6 percent of the increase in the underlying index, for a delta of .06.

From 186 to 188, the option might jump from 1 5/8 to 1 13/16, giving it a delta of .08. From 188 to 190, the option might jump from 1 13/16 to 2, for a delta of .10. A continued progression might look something like this:

Index	Option	Delta
190 to 191	2 to 2 3/16	.12
191 to 192	2 3/16 to 2 3/8	.14
192 to 193	2 3/8 to 2 9/16	.17
193 to 194	2 9/16 to 2 13/16	.20
194 to 195	2 13/16 to 3 1/16	.23
195 to 196	3 1/16 to 3 3/8	.27
196 to 197	3 3/8 to 3 11/16	.32
197 to 198	3 11/16 to 4 1/16	.37
198 to 199	4 1/16 to 4 1/2	.43
199 to 200	4 1/2 to 5	.50

It's not hard to see that delta is primarily a function of probability. In other words, each market advance of one point progressively increases the probability of profit on the option position. Thus, investors will bid up the price of the option at a rate that increases commensurate with the increased chance for profit.

COMMENTS ON OPTION SPECULATION

In the bull market legs since mid-1984, some investors have made ten or twenty times their investment in particular call options. This was especially true in August, 1984 and October-November, 1985, when implied volatilities were quite low and options were therefore relatively cheap.[7] By December of 1985, implied volatilities had risen considerably, so that a substantial market move was required before the option premium was recouped.

But it is big moves, particularly when coupled with low implied volatility, that make the purchase of at-the-money or out-of-the-money options so appealing. But remember, such circumstances do not occur

[7] Implied volatility refers to the volatility ascribed to the index in question by current option premiums. Thus, implied volatility reflects the collective judgment of traders regarding current and future volatility. This is distinguished from historical volatility, which measures past movement of the index.

regularly—or predictably. Nevertheless, I believe that technical analysis can improve your odds of getting in before major moves.

Taking Profits

An important question is when does one take profits on an option position? Some people have rather automatic rules of thumb that they will sell any time they double their money. Since such ironclad rules do not necessarily bear any relationship to current market trends, they may prevent you from maximizing profits. While such rote rules may be valid for one who can not afford to pay very close attention to the direction of the market, I maintain that greater profitability is available to one who sells profitable option positions not on the basis of percentage gain but rather on the basis of feelings about major trends and market direction as a whole, and identified support or resistance levels. Which isn't to say one should hesitate to take profits, at least a little bit at a time.

Finally, there are all kinds of strategies available to the options speculator. You can buy calls if you think the market is going up, or buy puts if you think it's going down. You can buy a bull spread if you think a rally will carry through one strike price but not a second strike price. The merits of such strategies are thoroughly outlined in the books by Mesler, McMillan, and Gastineau cited earlier.

I wish to add just one cautionary note regarding sexy-sounding strategies such as butterflies, iron butterflies, or boxes. Many of these strategies are often inappropriate for the individual speculator simply because transaction costs of establishing a multi-legged position are likely to cut substantially into one's expected profit. A strategy may be new, exciting, and different, but that does not make it wise from a risk-reward standpoint.

GUIDELINES FOR HEDGERS

Stock index options provide a hedging tool which might be more advantageous than stock index futures, depending upon market conditions and investor preferences. Several differences exist between hedging strategies using options rather than futures. Most critically, a futures hedge minimizes or even eliminates profit when the market rallies. Although a hedge through the purchase of put options will reduce upside profits to some extent, it allows far more profit from market rallies than would a futures hedge. Through the choice of strike price, an option hedger can select the amount of upside he wishes to preserve by paying lower options premiums in return for less downside protection.

Viewed another way, the cost and cash flow requirements of a futures hedge are uncertain, while the cost and cash flow requirements of a hedge with put options are fixed. A market rally will produce a request for maintenance margin on a futures position. The same rally may make a put option worthless, but the put premium is the most you can lose. This premium might be viewed as akin to any other insurance premium—an up-front "sunk cost" of portfolio insurance. Term insurance, not life insurance.

A much more aggressive strategy is writing call options rather than buying put options to hedge a portfolio. The principal advantage of this approach is that the hedger receives premium up-front which he keeps unless the market has a rally of sufficient magnitude to offset the deterioration in the time value of that premium. Therein lies the risk. If the market does have a sharp rally, a hedger can face even higher cash flow requirements than a hedger who is short futures contracts. Moreover, a call writer receives only limited protection (i.e., the amount of premium received) in the event of a substantial market decline. Thus, this strategy may be more attractive to portfolio managers for its income-generating potential than for protection against a substantial market decline. However, when volatility makes option premiums exceptionally high, granting call options may be a sound hedging strategy. Conversely, when volatilities are low, puts may be viewed as a "cheap" form of portfolio insurance. The following table summarizes the advantages and disadvantages of the three hedging strategies mentioned:

Short Futures	*Long Puts*	*Short Calls*
Variable Cost	Fixed Cost	Variable Cost
Minimizes Profit	Preserves Profit Potential	Profit Potential decreases the more the market rallies.
Substantial Protection in any market decline	Limited Protection in small market decline; substantial protection in large market decline.	Limited Protection in large market decline

Option-based hedges tend to involve higher commission and "slippage" costs than futures-based hedges, primarily because several options must generally be purchased to get the same protection afforded by one futures contract. For example, it takes ten at- the-money NYSE options to achieve the same initial protection as one would get from selling one NYSE future. If there is a 1/8 bid-ask spread in those options, a "slippage" cost of $125 may be incurred to buy ten put options. To sell one futures contract at the normal one-tick spread would involve slippage of only $25.

The same caveats set forth in Chapter 8 with respect to hedging one or a few stocks apply with equal force to index options. It can be quite risky to hedge a non-diversified portfolio with options on a broad-based market index.

APPENDIX B

Accounting for Stock Index Futures

Raymond E. Perry*

The following discussion first briefly summarizes accounting for marketable equity securities by various types of entities. This provides background for the discussion of accounting for stock index futures.

ACCOUNTING FOR MARKETABLE EQUITY SECURITIES

Accounting for marketable equity securities, in conformity with generally accepted accounting principles, is governed by *Statement of Financial Accounting Standards No. 12 Accounting for Certain Marketable Securities* (SFAS 12) issued by the Financial Accounting Standards Board in 1975. Variations from SFAS 12 apply to enterprises in industries that have specialized accounting principles, such as investment companies, brokers and dealers in securities, and insurance companies.

SFAS 12 applies to nonfinancial companies that hold marketable equity securities. The accounting differs between investments classified as current, because they are temporary, and those classified as non-current, because they are long-term.

*The author gratefully acknowledges the contribution of Raymond E. Perry. Mr. Perry is a partner in the Financial Services Center office of Touche, Ross & Co., New York, New York. He is the firm's Technical Director for Financial Services Industries.

Long-term investments are carried at cost, but reductions below cost are required when the market value of any investment is less than cost and this impairment in value is considered to be other than temporary. The adjusted amount establishes a new cost basis for the investment.

The total long-term investment portfolio is accounted for at the lower of cost or market. At each balance sheet date, the aggregate cost of all noncurrent marketable equity securities is compared with the aggregate market value of such securities. If aggregate market value is lower than aggregate cost, a valuation allowance equal to that difference is established. This valuation allowance, recorded as a reduction in the carrying value of the securities and as a reduction of stockholders' equity, is presented as a separate line item in the stockholders' equity section of the balance sheet. Subsequent changes in aggregate market value as compared to aggregate cost are recognized as increases or decreases in the valuation allowance. However, when aggregate market exceeds aggregate cost, the securities are carried at cost and no valuation allowance is recorded. Changes in the valuation allowance have no impact on income or expense.

Marketable equity securities classified as current assets are accounted for in the same manner with one important exception. The initial recording of a valuation allowance and changes in the valuation allowance are recognized in income and expense rather than in equity.

In the case of banks, thrifts, and some not-for-profit entities that do not classify assets as between current and noncurrent, marketable equity securities held in investment accounts are handled as described above for noncurrent assets. Securities held in trading accounts are generally recorded at current market with all changes recognized in income or expense.

Brokers and dealers in securities, investment companies, pension funds, and many not-for-profit entities carry marketable equity securities at market and recognize all changes in value in income and expense.

Insurance companies carry marketable equity securities at market; however, all unrealized differences between market and cost are recognized in equity and are not included in income or expense.

ACCOUNTING FOR STOCK INDEX FUTURES

Accounting for stock index futures was controversial until the Financial Accounting Standards Board issued its *Statement of Financial Accounting Standards No. 80, Accounting for Futures Contracts* (SFAS 80) in August 1984. This statement establishes generally accepted accounting principles for exchange-traded futures contracts for commodities and financial instruments contracts entered after December 31, 1984. SFAS 80 requires changes in the value of stock index futures contracts to be recognized as gains or losses at the time the changes occur, except in cases where hedge accounting applies. This is often referred to as ''market value'' or ''mark-to-market'' accounting.

The detailed application of mark-to-market accounting to stock index futures is as follows:

When a contract is initiated, the required margin deposit is recorded as an asset.

As the value of the contract changes, the margin account is increased or decreased and an offsetting gain or loss is recognized.

When the contract is closed, the balance in the asset account will represent the cash to be received on settlement before providing for commissions.

In theory, commissions should be expensed over the period of the contract. However, since the amounts of commissions are generally not material, the usual practice is either (1) to expense the full amount of the commission either when the futures contract is entered or when it is settled or (2) to expense half of the commission at initiation and half at settlement.

The accounting described in the preceding paragraphs applies in all cases where stock index futures contracts are entered as speculations. It also applies to contracts entered to hedge investment positions (''cash positions'') in the case of entities that carry investments at market.

However, entities that carry investment assets at cost or at the lower of cost or market and that enter stock index futures to hedge these investments use hedge accounting for stock index futures if certain requirements of SFAS 80 are met. The need for hedge accounting arises because the holder of the contract expects that gains or losses on the futures contract will offset opposite increases or decreases in the value of the cash position. Because the change in the value of the cash position is not included in determining income for a given period, (because the asset is carried at cost or the lower of cost or market), the futures gain or loss should also be excluded from the income statement for the same period. Thus, under hedge accounting, the gain or loss on the futures contract is deferred by recording it as an increase (for a loss) or decrease (for a gain) in the carrying amount of the hedged cash position.

The use of hedge accounting for stock index futures contracts is of theoretical rather than practical interest because many of the entities that use the cost or the lower of cost or market basis in accounting for cash positions—such as banks, thrifts, and insurance companies—are not generally allowed to invest significant amounts in common stocks or stock index futures contracts. Most other businesses, not so restricted, rarely hold diversified portfolios of common stocks. However, since hedge accounting is applicable in some cases and changes in regulations may some day expand the investment horizons of financial institutions, a brief explanation is provided in the following paragraphs.

In order for hedge accounting to be applicable under SFAS 80, certain conditions must be met.

First, high correlation between changes in value of the hedged item and changes in value of the futures contract must exist. Although not defined in SFAS 80, high correlation has generally been interpreted to mean that at least 80 percent to 90 percent of the change in the value of the cash position being hedged must be offset by a change in the value of the futures contracts designated as hedges. This will be met whenever a futures contract hedges an appropriate amount of an identical security. Thus, in the case of stock index futures, the sale of an appropriate amount of futures contracts would act as a perfect hedge of a portfolio of stocks exactly mirroring the stocks included in the index, a circumstance not likely to occur in real life. If stock index futures are intended to hedge a portfolio that is not an exact mirror image of the stocks included in the particular index, a cross hedge, then a clear economic relationship and a high correlation must be demonstrated between the index and the portfolio to be hedged.

An initial assessment of high correlation must be based on historical experience coupled with the expectation that the correlation will continue in the future. Additionally, SFAS 80 requires regular ongoing assessment of correlation. If high correlation ceases to exist, then hedge accounting must be discontinued and a gain or loss recognized to the extent that the futures results have not been offset by changes in value of the cash items being hedged since inception of the hedge. In addition, all subsequent gains and losses on the futures contracts must be recognized as they occur.

SFAS 80 also requires that (1) a company formally designate a futures contract as a hedge and (2) assess whether other circumstances, such as an existing commitment to sell the portfolio at a fixed price, obviate the need for the futures contract.

In cases where stock index futures qualify for hedge accounting, changes in the value of the futures are not recognized in determining income or expense, but are recognized as adjustments of the carrying value of the individual securities in the hedged portfolio based on their relative market values. The adjusted carrying values of the individual securities become their new "cost" bases and, when aggregated, the total is compared to aggregate market to determine if an adjustment in the valuation allowance for the portfolio is required.

SFAS 80 also permits hedge accounting for transactions that an enterprise expects to carry out in the normal course of business, although not obligated to do so. These are referred to as anticipatory hedges. In addition to the required characteristics described in the preceeding paragraphs, hedge accounting is permitted for anticipatory hedges only if the securities to be purchased or sold are identified as to type, amounts, and dates. Further it must be probable that the anticipated transactions will occur.

Index

Titles in Investment/Personal Finance

The Investor's Equation: Creating Wealth Through Undervalued Stocks, by William M. Bowen IV and Frank P. Ganucheau III. ISBN 0–917253–00–0.

Stock Index Options: Powerful New Tools for Investing, Hedging, and Speculating, by Donald T. Mesler. ISBN 0–917253–02–7.

Winning the Interest Rate Game: A Guide to Debt Options, by Frank J. Fabozzi. ISBN 0–917253–01–9.

Low Risk Strategies for the High Performance Investor, by Thomas C. Noddings. ISBN 0–917253–09–4.

Maximize Your Gains: Tax Strategies for Today's Investor, by Robert W. Richards. ISBN 0–917253–10–8.

Increasing Your Wealth in Good Times and Bad, by Eugene M. Lerner and Richard M. Koff. ISBN 0–917253–06–X.

The Insider's Edge: Maximizing Investment Profits Through Managed Futures Accounts, by Bertram Schuster and Howard Abell. ISBN 0– 917253–12–4.

Personal Economics: A Guide to Financial Health and Well-Being, by Robert A. Kennedy and Timothy J. Watts. ISBN 0–917253–08–6.

The New Mutual Fund Investment Advisor, by Richard C. Dorf. ISBN 0–917253–13–2.

Floating Rate Instruments: Characteristics, Valuation and Portfolio Strategies, by Frank J. Fabozzi. ISBN 0–917253–15–9.

Smarter Money: An Investment Game Plan for Those Who Made It and Want to Keep It, by Frank J. Fabozzi and Stephen Feldman. ISBN 0– 917253–16–7.

Warrants: Analysis and Investment Strategy, by Donald T. Mesler. ISBN 0–917253–25–6.

Mastering Your Money: The Complete Guide to Computerwise Personal Financial Management, by Colin K. Mick and Kerry Mason. ISBN 0– 917253–20–5.

Superhedging, by Thomas C. Noddings. ISBN 0–917253–21–3.

High Performance Futures Trading: Computerbased Strategies and Techniques, by William T. Taylor. ISBN 0–917253–22–1.

Executive Economics, by Timothy J. Watts. ISBN 0–917253–23–X.

Self-Directed IRAs for the Active Investor: Taking Charge of Building Your Nest Egg, by Peter D. Heerwagen. ISBN 0–917253–32–9.

The Investor's Desktop Portfolio Planner, by Geoffrey Hirt, Stanley Block, and Fred Jury. ISBN 0–917253–33–7.

The New Guide to Tax Sheltered Investments: How To Evaluate and Buy Tax-Favored Investments That Perform, by G. Timothy Haight and John C. Chanoski. ISBN 0–917253–30–2.

The Stock Index Futures Market: A Trader's Insights and Strategies, by B. Thomas Byrne, Jr. ISBN 0-917253-28-0.

The Trader's and Investor's Guide to Commodity Trading Systems, Software and Data Bases, by William T. Taylor. ISBN 0-917253-41-8.

Timing the Market: How to Profit in Bull and Bear Markets with Technical Analysis, by Weiss Research. ISBN 0-917253-37-X.

The Handbook of Mortgage-Backed Securities, by Frank J. Fabozzi. ISBN 0-917253-04-3.

Titles in Business

Revitalizing Your Business: Five Steps to Successfully Turning Around Your Company, by Edmund P. Freiermuth. ISBN 0-917253-05-1.

Compensating Yourself: Personal Income, Benefits and Tax Strategies for Business Owners, by Gerald I. Kalish. ISBN 0- 917253-07-8.

Using Consultants: A Consumer's Guide for Managers, by Thomas A. Easton and Ralph Conant. ISBN 0-917253-03-5.

Cutting Loose: Making the Transition From Employee to Entrepreneur, by Thomas A. Easton and Ralph W. Conant. ISBN 0- 917253-14-0.

What's What in American Business: Facts and Figures on the Biggest and the Best, by George Kurian. ISBN 0-917253-17-5.

Competing for Clients: The Complete Guide to Marketing and Promoting Professional Services, by Bruce Marcus. ISBN 0-917253- 26-4.

Compensating Your Sales Force: The Sales Executive's Book of Compensation Programs and Strategies, by W. G. Ryckman. ISBN 0-917253-38-8.

Leasing Industrial and Business Equipment: Strategies and Techniques for Lessors and Lessees, by Lloyd A. Haynes, Jr. ISBN 0-917253-31-0.

Not Heard on the Street: An Irreverent Dictionary of Wall Street, by Maurice Joy. ISBN 0-917253-40-x.

Public Relations for the Entrepreneur and the Growing Business: How to Use Public Relations to Increase Visibility and Create Opportunities For You and Your Company, by Norman R. Soderberg. ISBN 0-917253-35-3.

The Executive's Guide to Business and Economic Forecasting, by Charles E. Webster. ISBN 0-917253-36-1.

The Entrepreneur's Guide to Capital: More Than 40 Techniques for Capitalizing and Refinancing New and Growing Businesses, by Jennifer Lindsey. ISBN 0-917253-34-5.

The 101 Best Performing Companies in America, by Ronald N. Paul and James W. Taylor. ISBN 0-917253-39-6.

The Operating Executive's Handbook of Profit Planning Tools and Techniques, by Charles J. Woelfel and Charles D. Mecimore. ISBN 0-917253-24-8.

The Valuation of Privately-Held Businesses: State-of-the-Art Techniques for Buyers, Sellers and Their Advisors, by Irving L. Blackman. ISBN 0-917253-27-2.